Additional Praise for *The Option Advisor*

"Schaeffer covers all including how to choose an options broker and why you should trade on the Internet. Everything is suffused with the theory of Contrarianism."

—*Harrison Roth*
Senior Options Strategist, Cowen & Co.

"An excellent introduction to the world of options trading and technical analysis of the stock market. Experienced traders as well as newcomers to the option scene should find much of value."

—*Gerald Appel*
Publisher, Systems and Forecasts

"Bernie has written a must read book for anyone interested in the stock market. From the beginner to the professional, you will find this book insightful."

—*Jim Bianco*
Arbor Trading Group

"If you are looking for a straightforward explanation of options and profitable option trading strategies, look no further than this book."

—*Jon Najarian*
Managing Partner, PTI Capital Management

WILEY TRADING ADVANTAGE

THE OPTION ADVISOR

WEALTH-BUILDING TECHNIQUES USING EQUITY & INDEX OPTIONS

Bernie Schaeffer

JOHN WILEY & SONS, INC.

New York • Chichester • Weinheim • Brisbane • Singapore • Toronto

This book is dedicated to my father, Irving Jack Schaeffer, whose passion for the stock market I inherited, whose thirst for knowledge and love and respect for learning laced with skepticism in the face of "obvious" and popular viewpoints formed the foundation for my ability to accept and understand the power of the contrarian philosophy, and whose devotion to the principles of fairness and honesty has served as a source of life-time inspiration.

This text is printed on acid-free paper.

Copyright © 1997 by Bernie Schaeffer.
Published by John Wiley & Sons, Inc.

Library of Congress Cataloging in Publication Data:
Schaeffer, Bernie
    The option advisor : wealth-building techniques using
  equity & index options / Bernie Schaeffer.
      p. cm.—(Wiley trading advantage)
    Includes index.
    ISBN 0-471-18539-6 (alk. paper)
    1. Options (Finance) 2. Options (Finance)—Computer network
  resources. 3. Internet (Computer network) I. Title. II. Series.
  HG6024.A3S35 1997   97-17007
  332.63'228—dc21

Printed in the United States of America

10 9 8 7 6 5

Contents

Acknowledgments

Since December 1981 I have written all or a major portion of about 200 issues of *The Option Advisor* newsletter, a number of magazine articles, and countless speeches and presentations, and the so-called "writer's block" has always been a foreign concept to me. So when a friend in the publishing field approached me about the possibility of writing a book about options trading and my investment philosophy, and expressed the opinion that this book "has already been written" given my well-developed ideas in these areas and all that I'd already written about them, I felt 100 percent up to the challenge.

But seeds of doubt soon began to enter the picture. A respected colleague at a Market Technicians Association meeting described for me in great detail the huge time and energy commitment that his book had required. His conclusion was along the lines of "now that it's over I'm glad I did it, but if I had known before I had started the book what was in store for me, I may have decided to pass on it."

As work on the book commenced I began to realize that I was already stretched pretty far with my CEO responsibilities at Investment Research Institute and my need—as a timer, prognosticator, and analyst—to be involved in the day-to-day (and often hour-to-hour) fluctuations of the stock market. Plus, I realized that my expectations were very high, as I wanted this book to capture for the reader the knowledge and capabilities that I had accumulated over the years in two seemingly disparate areas—options trading and contrarian investment philosophy—in a coherent, logical manner.

In summary, this book has proven to be a monumental undertaking, and like all such challenges it would have been impossible to successfully complete without the inspiration and perspiration of a number of key people.

I'd like to first thank my wife, Kathy, for her support, her sacrifices, and her sage advice throughout this very difficult and intense period, while still attending to all of the needs and demands of our three young children.

First mention on the IRI staff belongs to Price Headley, my very capable research director, who was largely responsible for my original commitment to writing this book and who saw me through the toughest times during the writing process with his single-minded dedication to making this book a reality.

Next is my assistant, Denise Wilson, who enabled me to keep the project on course to completion during the critical "make or break" final months. And the other members of the IRI management team, Garry Phillips, Paula Trent, Bob Rack, and Dawn Woods, who saw to it that the company remained on course without a hitch as I became more and more consumed with completing this book.

Special thanks go to the research staff at IRI for their assistance and hard work, in particular: Todd Salamone, Brian Wire, Joe Sunderman, Mike Oyster, Moby Waller, Austin Griess, and Jerry Wang.

Finally, even a well-written, logically constructed book would be on shaky ground without a foundation of solid data, and for this I owe a debt of gratitude to *ILX Systems*, *Bridge Information Systems*, and *Omega Research SuperCharts*, whose data appear throughout this volume in the form of exhibits and tables.

Introduction

"If a man didn't make mistakes he'd own the world in a month. But if he didn't profit by his mistakes he wouldn't own a blessed thing."[1] These remarks appeared in Edwin LeFèvre's book *Reminiscences of a Stock Operator.* They have been attributed to Jesse Livermore, the famous turn-of-the-century stock speculator. As a teenager growing up in New York in the 1960s, fascinated by the world of Wall Street, I didn't realize that I was soon to discover for myself the wisdom of Livermore's view of mistakes.

My dad would often take me to visit the New York Stock Exchange and the American Stock Exchange, where I'd get caught up in the noise, excitement, and activity of the exchanges' trading floors. I'd also accompany him at every opportunity on his visits to our local brokerage firm. At that time, all of the transactions on the stock exchanges were actually printed on a long, narrow roll of paper called ticker tape, and this tape was then projected onto a screen so that brokers and their customers could conveniently view the latest prices. I'd watch this stock ticker for hours, nearly hypnotized by the continuous ebb and flow of stock prices.

As I began studying the financial section of the newspaper, I noticed some fascinating little advertisements like those in exhibit P.1 that regularly appeared in the *New York Times* and the *Wall Street Journal* in the late 1960s and early 1970s.

Although I had no idea what "options" actually were, the idea of being able to participate in the stock market for as little as $112.50 was a very powerful attraction to a middle-class teenager, particularly when the rewards for successfully investing that $112.50 could be thousands of dollars!

My fascination with the profit potential of options trading combined with my degree in mathematics helped me to learn the princi-

---

1. Edwin LeFèvre, *Reminiscences of a Stock Operator* (New York: John Wiley & Sons, 1994, 97).

Exhibit I.1 **PRE-OPTIONS EXCHANGE ADVERTISEMENTS**

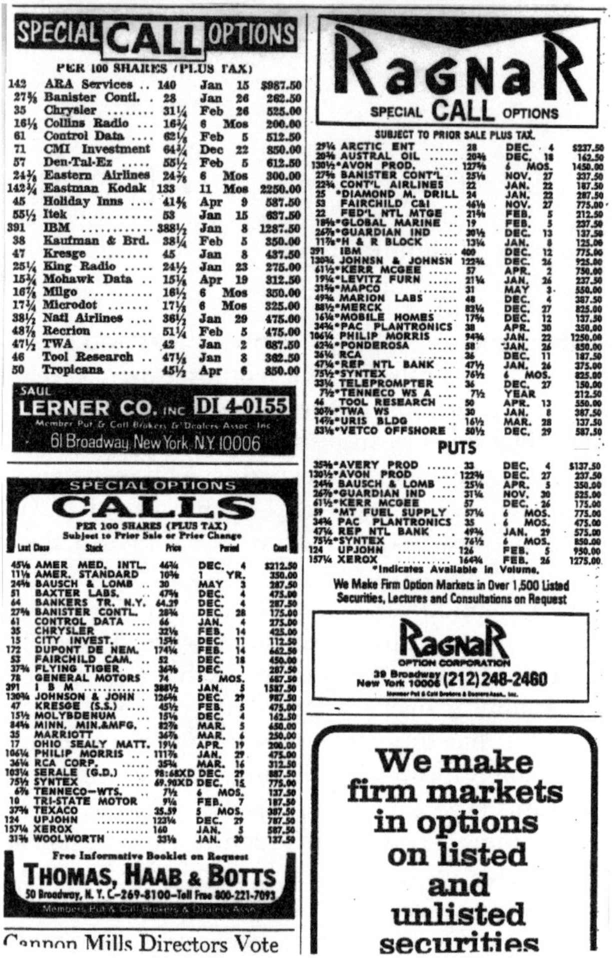

SPECIAL CALL OPTIONS

PER 100 SHARES (PLUS TAX)

142	ARA Services ..	140	Jan 15	$987.50
27⅝	Banister Contl. .	28	Jan 26	262.50
35	Chrysler	31¼	Feb 26	525.00
16⅛	Collins Radio ...	16¾	6 Mos	200.00
61	Control Data	62⅛	Feb 5	512.50
71	CMI Investment	64¾	Dec 22	850.00
57	Den-Tal-Ez	55½	Feb 5	612.50
24⅛	Eastern Airlines	24⅞	6 Mos	300.00
142¾	Eastman Kodak	133	11 Mos	2250.00
45	Holiday Inns	41⅝	Apr 9	587.50
55½	Itek	53	Jan 15	637.50
391	IBM	388½	Jan 8	1287.50
38	Kaufman & Brd.	38¼	Feb 5	350.00
47	Kresge	45	Jan 8	437.50
25¼	King Radio	24½	Jan 23	275.00
15¾	Mohawk Data ..	15⅛	Apr 19	312.50
16⅞	Milgo	16½	6 Mos	350.00
17¾	Microdot	17⅛	6 Mos	325.00
38½	Natl Airlines	36½	Jan 29	475.00
48⅞	Recrion	51¼	Feb 5	475.00
47½	TWA	42	Jan 2	687.50
46	Tool Research ..	47⅛	Jan 8	362.50
50	Tropicana	45½	Apr 6	850.00

SAUL
LERNER CO. INC DI 4-0155
Member Put & Call Brokers & Dealers Assoc. Inc
61 Broadway, New York, N.Y. 10006

SPECIAL OPTIONS
CALLS
PER 100 SHARES (PLUS TAX)
Subject to Prior Sale or Price Change

Last Close	Stock	Price	Period	Cost
45⅛	AMER MED. INTL.	46¾	DEC. 4	$212.50
11⅛	AMER. STANDARD	10⅝	1 YR.	350.00
24⅝	BAUSCH & LOMB ..	30	MAY 3	287.50
51	BAXTER LABS. ..	47⅝	DEC. 4	475.00
64	BANKERS TR. N.Y.	64.29	DEC. 4	287.50
27⅝	BANISTER CONTL.	28¾	DEC. 28	175.00
61	CONTROL DATA	66	JAN. 4	275.00
35	CHRYSLER	32⅛	FEB. 14	425.00
15	CITY INVEST. ...	15⅝	DEC. 11	112.50
172	DUPONT DE NEM.	174¼	FEB. 14	662.50
53	FAIRCHILD CAM. ..	52	DEC. 18	450.00
37¾	FLYING TIGER ..	36⅝	DEC. 1	287.50
78	GENERAL MOTORS	74	5 MOS.	687.50
391	I B M	388½	JAN. 5	1587.50
130¾	JOHNSON & JOHN .	126⅝	DEC. 29	987.50
47	KRESGE (S.S.)	45½	FEB. 5	475.00
15½	MOLYBDENUM ...	15⅛	DEC. 4	162.50
84⅝	MINN. MIN.&MFG. .	82⅞	MAR. 5	650.00
35	MARRIOTT	36⅞	MAR. 6	250.00
17	OHIO SEALY MATT.	19⅛	APR. 19	200.00
106¼	PHILIP MORRIS ...	111⅞	JAN. 29	475.00
36¼	RCA CORP.	35¾	MAR. 16	312.50
103¼	SERALE (G.D.)	98:68XD	DEC. 29	887.50
75½	SYNTEX	69.90XD	DEC. 15	775.00
6⅝	TENNECO—WTS. ..	7½	6 MOS.	137.50
10	TRI-STATE MOTOR	9⅛	FEB. 7	187.50
37⅜	TEXACO	35.59	5 MOS.	387.50
124	UPJOHN	123¼	DEC. 29	787.50
157¼	XEROX	160	JAN. 5	587.50
31⅞	WOOLWORTH	33⅛	JAN. 30	137.50

Free Informative Booklet on Request
THOMAS, HAAB & BOTTS
50 Broadway, N. Y. C—269-8100—Toll Free 800-221-7093

Cannon Mills Directors Vote

RagnaR
SPECIAL CALL OPTIONS

SUBJECT TO PRIOR SALE PLUS TAX.

29¼	ARCTIC ENT	28	DEC. 4	$237.50
20⅝	AUSTRAL OIL	20⅝	DEC. 18	162.50
130½	*AVON PROD.	127⅝	6 MOS.	1450.00
27⅝	BANISTER CONT'L ..	25⅛	NOV. 27	337.50
22¾	CONT'L AIRLINES	22	JAN. 22	187.50
25	*DIAMOND M. DRILL	24	JAN. 22	287.50
53	FAIRCHILD C&I ...	46⅛	NOV. 27	775.00
22	FED'L NTL MTGE .	21⅝	FEB. 5	212.50
18⅝	*GLOBAL MARINE ..	19	FEB. 5	237.50
26⅞	*GUARDIAN IND	30½	DEC. 13	137.50
11⅞	*H & R BLOCK	13¼	JAN. 8	125.00
391	IBM	400	DEC. 12	775.00
130¾	JOHNSN & JOHNSN	122¾	DEC. 26	925.00
61½	*KERR MCGEE	57	APR. 2	750.00
19¼	*LEVITZ FURN	21¼	JAN. 26	237.50
31⅝	*MAPCO	31	MAY 3	550.00
49¾	MARION LABS	48	DEC. 4	387.50
88½	*MERCK	82⅛	DEC. 27	825.00
16⅛	*MOBILE HOMES .	17⅝	DEC. 12	137.50
34¾	*PAC PLANTRONICS	38	APR. 30	350.00
106¼	PHILIP MORRIS	94¾	JAN. 22	1250.00
62¾	*PONDEROSA	58	JAN. 26	850.00
36¼	RCA	36	DEC. 11	187.50
47⅛	*REP NTL BANK ...	47½	JAN. 26	375.00
75½	*SYNTEX	76½	6 MOS.	825.00
33¼	TELEPROMPTER ..	36	DEC. 27	150.00
7½	*TENNECO WS A	7½	YEAR	212.50
46	TOOL RESEARCH ...	50	APR. 13	550.00
30⅞	*TWA WS	30	JAN. 8	387.50
14⅞	*URIS BLDG ..	16½	MAR. 28	137.50
53⅛	*VETCO OFFSHORE .	50½	DEC. 29	587.50

PUTS

35⅝	*AVERY PROD	33	DEC. 4	$137.50
130½	*AVON PROD	122⅝	DEC. 27	237.50
24⅝	BAUSCH & LOMB ...	25⅛	APR. 5	350.00
26⅞	*GUARDIAN IND	31¼	NOV. 30	525.00
61½	*KERR MCGEE	57	DEC. 26	175.00
59	*MT FUEL SUPPLY .	57¼	6 MOS.	775.00
34¾	PAC PLANTRONICS	35	6 MOS.	475.00
47¼	REP NTL BANK .. .	49¾	JAN. 29	575.00
75½	*SYNTEX	76½	6 MOS.	850.00
124	UPJOHN	126	FEB. 5	950.00
157¼	XEROX	164¾	FEB. 26	1275.00

*Indicates Available in Volume.

We Make Firm Option Markets in Over 1,500 Listed Securities, Lectures and Consultations on Request

RagnaR
OPTION CORPORATION
39 Broadway
New York 10006 (212) 248-2460

We make firm markets in options on listed and unlisted securities

This page of options advertising is typical of those that appear in the *Wall Street Journal* and the *New York Times* in the late 1960s and early 1970s, prior to the formation of the Chicago Board Options Exchange (CBOE). Supplied through the courtesy of the Committee on Options Proposals (COOP), Memorabilia Collection.

ples of options at breakneck speed. I very quickly understood that "call" options gave me the right to buy a stock at a specified price for a specified period of time, and that "put" options gave me the right to sell rather than to buy a stock.

I also learned that if I were very *bullish* on a particular stock, I wanted to buy a *call* option, because if I was correct and the stock rose significantly in price, my call option would allow me to buy that stock well below the market price. I could thus "buy low" (by exercising the terms of my call option and buying the stock at the specified price) and then "sell high" (by selling the stock that had rallied). And relative to my small initial investment, my profits could be huge. Of course, all of this favorable stock movement needed to occur before the option "expired," and if the necessary rally in the stock did *not* occur by the expiration date, I would lose the entire sum I paid for the option.

At the other end of the spectrum, I learned that if I were very *bearish* on a stock, I wanted to buy a *put* option, because if I was correct and the stock declined significantly in price, my put option would allow me to sell that stock well above the market price. Again, I would be "buying low" (by buying the stock that had declined) and "selling high" (by exercising the terms of my put option and selling the stock at the specified price).

My fascination with the ads offering various call and put options grew, but there was a significant stumbling block for me: While I had the $100 or $200 required to purchase many of these options, the process of actually "exercising" the options (should the stock move as I had expected) was far beyond my reach as a teenager. At that time, the only way to realize the value of a purchased call option was to buy the stock from the options dealer and then sell the shares on the exchange. While I had enough capital to buy the option, I was far short of the capital I would need to exercise it.

So options remained an enticing but unrealizable dream for me until 1973, when the Chicago Board Options Exchange (CBOE), the first exchange devoted exclusively to trading equity options, began operation. On the CBOE, options transactions occurred on a trading floor in a manner similar to how stocks were traded on stock exchanges. Options investors enjoyed exchange and regulatory protections similar to those afforded stock investors. And most important for me, options could be purchased and sold on the exchange at any time (the technical term is *full fungibility*), so that I, as an options buyer, needed no additional capital beyond that required to purchase the option. I was in business.

Or so I thought. I spent most of the remaining part of the 1970s making every mistake possible by a beginning options trader. To add insult to injury, I repeated some mistakes with numbing regularity. Many of these mistakes involved ignoring sound *money management principles.* Too much of my total investment capital was tied up in my options trading, and too much of what I was investing in the options market was in just one or two situations. Another mistake was in trading options in the exact same manner as I would trade stock, thereby ignoring the two most important words in options investing: "options expire."

By the end of the 1970s, I had put together some extensive notes on what I had learned from my options trading experiences. I began to approach options trading in a much more serious, intelligent, and intense manner. At the time, I was vice-president and actuary for a major midwestern insurance company, and a career change appeared to be in order.

Like most investors of that era, I had subscribed to a number of market letters. These newsletters published the investment advice of entrepreneurs whose work was generally steeped in technical analysis (the analysis of stock price and volume patterns). Even though there were hundreds of these market letters, and many were very valuable sources of advice for stock traders, I was amazed to discover that there was little available in these publications for the options investor.

Although it was possible for the options investor to gain some value from these stock-oriented market letters, I was already well aware of the pitfalls of trying to adapt a stock trading approach to the options market. It became clear to me that the needs of the options investor were not being served by the investment newsletter industry. And I realized that I was at a juncture in life where I could fill that void for the options investor.

What were my qualifications for this role of "market-letter writer for the options trader"? I had a thorough understanding of the stock market and the mathematics and practicalities of the options market, and I had spent the better part of a decade learning from the mistakes most investors make in trading options. Plus, I had good communications skills. Finally, I was just plain fascinated with options—their profit potential, their low capital requirement, and the excitement of trading them. I wanted to share my enthusiasm with other investors and show them how to benefit from my experiences so that they could trade options intelligently and, thus, profitably.

But I needed more than a solid foundation and enthusiasm about options. Successful options trading is ultimately about successful timing—of the market, of industry sectors, and of individual stocks. I learned that to be successful at timing in the stock market, an investor needs an "edge"—a set of indicators or a methodology that is both unique and effective.

Many stock market indicators have proven effective over the years, but they share a common shortcoming: They lose their effectiveness as they gain in popularity. Too many market participants begin to use these indicators in their trading decisions, and then the "Heisenberg Uncertainty Principle" comes into play. Simply put, this tells us that an indicator that becomes too popular will, by definition, lose its effectiveness. The difficulty is compounded by the fact that the unique indicators that avoid the consequences of the Heisenberg Uncertainty Principle are almost uniformly afflicted with the malady of ineffectiveness.

It also became obvious to me that following the conventional wisdom on Wall Street was a sure recipe for investment mediocrity. Time and again I would listen to the "experts" who were quoted in the pages of the leading financial publications, only to be led down the path to investment losses. But, like the fly who continually bumps into the windowpane in its "logical" attempt to get outdoors, I just couldn't seem to stop heeding all the expert advice, despite the losses I had sustained. How could the best minds on Wall Street be so consistently wrong when they were in agreement?

Fortunately, I took heed of the wisdom of those around me. I learned from reading the wry wit of Alan Abelson's weekly column in *Barron's* that research churned out by Wall Street firms was as often a subject for ridicule as it was an object of reverence. Joe Granville stimulated my skepticism even further with his simple yet profound trademark phrase: "The obvious is obviously wrong."

But I still needed a logical explanation for why skepticism was the proper approach to the investment world. My breakthrough came when I read John Kamin's pioneering iconoclastic newsletter, *The Forecaster*, which boldly stated on its masthead that "The Theory of Contrary Opinion Has Never Been Disproved." Kamin's opinions tended to diverge significantly from the conventional wisdom that had so often disappointed me, and I became intrigued with what this "contrary opinion" theory, which Kamin attributed to one Humphrey B. Neill, was all about. I then read Neill's masterpiece, *The Art of Contrary Thinking*,[2] full of revelations that completely changed my approach to investing forever.

In this outstanding book, Neill revealed the reasons why the conventional wisdom on Wall Street was constantly letting me down. I began to understand that when market participants develop a strong consensus opinion, an atmosphere of vulnerability is created, rather than the atmosphere of safety that I first envisioned.

For example, a widespread bullish consensus on a stock indicates that most of the buying power to propel this stock higher has already been used to purchase the shares. The stock price then becomes vulnerable to selling based upon disappointing developments or from simple profit-taking, as there are few buyers remaining to step up when sellers wish to get out. I began to refer to such stocks as "high-

---

2. Humphrey B. Neill, *The Art of Contrary Thinking* (Caldwell, Idaho: Caxton Printers, 1985), 134.

expectation stocks," which, by definition, are stocks to avoid or to consider for shorting or, better yet, for put buying.

"Low-expectation stocks," on the other hand, are ripe for big gains on any positive developments, as there are very few buyers who have committed to these shares. These stocks should therefore form the core of my "call buying list."

I was very excited about this "expectational approach," but I still didn't have my "edge." I recalled very vividly Neill's warning, "We need accurate sentiment measures, otherwise we will conclude that the consensus is what we wish it to be." In other words, if I wanted to know which stocks were truly high-expectation or low-expectation situations, I needed to have an objective way of measuring the sentiment on those stocks.

Once again, the options market provided my inspiration. I recalled that in the old days, prior to widespread options trading, the "odd-lot traders" (those who traded stocks in lots of less than 100 shares) were small speculators who were considered to be almost always incorrect when they agreed in large numbers. These were unsophisticated investors who tended to trade on rumors or on old news, and who thus were almost always buying late into trends or chasing ill-fated hot tips.

But once listed options trading became popular, the odd-lotters gave way to option speculators, who had the same propensity to be wrong. And the beauty of analyzing data from the options market was that it was available separately for puts and for calls, by expiration date and striking price. I could see at a glance which stocks the speculators were enthusiastic about through heavy call buying (my high-expectation stocks) and which stocks they were pessimistic about through heavy put buying (my low-expectation stocks).

I now had an effective methodology (expectational analysis) and unique and objective indicators (option-trader activity) and I was prepared to begin publishing my options newsletter. I cofounded Investment Research Institute in 1981; the first issue of *The Option Advisor* newsletter was published in December of that year.

Over the course of the ensuing fifteen years, equity options trading has continued to grow by leaps and bounds, with only a brief pause in the aftermath of the 1987 stock market crash. This growth has accelerated during the 1990s (see table P.1), fueled by increasing participation of individual investors.

I believe that two major factors have helped drive this explosive growth in options trading. First, today's investors are increasingly aware of the benefits of adding an options trading component to their investment arsenal. Most investors are attracted to options because they can be used as a cheap, leveraged vehicle to profit handsomely

Table I.1   CBOE EQUITY OPTION GROWTH, 1990–1996

Year	Contract Volume	Growth Since 1990 (%)	Open Interest	Growth Since 1990 (%)
1996	88,456,579	95.46	9,122,520	270.88
1995	77,040,466	58.89	7,350,437	198.84
1994	68,974,809	42.26	6,028,581	145.09
1993	58,710,818	21.09	5,642,471	129.40
1992	44,918,235	–7.36	3,781,653	53.74
1991	45,255,301	–6.66	2,783,155	13.15
1990	48,486,402		2,459,695	

from the movement in an equity. But options can also be used to protect a portfolio from a major decrease in value or to provide additional income, and these more conservative uses are attracting more and more attention in an increasingly nervous investment environment.

Second, the equity options industry has moved out of the back rooms and into the investment mainstream. As recently as twenty-five years ago, equity options transactions were performed for investors by a small group of obscure firms without the benefit of an options exchange. As a result, options tended to be very expensive. Compounding this problem was the fact that options buyers could not take immediate advantage of changes in the value of their contract, as its terms could not be exercised until the day the option expired. It is not surprising that the tiny options industry sported something of an outlaw reputation.

Today, options are traded on the options floor of four exchanges (the CBOE, the American Stock Exchange, the Philadelphia Stock Exchange, and the Pacific Stock Exchange) in virtually the same manner that stocks are traded on stock exchanges. Plus, options investors have protections analogous to those traditionally enjoyed by stock investors. And options are now fully fungible, which simply means that an options buyer can turn around and sell his contract on the options exchange at any time up to and including the date that it expires.

When I look back over my fifteen years of providing advice and analysis to investors, there are a number of accomplishments of which I am particularly proud. I'm proud of the fact that *The Option Advisor* has grown to become the nation's largest-circulation newsletter specializing in equity options recommendations. We have had the privilege of helping tens of thousands of investors to understand the principles of an intelligent approach to options trading and to avoid the common mistakes that have tripped up most options investors over the years.

I'm also proud that I have kept my subscribers on the right side of all of the major moves in the market. I was bullish until the exact market top two months ahead of the 1987 crash, and then maintained a bearish posture until the day after the crash. And I have since remained bullish throughout most of what has proven to be one of the greatest bull markets in history.

I'm convinced that my market timing success has been the result of my ability to analyze investor sentiment and expectations and to combine this analysis with a sophisticated approach to technical and fundamental analysis. This unique approach is also a cornerstone of the advice I provide to institutional investors.

My approach to selecting options, which emphasizes the importance of determining the correct underlying stock and places lesser emphasis on the "probabilistic" approach to options trading, is also key. This latter approach is predominant in the options advice industry. It assumes that stock price movements are random and relies instead on an analysis of the "cheapness" or "expensiveness" of individual options. Investors (and their advisors) often forget that options are only cheap or expensive in relation to the actual future price movement of the underlying stock, and that "cheap" options can get cheaper and "expensive" options can become more expensive.

I had a threefold purpose in writing this book. First, I wanted to provide beginning and intermediate options traders with a resource that explains basic options principles in an understandable yet thorough manner. The literature on options trading is replete with oversimplified, "gee-whiz"–type works that do little to prepare the reader for the real world of options trading. At the opposite end of the spectrum, there are a number of fine options books that are extremely thorough and comprehensive but are also extremely complex and intimidating, even to the intermediate trader.

Second, I wanted to break some new ground in the world of options literature by thoroughly explaining why equity options cannot be successfully traded in the same manner as stocks, nor can they be successfully traded in a mathematical void without regard to the short-term prospects for the underlying stock. I have a simple reason for this emphasis, for I believe that the biggest component of any individual's lack of success in trading options is not a poor understanding of basic options concepts, but serious misconceptions that options trading and stock trading can be approached in an identical manner or that options trading can be reduced to a probabilistic computer model. The intermediate trader may prefer to concentrate on these sections of the book, and even the advanced trader would likely benefit from such a review.

Finally, I wanted to help "de-mythify" the options world and allow investors to make intelligent choices without falling prey to the misconceptions underlying the vast folklore about options. Myths about options trading abound. Most of them date from the old "cottage industry" days, and the fact that they are still with us is testimony to the enduring power of folklore.

It is my fervent hope that this book will not only help you to better appreciate the essentials of options, but that it will also help you to achieve success in equity options trading. Such success is dependent upon an understanding that options trading must be approached differently from stock trading and that an analysis of the attractiveness of an options trade is meaningless without a solid appreciation of the short-term prospects of the underlying stock. And it is with this success model in mind that the first chapter explains the concept of analyzing investor expectations, which, in my view, is the key to success in the equities market and the key to success in trading options.

Bernie Schaeffer
March 1997

Part 1

Theory and Foundation

1

Expectational Analysis

INTRODUCTION

The words of the great contrarian Humphrey B. Neill, in his book *The Art of Contrary Thinking*, have great relevance to the options trader: "The 'crowd' is most enthusiastic and optimistic when it should be cautious and prudent; and is most fearful when it should be bold".[1] As you will soon see, measuring and evaluating the sentiment of the crowd can make the difference between mediocre and successful trading. And success in trading options depends on understanding that the results from your options strategy are a function of your ability to correctly predict both the direction and the timing of a move in the underlying stock.

This idea that "the underlying stock comes first" will be discussed in detail in chapter 2, but it is also important to our present discussion. One of the biggest pitfalls for beginning options traders is jumping right into learning the fundamentals of options without a firm foundation in how to judge the prospects for the underlying stock. These new traders concentrate instead on the specific characteristics of the options, including such factors as whether the options are "underpriced" or "overpriced." An understanding of the mathematical esoterica of options without an understanding of the dynamics of stock price movement is a disastrous recipe for options trading. It is equivalent to an attempt to become a successful horse-and-buggy driver by becoming expert at every aspect of the buggy without any understanding of the behavior of horses and what makes them run (or trot). It is my contention that stock behavior ultimately drives the success of options strategies, just as the horse determines the ultimate position and movement of the buggy.

---

1. Humphrey B. Neill, *The Art of Contrary Thinking* (Caldwell, Idaho: Caxton Printers, 1985), 134.

The purpose of this chapter is to demonstrate why measuring investor expectations is so important for your success in determining the future price movement of the underlying stock; it therefore becomes a critical factor for your success as an options trader. In this process, I will also define my conception of the contrarian approach to investing.

Most do-it-yourself investors focus on the two traditional approaches to stock selection: *fundamental analysis*, which uses factors such as earnings, dividends, and economic projections to forecast stock prices, and *technical analysis*, which focuses on historical price patterns and volume characteristics to predict future performance. The difference in my approach to trading options is that I also use *expectational analysis* to evaluate the opinions and sentiments of the investing community and then use that evaluation to help predict stock price movement.

"IN THE BEGINNING, THERE WAS FUNDAMENTAL ANALYSIS"

Although the world of great traders has always been replete with those who looked at factors well beyond the "fundamental" earnings prospects and financial condition of the companies whose shares they bought and sold, the language of Wall Street securities analysis was for all practical purposes 100 percent fundamental until the past decade or so.

Great tomes were written by the major brokerage firms in the form of "research reports" about a company or an industry group, complete with detailed statistics, ratios, and projections of sales, profits, balance sheets, and relevant economic factors. The basic conclusion of these reports tended to be: "Buy this stock because this is a great company."

Inspired by the 1948 classic work *Technical Analysis of Stock Trends* by Edwards and Magee, in the late 1950s and early 1960s some bright, young Wall Street analysts led by James Dines and Joseph Granville began to actively challenge the conventional fundamental approach to deciding which stocks to buy. They began pointing out what sharp traders had known for years—the prices of stocks in "good" companies can decline precipitously, particularly over the short-term, and the shares of "bad" companies, which are demonstrating very little earnings power and whose prospects are deemed to be unfavorable by Wall Street, can be among the market's best performers at various points in time.

Both Granville and Dines wrote books explaining these phenomena that were instrumental in the further development and popularization of the alternative approach to stock selection known as technical analysis. But it should be noted that each left their respective Wall Street firms to begin publishing independent newsletters (still published today), as Wall Street was far from ready to embrace any thoughts that challenged its comfortable fundamental approach, despite its shortcomings.

Although each of these pioneering technical analysts had a different area of specialization (Dines in "point and figure" charting and Granville in "on balance volume"), there was much common ground in their discomfort with the fundamental approach. In particular, they noted that there were historical price and volume patterns that were characteristic of stocks that would consistently outperform or underperform the market, and that these patterns were often completely independent of Wall Street's version of the "fundamentals" of these stocks. It was as if the collective actions of thousands of investors, which manifested itself in the price and volume patterns that appeared on the charts of the technicians, provided better forecasts for the future price action of a stock than did the lengthy research reports. While this concept raises few eyebrows in the more eclectic 1990s and had previously been detailed by Edwards and Magee, it was close to heretical in the era of Dines and Granville.

One of the rejoinders of the fundamentalists was that there was no "logic" to technical analysis and that it was the stock market equivalent of reading tea leaves. But this argument ignores the deep gaps in the logic of the fundamental approach. It is difficult to argue with the facts presented in research reports. But it is very easy to argue with the projections that result from those facts, and even easier to argue with the conclusions on how these projections will translate themselves into future stock prices.

For example, let us assume that a hypothetical company, Silicon Computer, is being analyzed on the basis of its fundamentals. The analyst has gathered and presented in a report all of the company's relevant financial data for the past five years. His next step is to project Silicon's sales and earnings over the next three years. But the computer industry is extremely competitive, and the demand for computers can be highly volatile. Does the analyst know for sure whether some or all of Silicon's competitors will cut prices drastically, thereby forcing Silicon to either match the price cuts and hurt their profit margins or to lose significant market share? In addition, the technological backdrop is constantly changing. Does the analyst know whether a new technology or manufacturing process will put Silicon at an extreme disadvantage?

The answers to the above questions are clearly "no," but the typical research report then proceeds to add yet another level of assumptions by attempting to predict how the stock market will value the shares of Silicon in the future, assuming that the analyst's first level of assumptions are correct. Not only are future earnings being predicted with a set of assumptions that may not be accurate, but then the future stock price is predicted based upon an assumption of how the market will value those very iffy future earnings projections.

A look at exhibit 1.1 will help illustrate the extent to which a dichotomy can exist between assumptions in Wall Street's research reports and the reality of the stock market. Wal-Mart Stores has consistently been one of the most admired organizations in the United States. Founder Sam Walton became a folk hero for the "friendly folks" atmosphere he encouraged in his stores and for his success at motivating his employees by treating them with respect, eliciting their suggestions, and providing them with shares in the company. By the end of 1992, Wal-Mart had achieved sales of $55 billion and a market capitalization of $73 billion. By early 1993 Wal-Mart shares reached an all-time high price of $34, but as of this writing in 1997 this price has still not been surpassed.

Wall Street was almost unanimously bullish on Wal-Mart shares late in 1992, based upon a variety of assumptions that the company's heady growth rate would persist and that the stock market would continue to value Wal-Mart shares at a very high multiple of its earnings per share. But notice how the price of Wal-Mart has stagnated from 1993 to date, even as the overall market has rallied sharply to all-time highs. Was the chorus of bullish analysts incorrect that

Exhibit 1.1   WAL-MART MONTHLY CHART

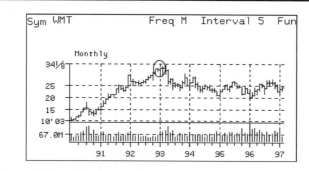

Reprinted with permission. Compliments of ILX Systems.

Wal-Mart was a "very good company"? Certainly not, as the company has continued to gain market share and produce respectable earnings growth.

The reason that the shares stagnated, as any analyst will now tell you, is related to the fact that there was a slight slowing in the earnings growth rate, and as a result investors were no longer willing to value the company at such a high ratio to earnings. But once again, the weakness of fundamental analysis is revealed, as it proved to be a poor predictor of Wal-Mart's future share price performance and could only subsequently explain that price performance on a "look back" basis.

This seems to be a harsh critique of fundamental analysis, and one could argue that it does not jibe with the fact that, over the long term, almost 100 percent of stock price movement can be explained by the level of earnings. In fact, Stephen Todd of the *Todd Market Timer* recently stated that from 1935 to 1995 the Dow Jones Industrial Average increased by 4,400 percent while earnings growth for the component stocks in this average grew by 4,200 percent, a remarkable correlation.[2]

The problem with fundamental analysis is that it is a good reflective tool but it is *not* a forecasting tool for stock prices, particularly for the short-term time frame in which option traders operate. There are simply too many assumptions underlying the projections and too many possible outcomes. In my opinion, it is impossible to construct a model that will consider all of the company-specific and economic factors that will affect future earnings, and the appropriate weights that should be assigned to them. And even if this could be accomplished, it is impossible to then determine how the market will price the stock in the future, based on these factors.

Although technical analysis is certainly not the "Holy Grail" for predicting stock price movement, it offers an advantage in that analyzing price and volume patterns is grounded in the "real world" of how investors are currently viewing a stock or a market. No one technical indicator "works" in all cases as a forecasting tool, and many a "nice" chart can deteriorate very quickly. But technical analysts would be unlikely to fall into the same trap as did the fundamentalists with regard to Wal-Mart. The price action was clearly deteriorating despite the chorus of Wall Street "buy" recommendations, and it was only in hindsight that the fundamentalists realized that the market was thereby reflecting a future trend of slowing earnings growth layered on top of a valuation that by 1992 had reached unsustainable

---

2. *The Todd Market Time,* December 16, 1996, Volume 12, Issue 18, p. 1, 26861 Trabuco Rd., Mission Viejo, CA 92691.

levels. In other words, in this instance and in many others, it paid to listen to the market as opposed to listening to the research reports.

It does not always pay to listen to the market, however, as technical analysis has its own limitations. There is a strong tendency in the technical approach to extrapolate and to assume that past price patterns will repeat themselves. Five different technical analysts may offer five different opinions based upon a review of the same chart. But technical analysis does provide a very important, real-world perspective. To quote Humphrey Neill: "I am not opposed to the intelligent use of charts. They have their worthwhile usages, especially as checker-uppers to preconceived ideas or tips. It is the 'depend-all' form of chart usage I'm afraid of."[3]

Mainstream analysis seems to have heeded Neill's words, as many fundamentalists now employ some technical analysis tools, and most technicians are now keenly aware of anticipated quarterly earnings releases, product announcements, and other key fundamental factors. The Market Technicians Association has become an important voice in market analysis, and the Certified Market Technician (CMT) designation is the technical analysis parallel of the more familiar, fundamentally based Chartered Financial Analyst (CFA) designation. In fact, there are some individuals who now have both designations.

If you or your advisor is one of these "fundatechnicians," I have good news and bad news for you. The good news is that strong fundamentals and strong technicals are usually a *necessary* condition for a stock to move higher. The bad news is that the confluence of strong technicals and strong fundamentals is not a *sufficient* condition for future strength.

This concept is so basic to options trading success that it warrants restating: Although it is usually necessary for a stock or an industry sector purchase candidate to have strong fundamentals and strong technicals, it is not enough. Investor expectations affect the power and the importance of technicals and fundamentals.

Let us expand on the discussion begun in the preface on the view of investor expectations known as "contrary opinion," and how it is vital to options trading success. Note that you are not expected to become a master of the techniques for measuring investor expectations, but simply to be aware of the importance of this expectational element in forecasting future stock prices, as such an awareness is rare among options traders and will always give you an important trading edge no matter which options strategies you choose to employ.

---

3. Neill, *Art of Contrary Thinking,* 180.

CONTRARY OPINION THEORY

The Art of Contrary Thinking profoundly changed the way I approached investing. Humphrey Neill emphasized the importance of measuring the sentiment of the investing "crowd," as the actions of the vast majority of investors is characteristic of crowd behavior. And, according to Neill, "because a crowd does not think, but acts on impulses, public opinions are frequently wrong."[4]

Neill also stressed the importance of thinking critically and thoroughly in developing investment decisions. This gives you an immediate advantage over the average investor, who Neill claims "does not think—and does not wish to think."[5] And when the average investor does feel compelled to think, it tends to involve "obvious thinking" or "thinking the same way in which everyone else is thinking," which "commonly leads to wrong judgements and wrong conclusions."[6]

The proper application of Neill's approach helps you to avoid thinking like the crowd, because you tend to think critically and independently and are not seduced by the obvious. It also leads you to measure the sentiment of the crowd so you can adopt a contrarian or opposite viewpoint to that of the crowd, but only when appropriate. You must remember that the crowd is not always wrong. In fact, it tends to be right during the heart of a market trend, but decidedly wrong at the tops and the bottoms. As Neill states: "The public is perhaps right more of the time than not. In stock market parlance, the public is right *during* the trends but wrong at both ends."[7]

The fact that the public is not always wrong is one of several major misconceptions about contrarian theory, and is also one of the major factors that has tripped up so many analysts concerning the bull market of the 1990s. Time and again, the public's infatuation with the stock market, as manifested by the huge dollar inflows into equity mutual funds, has been trotted out by the bears as an argument that the end of the bull move is at hand. A severe price has been paid by those who have ignored Neill's maxim that the public is right most of the time. The public will be overly enthusiastic and overly invested at the ultimate top, but such enthusiasm is merely a necessary, and not a sufficient, condition for a top to be in place.

There are other misconceptions about what contrary opinion really means, which are discussed in greater detail in chapter 12. For ex-

---

4. Ibid., 35.

5. Ibid., 54.

6. Ibid., 1.

7. Ibid., 44.

ample, contrary opinion is not about buying low prices or cheap stocks. "Cheap" can always become "cheaper," and it is just as dangerous to mindlessly "bottom fish" in a stock that is in a free fall as it is to buy a stock just because it is achieving new highs. But as a "sentimentician," you would tend to be attracted to stocks on which expectations are low, so you would generally be avoiding the crowd; and if a stock or a sector were overly loved by the crowd, you would tend to avoid it.

To summarize, true contrary opinion is about buying low expectations, not about buying low prices. In fact, as will be shown in chapter 3, it is often best to have a philosophy of "buy high and sell higher." And since low expectations often accompany strong technicals and strong fundamentals, a contrarian approach can be successfully implemented without the dangers of bottom-fishing in weak stocks and sectors.

HOW EXPECTATIONS AFFECT STOCK PRICE MOVEMENT

It is vitally important to remember that the "price" of a stock is the sum total of investors' expectations of reality. If these expectations are too low, a stock will have a tendency to rally. This is because the gap will eventually narrow between the stock price that reflects these low expectations and the stock price that reflects the real world. Similarly, if expectations are too high, there is a tendency for a stock to decline in price, as these high expectations are eventually adjusted downward to better reflect the real world.

There are instances in which this "expectation gap" is bridged almost instantaneously. For example, we have all seen highly touted stocks report a "positive earnings surprise" after a big run-up in the shares, only to decline in price just after this positive earnings report is released. "Profit-taking" and "selling on the news" are reported in the financial press as explanations for this seemingly aberrant price behavior. But the real answer is that investor expectations were too high ahead of the release of the report. High expectations generally equate to little sideline money, as nearly all those investors who would have committed their capital to that stock are likely to have already made that commitment. So when the favorable report is released and the inevitable profit-taking on the news occurs, there is not enough sideline money being deployed into the stock to absorb the selling, and the stock moves lower.

If expectations were modest, or better yet, low, the stock would likely have rallied on the good report despite the fact that some people would be "taking profits."

Why would this be so? Because modest expectations are an indication of potential buying power, as there are likely to be many skeptical investors on the sidelines. When a positive earnings surprise is reported, enough of this sideline money will likely move into the stock and sop up supply from the profit-takers. And the result is that the stock moves higher.

APPLYING EXPECTATIONAL ANALYSIS AND THE CONTRARIAN APPROACH

Let us take a look at the chart of Telmex in exhibit 1.2 and focus on the month of December 1994. Note how Telmex had already declined by about 50 percent from its highs of earlier that year. But was Telmex "cheap"? My expectational analysis said "no way," and I admonished my subscribers to stay away no matter how seductive this "low" price appeared.

How did I know that there was likely to be additional downside in Telmex? One way was by simply reading the financial media. In December 1994 the media was dutifully reporting the opinions of the Wall Street community on the Mexico market. Despite the fact that this market had virtually collapsed, Wall Street was screaming "buy, buy, buy" to anyone who would listen.

While extreme reactions to market conditions are fairly easy to spot, it is also important to note *complacency* in the media—a sure way to know that a weak stock or sector has not yet bottomed. In fact, nothing is more dangerous in a falling market than a calm reaction to

Exhibit 1.2   **TELMEX WEEKLY CHART**

the decline, as this calm is a strong signal that expectations are still too high, despite the "low" price.

There was a confluence of other disturbing factors on the expectations front. In an attempt to call a bottom, options traders were buying call options heavily on Telmex as the shares continued to decline. At the true bottom, options players would be strongly biased toward buying put options, as these wrong-way players would be convinced that disaster lay ahead. And it would also be expected that the mutual fund switchers would be bailing out of the Latin American funds by December 1994 as a result of the miserable performance of those funds that year. But there was no such bailout, as investors confidently awaited the turnaround they saw as inevitable.

The bottom line is that expectations were way too high on Telmex and on the Latin American markets for December 1994 to have marked a true bottom. And sure enough, there were substantial declines ahead in 1995 before the situation began to stabilize.

THE MAGAZINE-COVER PHENOMENON

No discussion of contrarian theory and the importance of measuring investor expectations would be complete without a look at magazine covers and their implications.

The covers of business magazines are often amazingly accurate contrary indicators, and when a business story is featured on the cover of a general news magazine, the contrarian implications are even stronger. Quite simply, when a magazine cover features a stock or an investment trend in a bullish light, it is very likely that this stock or investment trend is at or near its peak. Or, conversely, when a cover is bearish on a stock or an investment trend, that stock or investment is very likely at or near its bottom.

Why do magazine covers work so well as contrary indicators? Because they provide us with strong insight into those situations in which investor expectations are at an extreme.

Only when a trend has been in place long enough to become widely known and almost universally accepted will it be featured on a magazine cover, as magazine editors are focused on selling their product on the newsstands. Editors are looking for the "Aha!" not the "Huh?" reaction from prospective buyers. There is nothing to be gained and much to be lost from a cover story about an obscure business trend of which few are aware and perhaps even fewer care.

So if we understand that magazine covers feature only those trends that have been in place for a long time and are widely known and almost universally accepted, what are the implications for those trends after the magazine hits the newsstand? In the vast majority of cases, those trends have peaked and are about to reverse.

In the world of investing, it has always been the case that the "smart money" identifies and buys into trends very early, way before these trends attract the attention of the media. As media awareness spreads, the general public—who invariably arrives late in the trend—gets involved. Once a trend reaches the magazine-cover level of awareness, it is almost certainly at its peak, as the last to know in the investing public finally gets the word. In fact, the smart money is very likely to be selling its shares to these eager, but very late, magazine-cover buyers.

A classic example of the contrarian power of magazine covers is provided to us by *Time* magazine. On November 9, 1992, *Time's* cover queried "Can GM Survive in Today's World?" The implications of the cover and of the feature article were very dire for General Motors. Exhibit 1.3 shows the historical price movement in GM shares. Note the price of GM at the time of the November 1992 *Time* cover. Now fast-forward to December 13, 1993, when *Time* featured a triumphant photograph of the CEOs of each of the Big Three automakers. The feature

Exhibit 1.3   **GENERAL MOTORS MONTHLY CHART, SHOWING MAGAZINE-COVER PHENOMENON**

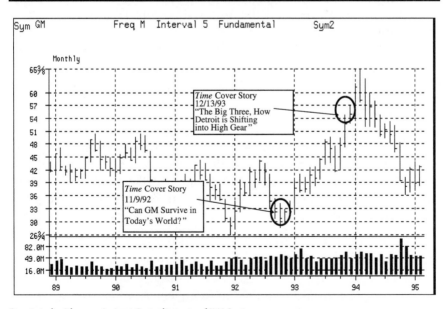

Reprinted with permission. Compliments of ILX Systems.

article was a glowing tribute to the comeback of the U.S. auto industry and was very optimistic in its implications.

What's wrong with this picture? Any investor who would have sold their GM shares in November 1992 based upon the bearish *Time* cover story, and then bought in December 1993, based upon the bullish *Time* cover story, would have done the wrong thing at the wrong time in both cases.

Is the perverse result in the aftermath of these cover stories surprising? Only to the vast majority of investors who have no understanding of contrarian implications. The cover in November 1992 came at a time of maximum bearishness on GM and the auto industry. It was the final warning to the investing public to bail out of their GM shares before it was too late, which they dutifully heeded. But it was also a clarion call for the smart money to begin buying GM shares from a panic-stricken public.

By December 1993, sentiment had taken a decidedly bullish turn. Auto stocks had rallied sharply, and the prospects for the U.S. auto industry appeared to be much brighter. It thus became a safe bet for the media to lionize the CEOs of the Big Three on a magazine cover. But was it also a safe bet for the public to buy the shares of these companies? Most definitely not, as exhibit 1.3 clearly shows. In fact, it was time for the smart money to start *unloading* its shares to a now-enthusiastic public.

None of this discussion of cover stories and their contrarian implications is meant to impugn the editorial quality of the publications under discussion. In truth, the very fact that these publications are known for their high editorial quality gives them the credibility and respect necessary for such contrarian conclusions. The point here is one of timing. The articles themselves were highly informative and factual, but because of the nature of the magazine business (or, for that matter, any media business), the timing of these articles as cover stories was almost by definition a contrarian indicator for investors.

In our increasingly sophisticated investment world, the magazine cover phenomenon seems almost silly. But if you understand that the expectational element is often the missing link in forecasting future stock prices, the concept of using magazine covers as a forecasting tool becomes quite logical.

THE CONSENSUS FORECAST

The consensus forecast provides us with yet another contrarian insight from the media. These forecasts are usually issued at the end of a calendar year, when media editors feel compelled to provide us with predictions for the coming year. Why? Because these are among the best-selling issues over the course of the entire year, as many people can be enticed into buying into the crystal ball of "the experts."

These consensus forecasts will, almost without exception, be extrapolations of the most recent trends, which means that by definition they will be wrong if a turning point is at hand. And as we shall see shortly, turning points have an uncanny knack for occurring in conjunction with a new year.

But, you might say, those who contribute to these year-end forecasts are among the best minds in the business. Why would we be drawing contrarian conclusions from such forecasts?

Neill provides a great insight into this seemingly paradoxical situation:

> I hold [that] one goes out on the guessy limb when he extrapolates from an observation or from what happens to be occurring in "crowd activities."
>
> Countless forecasts (I'd be willing to assert that the *majority* of predictions) are made largely upon projecting into the future what is happening in the present. Today's trends are expected to continue tomorrow and into next week.[8]

Let us review an outstanding real-life illustration of the contrarian power of the year-end forecast. The bond market was very strong in 1993, which means that long-term interest rates were low and declining. At year-end 1993, *Business Week* polled a group of 50 distinguished economists for their forecasts for 1994, including their forecasts for long-term interest rates. Table 1.1 shows the highest and lowest forecasts for long-term interest rates for 1994 as contained in this *Business Week* survey. Most of these forecasts were extremely optimistic, reflecting the good year that bonds were having in 1993 and the extrapolation principle just discussed. As it turned out, however, 1994 was the single worst year for the bond market since 1927, and even the most pessimistic year-end 1993 forecasts fell far short of the mark, as long-term interest rates soared as high as 8.5 percent in 1994.

Now let us look at year-end 1994. As you can see from table 1.2, the *Business Week* forecasters "learned their lesson" from the soaring long-term interest rates of 1994, and their forecasts for 1995 were quite pessimistic, based upon the extrapolation principle. Once again they missed the mark by a wide margin, as 1995 was one of the best years ever for the bond market, resulting in long-term interest rates that were lower than the expectations of even the most optimistic year-end 1994 forecasters.

---

8. Ibid., 169.

Table 1.1   **WHAT ECONOMISTS PREDICTED FOR 1994**

	30-Year Treasury Yields (%)
Dean Witter Reynolds	7.00
Tokai Bank	5.80
C.J. Lawrence	5.00
Deutsche Bank	7.10
Bear Sterns	7.00
Mellon Bank	5.75
A.Garry Shilling & Co.	5.00
DKB Securities	5.50
Robert H. Parks & Assoc.	5.00
Consensus of 50 economists	**6.30**

Portion of graph from *Business Week*, December 27, 1993.

Table 1.2   **WHAT ECONOMISTS PREDICTED FOR 1995**

	30-Year Treasury Yields (%)
Tokai Bank	9.00
Georgia State University	8.65
Weyerhaeuser	9.00
Argus Research	9.00
Univ. of North Carolina	5.65
Bankers Trust	7.00
First Chicago	8.90
Shawmut National	7.20
Chemical Bank	7.25
Consensus of 50 economists	**7.86**

Portion of graph from *Business Week*, December 26, 1994.

USING THE OPTIONS MARKET TO GAUGE EXPECTATIONS

Tracking the activity of options traders can provide a very effective measurement of investor expectations. Such a tracking system is the cornerstone of my own expectational analysis.

Iomega (IOM) and Micron Technology (MU), two high-flying technology stocks that ultimately dropped sharply from their highs, provide us with a recent illustration of the powerful contrarian implications of option trader behavior when juxtaposed against the price action of the underlying stock. During the rallying phases in IOM and MU, options speculators were attempting to call a top via heavy purchases of put options as reflected in the high put/call ratios in circle 1 on exhibits 1.4 and 1.5. The fact that these speculators were going against the trend was a powerful contrarian indicator, and it argued for a continuation of the rallies in these stocks.

But note that the speculators eventually "caught on" and became more bullish as these stocks continued to rally toward their ultimate tops, as evidenced by the decline in the put/call ratios during this phase (see circle 2 on exhibits 1.4 and 1.5). It is during this period that the crowd was right and their behavior became consistent with the uptrend in these stocks. Such a phase provides little insight for the contrarian.

But the behavior of these options speculators once again assumed contrarian implications as these stocks peaked and began to roll over to the downside, and call options speculators continued to be very aggressive despite the weakening share prices. Options speculators now believed that these stocks would resume their uptrends rather than continue to move lower, so they stepped up their buying of calls, as

Exhibit 1.4   **IOMEGA (IOM) PUT/CALL OPEN INTEREST**

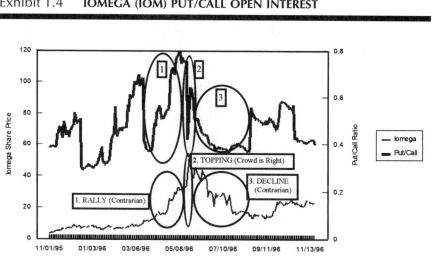

Exhibit 1.5   MICRON TECHNOLOGY (MU) PUT/CALL OPEN INTEREST

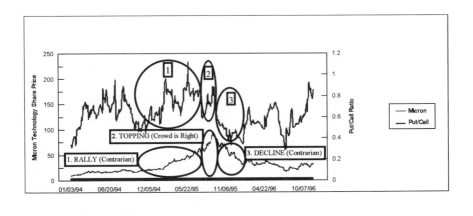

reflected in the declining put/call ratios in circle 3 on exhibits 1.4 and 1.5. Once again the counter-trend activity of options speculators proved to be excellent contrarian indicators, as both IOM and MU proceeded to decline substantially from their highs.

THE POWER OF BUYING LOW-EXPECTATION INDUSTRY SECTORS

As a final illustration of the importance of accurately reading investor expectations let us look at that "best of all worlds" situation for bullish investors, in which expectations are clearly low, yet the technicals and the fundamentals are relatively strong. This situation can best be illustrated by the retailing sector, as exemplified by the chart of the Fidelity Select Retailing Fund in exhibit 1.6.

In late 1990, the nation was in a glum mood as hostilities in the Gulf grew inevitably closer. And nowhere was this glum mood more evident than in the attitude on Wall Street toward the retailing sector. Article after article in the media proclaimed the "death of the shopping mall" and the end of the "shop till you drop" mindset. Consumers were said to be overextended and depressed, and the retailing industry was expected to pay a terrible price for this consumer malaise in the 1990 Christmas shopping season and well into 1991.

Were conditions all that bad? Definitely not. Although Christmas holiday sales in 1990 were not in the robust category, they certainly exceeded the expectations of the "doom and gloomers." And the na-

Exhibit 1.6   **FIDELITY SELECT RETAILING FUND MONTHLY CHART**

Reprinted with permission. Compliments of ILX Systems.

tion soon received a huge psychological boost as it became clear that the Gulf War was destined to be a triumph for the Allied forces.

How did the Fidelity Select Retailing Fund perform in 1991? Amazingly, this normally conservative sector fund produced a return of about 68 percent (see circled area in exhibit 1.6). This is actually not very surprising, given the crescendo of media bearishness, put option buying, and frenzied short-selling that accompanied this sector in late 1990.

On Christmas Day 1995, the *New York Times* featured a front-page headline, "Retailers Report a Shopping Season Worth Forgetting—Bleak Forecast for 1996." Note that the expectational significance of a business-related front-page story in general is always huge, because most business matters are restricted to the business section. So when a business-oriented piece is featured on the front page, you know that sentiment is at an extreme.

Then the *Wall Street Journal* proclaimed in its January 31, 1996, edition: "Retailers Register a Dismal December."

Was the holiday season of 1995 in fact so terrible for retailers? Once again, the answer is "no." There were certainly individual retailers who suffered over this period, but sales in December 1995 actually exceeded those for December 1994.

So once again we had overly negative expectations on the retailing sector as we approached a new year, and once again this sector responded by posting outstanding gains over the course of that year, as the Fidelity Select Retailing Fund was up 21 percent in 1996, with the bulk of this gain achieved in the first quarter (see circled area in exhibit 1.6).

CONCLUSION

By now it should be clear that measuring investor expectations is a cornerstone for investing success. And it should also be clear that contrarian theory is not a simple-minded approach for buying beaten-down stocks, but rather an approach that requires you to think critically about all you read and hear and to heed the timeless words of Sir Francis Bacon: "Doubt all before you believe."

Will an understanding of the importance of the expectational element guarantee you success in your options trading? No, as there are no guarantees in investing and, as you will be reminded throughout this book, successful options trading involves the confluence of many different disciplines. But an understanding of investor expectations will give you a *major edge* over the vast majority of options traders who have no conception of how this critical factor affects their probability of success. With this foundation in expectational analysis, let us next examine in detail how to select the right underlying stock for your options trades, which is the most important factor in profitable options trading.

2

Selecting the Right Stock

INTRODUCTION

Mark Twain wrote in 1888, "The difference between the *almost*-right word and the right word is really a large matter—it's the difference between the lightning bug and the lightning." Twain's idea of rightness certainly applies to trading stocks and options. Choosing the right stock to support an option strategy *can* create lightning in generating profits, and choosing the wrong stock too often can eliminate the trader from the options game.

Your success as an options trader hinges first on your ability to select the right underlying stock. You need to be able to determine a stock's personality and then pair it with an appropriate options strategy. A stock's personality includes the long-term direction of the stock, whether the stock is trending or in a trading range, how the stock is viewed by the investment community at large, and the expectations surrounding the stock that create high (or low) reward potential relative to risk. This chapter presents useful indicators for selecting the right stock so you can then tailor an appropriate options strategy relative to the timing and magnitude of that stock's anticipated move.

DIRECTIONAL TRADING

As a directional trader, you want to create your option strategy based on a realistic assessment of the underlying stock's expected value at a certain point in the future. Many scoff at efforts to time the market or individual stocks. But my experience suggests that there are significant opportunities to profit from market inefficiencies, as long as you know where to look. Having followed the standardized options markets since their inception, I believe that although it is a big challenge to predict future stock prices, the rewards in the options market for the successful directional trader are well worth the effort.

TRENDS VERSUS TRADING RANGES

There is money to be made in both trends and trading ranges, but trending phases offer far greater profit potential for the options trader. In a trading range, a stock will trade up to a previous high or down to a previous low, but will not move outside of this range. On the other hand, trends are not constricted by previous highs or lows. In fact, an uptrend is defined by a series of higher highs, and a down-trend is typically in place as a stock makes a lower low vis-à-vis a pre-vious significant low. Whereas the best "buy" signals are generated during oversold periods within a bull market, an uptrend can fix less than optimal buy signals made in temporarily overbought periods, because consolidations after advances tend to be resolved to the up-side. As an options buyer, you need a directional trend's favorable bias to help you overcome the *time decay* (discussed in chapter 3) that eats into the option's value with each passing day.

Coca-Cola (KO) is an excellent example of a steadily uptrending stock. Each run higher in KO shares since the mid-1994 lows has been worked off with a consolidation, followed by a run to even higher share prices. Exhibit 2.1 shows a 100-day moving average, which has

---

Exhibit 2.1   **COCA-COLA (KO) WEEKLY CHART, 1994–1997, SHOWING CONSOLIDATIONS AND UPTREND**

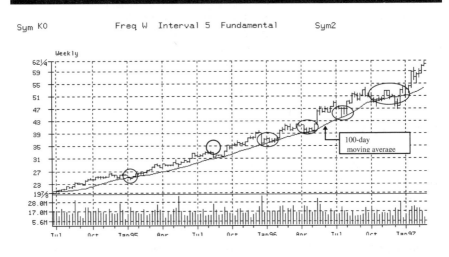

Reprinted with permission. Compliments of ILX Systems.

contained these consolidations and has generally marked excellent buying points (see circles) within the uptrend. A simple moving average is a series of data points calculated by averaging a specific number (here 100) of a security's most recent closing prices.

In contrast to the Coca-Cola example, Home Depot (HD) made no net progress over the same period, despite one brief run early in 1996. The nature of stocks stuck in trading ranges is such that direction will be more difficult to predict, due to the more random nature of the price action in such nontrending situations. Also, profit potential will usually be less in a trading range than in a trending situation, even if by chance you should catch the trading range stock at its lows.

For example, if you happened to have picked the week of the low in HD (October 27, 1995; see exhibit 2.2), purchased a 1997 January 40 call with the stock at $36\frac{7}{8}$ and closed it on the expiration date on January 17, 1997, with the stock at $50\frac{7}{8}$, you made a 38 percent profit on the stock and 146 percent on the HD option. But if you purchased the KO 1997 January 40 call with the stock at $35\frac{13}{16}$ (split adjusted) on that same date and sold on January 17, 1997, with KO shares at $58\frac{3}{4}$, you made an even greater profit of 64 percent on the stock and 322 percent on the KO option. So even in the unlikely event that you magically buy the low on a trading range stock, you are still likely to miss greater opportunities with trending stocks over the same time period.

The best policy is to avoid bullishly oriented option strategies in downtrends, and avoid bearishly oriented option strategies in uptrends. Surprisingly, some options players actually have an emotional need to fight the trend and be heroes by trying to pick a top or bottom, and although such feats are occasionally accomplished, the ma-

Exhibit 2.2   **HOME DEPOT (HD) WEEKLY CHART, JULY 1994–APRIL 1997**

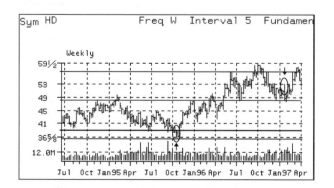

jority of bets against the trend are likely, by definition, to fail. Unfortunately the human psyche is expert at remembering the few instances of correctly predicted long-shot bets against the trend. Remember from chapter 1 that being a contrarian is not about buying cheap stocks in downtrends, but is rather about buying low-expectation stocks that often are in uptrends. For example, throughout the uptrend in Coca-Cola, the stock has been widely derided as overvalued and there has been a strong tendency for put buyers to bet against this trend, thus creating a bullish low-expectation environment that is ideal for the call buyer.

Nowhere is trend-fighting more painful than in options trading. As a stock trader, if you bet against an uptrend by shorting a stock, you can at least hang close to break-even if the stock goes into a consolidation before its next run higher. But a put buyer loses money not only when the underlying stock rises, but also when the security goes flat in a consolidation. This should reinforce the importance of following, predicting, and staying with the trend—or at least not betting against it until evidence materializes regarding a change in its direction.

DIFFERENCES IN TRADING PUTS VERSUS CALLS

The call buyer can ride the slower, steadier trends, given the longer-term upward bias in the market. The put buyer can potentially make more money more quickly on panicky downdrafts, but put traders must be more nimble in getting out fast if the position is not working or if windfall profits occur.

Bearish trades require a completely different methodology to be successful. If you try to establish the same number of bearish positions as bullish positions in the midst of a general market uptrend, your losses on bearish trades will counterbalance your profits on bullish positions.

In a bull market, be prepared for less inspiring results from put trades. Expect to find selected bearish opportunities even in bull markets, but keep in mind that a rising tide lifts all boats. The lesson here is that time stops—whereby you close out an options trade in a preselected number of days—are even more critical on put trades. If the security is not declining relatively quickly after a put position is entered, a quick exit is usually a good idea (see chapter 4 for a further discussion of time stops).

Call positions on stocks leading the market tend to work out best during bull markets, yet these stocks usually incur the heaviest profit-taking on brief market downdrafts. At the same time, these stocks can be dangerous for put buying unless they are clearly breaking down in relative strength versus the broader market.

The chart of Ascend Communications (ASND) shown in exhibit 2.3 provides an example in which the change in relative strength versus the S&P 500 Index (SPX) signaled a short-term change in the trend. Relative strength measures how well a stock is performing in comparison to the market. Clearly, you want to be bullish on stocks that outperform the market, and look for bearish opportunities when a stock underperforms the market. From ASND's lows around 1½ in 1994, the stock moved steadily higher to reach 71¼ by late May 1996. Yet two weeks later, as ASND declined to close at 62¼, it broke below the 10-week moving average of the relative strength line that had held perfectly the entire way up. At the time, I was concerned that ASND's 100-day moving average would still provide support as it had done in earlier situations during the bull run. Yet the relative strength breakdown foreshadowed the breach of the 100-day trendline, and the retest of the 100-day moving average as new resistance proved an excellent put buying opportunity, as ASND shares dropped from the 60 area to just under 40 in only two weeks. The rally back *above* the 10-

Exhibit 2.3   **ASCEND COMMUNICATIONS (ASND) WEEKLY CHART WITH 20-WEEK MOVING AVERAGE AND 10-WEEK RELATIVE STRENGTH VERSUS S&P 500 INDEX, 1992 TO END OF 1996**

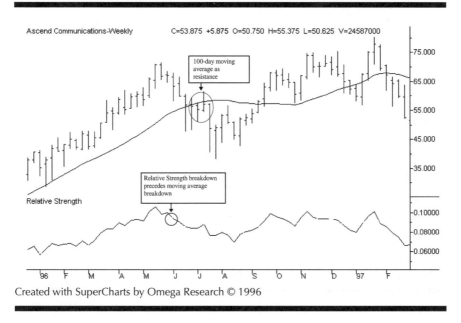

Created with SuperCharts by Omega Research © 1996

week relative strength line in late August 1996 signaled the end of this downtrend.

I prefer not to bet against certain powerful stocks, such as Microsoft (MSFT). As shown in exhibit 2.4, MSFT's breakdowns below its 10-week relative strength line versus the S&P 500 Index have only led to consolidations, not major declines, which is a sign of great strength. If past patterns say a stock does not decline significantly even when relative strength turns down, I won't buy puts. In fact, those are likely to be the best stocks on which to buy calls when relative strength again turns up.

At the other end of the spectrum, stocks that have been big underperformers may not deteriorate in price if the market breaks down, as value hunters will often rotate into these stocks as the higher fliers get hit on profit-taking. For example, on December 21, 1995, I recommended the long-term EMC Corp. January 1998 15 put. EMC shares had declined in 1995 despite a strong stock market, and as shown in exhibit 2.5, they still appeared to be in a relative strength downtrend versus the S&P 500 Index. But in the weeks following my recommen-

---

Exhibit 2.4   **MICROSOFT (MSFT) WEEKLY CHART WITH 20-WEEK MOVING AVERAGE AND 10-WEEK RELATIVE STRENGTH VERSUS S&P 500 INDEX, 1996–MARCH 1997**

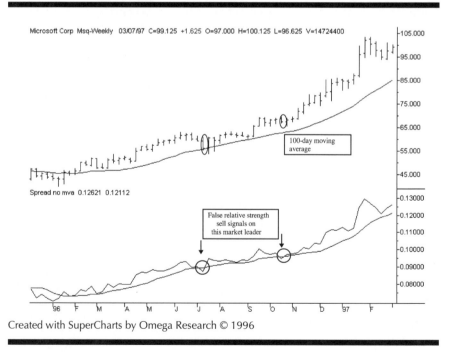

Created with SuperCharts by Omega Research © 1996

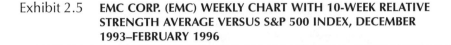

Exhibit 2.5   EMC CORP. (EMC) WEEKLY CHART WITH 10-WEEK RELATIVE
STRENGTH AVERAGE VERSUS S&P 500 INDEX, DECEMBER
1993–FEBRUARY 1996

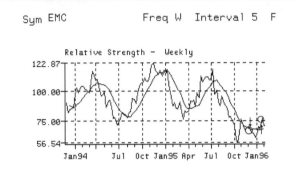

Reprinted with permission. Compliments of ILX Systems.

dation, EMC shares rallied above the 10-week average of this relative strength line, and I closed the position at a 23 percent loss. The lesson from this trade is that lagging stocks can provide traps for put buyers who enter too late in the underperformance cycle.

The optimal put buying candidates are stocks in the middle of this relative strength spectrum that have incurred a fresh breakdown but have not been in an obvious downtrend. You get the benefit of these midrange stocks moving lower in conjunction with a market break, but you don't get "killed" if the market stays firm for longer than expected. For example, I recommended the March 1997 45 put on Viasoft (VIAS), a "Year 2000" company, on February 18, 1997. The stock had just broken its 10-week relative strength average versus the SPX (see exhibit 2.6). My recommendation benefited from the quick plunge in VIAS shares from 46 to 38 over the next two trading days, and I recommended a quick exit on February 20 for a 78 percent profit on the put option.

A typical newcomer to options may say, "I've used methods to predict direction. I read a bullish cover story on XYZ Corp. and thought surely the stock would go up. So I bought short-term calls. After an initial brief rally, the stock reversed and my call option position was wiped out. I may never trade options again." Don't fall into this typical trap. First, don't trade options in the same direction as the crowd at key turning points (as noted in chapter 1, magazine covers usually mark extremes that signal the end of a price trend). Second, and more important, don't trade options without a defined strategy

Exhibit 2.6   VIASOFT (VIAS) WEEKLY CHART WITH WITH 10-WEEK
RELATIVE STRENGTH AVERAGE VERSUS S&P 500 INDEX,
JANUARY 1996–MARCH 1997

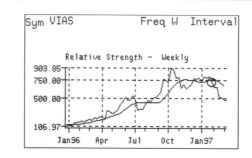

Reprinted with permission. Compliments of ILX Systems.

within a specific time frame—the simple statement "the stock must go up" provides no specific price or time target. Even if it does go up initially, a reversal inevitably will hurt a trader who hasn't defined a specific exit price or closeout date.

Proper trading discipline requires the specific definition of entry and exit parameters, such as: "If in ten trading days, XYZ Corp. shares close below the 50 level they traded at on the day of the cover story, target a 10 percent decline over the next twenty trading days. Buy the two-month on-the-money put to hold for no more than twenty days. Take profits should XYZ trade at 45, with a mental stop to close the put position if XYZ trades at 51½." Of course, you must be sure to test any methodology for its profit potential over time, and then follow winning methods specifically. In this case, you would study the downside potential for stocks over a certain number of days after positive mention in a major financial publication's cover story.

INDICATORS TO PREDICT STOCK MOVEMENTS

Before discussing my favorite indicators, I must again warn you there is no Holy Grail indicator that can be relied upon 100 percent of the time. Why? Because market conditions change, which means that your indicators must be adapted to these changing conditions. The options trader with a flexible portfolio of indicators is far more likely to be successful than the "seat of the pants" trader.

SENTIMENT INDICATORS

Indicators that gauge the expectations of investors are among my favorite measures because this area remains among the least understood and least quantified realms of market analysis. Some of my preferred sentiment indicators are discussed next.

Put/Call Ratios

The put/call ratio (the ratio of the trading volume in puts to the trading volume in calls) is an important sentiment indicator. As a contrarian, my belief is that when too many speculators are bullish (exemplified by a low put/call ratio), the market is poised to fall, or at least consolidate within a bull trend. And just as this "wrong-way" crowd becomes exuberant at market tops, it feels gloomiest at market lows. As demonstrated in exhibit 2.7, when the market was hitting its lows in late 1994, the crowd was reaching a multiyear extreme pessimistic condition, and this high CBOE equity put/call ratio signaled the upcoming powerful 1995–1997 bull market.

I am especially interested in the extreme readings in the put/call ratio, as these tend to be the most reliable indicators. Just as a high put/call ratio indicates speculator pessimism and thus signals significant lows in the market to contrarians, a very low put/call ratio is similarly a bearish omen to contrarians. But note that whenever senti-

Exhibit 2.7   **CBOE EQUITY PUT/CALL RATIO AND S&P 100 INDEX, 1991–1995**

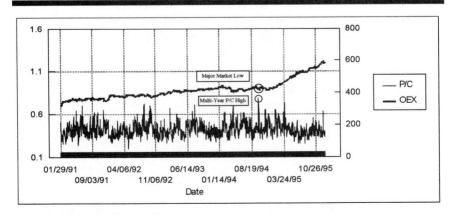

Exhibit 2.8   **CBOE EQUITY PUT/CALL RATIO AND S&P 100 INDEX (OEX), 1996**

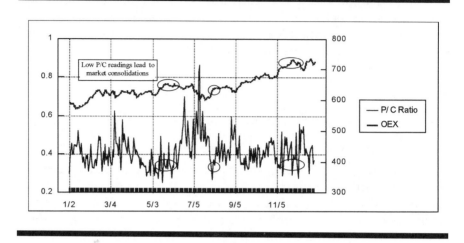

ment became too bullish in 1996, fear quickly re-entered the picture on minor pullbacks. The result, as shown in exhibit 2.8, was a market consolidation within the uptrend during these brief periods of speculator bullishness, readying the market for the next run to new highs. This fear-driven investor psychology is one reason the market has enjoyed such a steady and impressive rally in the 1990s, as markets do not top out until they become driven by greed.

As Humphrey Neill wrote, "The public is right *during* the trends but wrong at both ends!"[1] By identifying extremes in public opinion, put/call ratios offer one of the most valuable tools available today to tell you where the major market turning points are likely to occur. This then allows you to buy calls on more aggressive growth stocks when the market is poised to make a significant run higher, as these stocks benefit the most during rallies. On the other hand, when speculator optimism appears and a "cooling off" period is warranted, this allows you to rotate out of market leaders, which get hit the hardest during market consolidations or pullbacks. Often when I see such higher expectations from the options crowd, I'll either lighten my number of call positions, or moderate my portfolio's call exposure by finding more put positions, to benefit from any short-term decline I might expect.

---

1. Humphrey B. Neill, *The Art of Contrary Thinking* (Caldwell, Idaho: Caxton Printers, 1985), 44.

Implied Volatility

Implied volatility is the option market's assessment of the expected future volatility of the underlying stock. Exhibit 2.9 shows the daily implied volatility of the options on Federal National Mortgage Association (FNM), with the 10-day and 30-day moving averages of FNM's implied volatility. For example, if FNM options have an implied volatility of 35 percent, this suggests that the shares have a two-thirds chance of trading within 35 percent of the current stock price over the course of the next year. The S&P 500 Index has historically tended to have an implied volatility assumption in the area of 12–15 percent, whereas some technology stocks have implied volatilities of more than 50 percent. At-the-money options on technology stocks that are four times more volatile than the market would tend to be priced at approximately four times the price of an option on the index. The higher the volatility assumption, the higher the premium of the op-

Exhibit 2.9   **FEDERAL NATIONAL MORTGAGE (FNM) IMPLIED VOLATILITY "SPIKES" WITH 10-DAY AND 30-DAY MOVING AVERAGES, AUGUST 1996–FEBRUARY 1997**

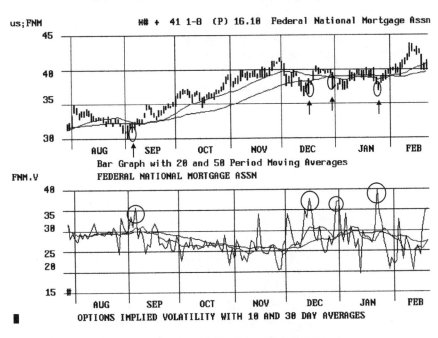

Reprinted with permission. Compliments of Bridge Information Systems.

tion (see chapter 3 for a detailed discussion of volatility and option premiums).

I look at spikes (sudden, sharp increases) in the implied volatility reading to anticipate large moves in the stock. In the case of FNM's options, a spike in the implied volatility assumption above 35 percent was followed by a significant rally in the stock in three of the four instances in exhibit 2.9 (see circles).

Spikes in implied volatility in the 1990s typically occur as a stock is plunging. Option premiums skyrocket as the demand for puts by fearful investors reaches climactic levels. By contrast, at tops, implied volatility tends to be low, as complacency sets in and few expect a decline. This ultimately suggests a pullback as buying power evaporates. Note that if fear and greed were equally balanced, you would expect "greed spikes" in implied volatility as a stock rallies to new highs and greedy call buyers bid up option premiums. But this has been very uncommon in the 1990s, with the exception of rumored takeover stocks. As a contrarian, I have interpreted this lack of greed-driven extremes bullishly, as stocks and markets do not top out without a preponderance of greed-driven behavior.

Option Volume and Open Interest

To predict short-term price movements in stocks, one of my favorite indicators is derived from equity option volume and corresponding open interest adjustments. One of the most overlooked areas in options analysis is the call and put open interest changes that result from the more widely watched option volume figures. Open interest is the most accurate measure of cumulative demand for an option and can be very helpful in predicting future stock direction.

Volume can be defined as the number of option contracts that trade on a particular day or in any time period. Option volume provides an easy "snapshot" of the activity in an option, but it is not as "clean" an indicator of demand as open interest.

Open interest is the number of outstanding contracts on a particular option class or series. What can cause open interest to change? Open interest will increase by one contract when a buyer is entering a new long position and the seller is entering a new short position. When a buyer is entering a new long position but the seller is simultaneously closing an old long position, open interest remains the same. Open interest also remains the same when the seller is establishing a new short position but the buyer is closing an old short position at the same time. Finally, if the buyer is closing an old short position and the seller is closing an old long position, open interest will drop by one contract.

An awareness of unusual option activity in a stock can give you a significant edge in the prediction of the stock's short-term direction. Very profitable opportunities can be uncovered by observing what inexperienced option traders frequently do and then fading (trading against) their activity. For instance, the small speculator who purchases a few cheap out-of-the-money options tends to be wrong with great regularity. This trader often reacts to widely published news stories and inevitably jumps on the trend too late. When these small speculators are in agreement en masse, they generally send a powerful contrarian signal.

In April 1996, big rallies were taking place in U.S. Robotics (USRX) and Iomega (IOM) shares. These strong upmoves were accompanied by significant skepticism as put speculators attempting to pick a top were very active relative to call speculators (see exhibits 2.10 and 2.11). Note how the options' open interest configuration changed dramatically on these stocks as they surged higher over time. Then option players finally caught on to the upward trend and started buying calls in large quantities. By mid-June 1996, call open interest quickly rose, and the put/call open interest ratios plunged in a very short time. Such an enormous shift from bearish to bullish sentiment by the crowd that was wrong all the way up was a strong sign of a top in the shares.

Exhibit 2.10 U.S. ROBOTICS (USRX) WEEKLY CHART AND PUT/CALL OPEN INTEREST

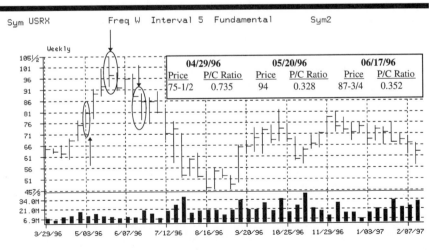

Reprinted with permission. Compliments of ILX Systems.

Exhibit 2.11   **IOMEGA (IOM) WEEKLY CHART AND PUT/CALL OPEN INTEREST**

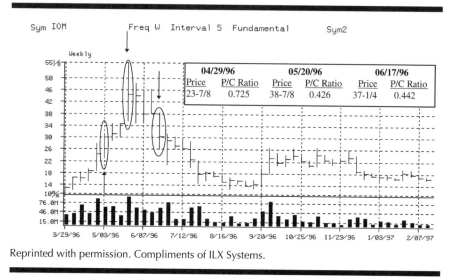

Reprinted with permission. Compliments of ILX Systems.

In both cases, the stocks that had rallied so quickly on the way up fell just as swiftly on the way down. And the common denominator in each case was that the small option speculator was on the wrong side of the market both on the way up and on the way down.

Was it an aberration that option market activity correctly predicted the rally and subsequent sell-off on these high-flying technology names? Hardly. During the same April–June 1996 period, when option speculators were attempting to fade the strength in these momentum stocks, these "wrong-way Corrigans" were also enamored of the potential luster of gold stocks. In fact, exhibit 2.12 shows how put activity was dwarfed by call activity on major gold stocks such as Barrick Gold, Homestake Mining, and Placer Dome, which are important components of the Philadelphia Exchange's Gold & Silver Index (XAU). The put/call open interest ratios for the options on gold futures were also at very low levels. Such speculator optimism in the face of gold's poor price action was a strong contrarian bearish signal. Exhibit 2.12 shows that option players were again caught on the wrong side of the market as gold plummeted.

Excessive option speculation on one side of the market often marks classic turning points for individual stocks. Perhaps the most memorable example is provided by Micron Technology (MU). Micron's 1995 surge, which took the shares from 25 to 92¾ in thirty-two weeks (see exhibit 2.13), was accompanied by consistently heavy put activity by skeptical option players. However, this herd mentality

Exhibit 2.12   **PHILADELPHIA EXCHANGE GOLD & SILVER INDEX (XAU)
WEEKLY CHART AND PUT/CALL OPEN INTEREST**

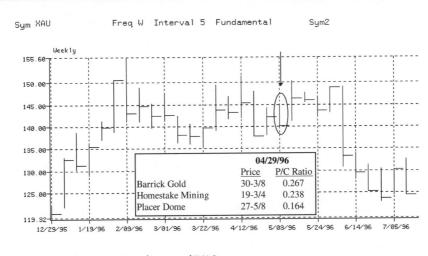

04/29/96		
	Price	P/C Ratio
Barrick Gold	30-3/8	0.267
Homestake Mining	19-3/4	0.238
Placer Dome	27-5/8	0.164

Reprinted with permission. Compliments of ILX Systems.

shifted dramatically in late September 1995. Just before Micron's quarterly earnings release, put activity dried up and call activity surged as option speculators finally capitulated and switched to a bullish posture. And despite Micron's poor reaction to "strong" earnings, the call accumulation continued, thereby giving the classic contrarian "sell" signal. Just as option speculators wrongly purchased puts during Micron's explosive rally, they wrongly accumulated calls throughout most of its decline. The stock that had looked expensive to option players on the way up now looked cheap on the way down, and tens of thousands of call positions were incinerated throughout the 1996 decline.

Delta Hedging

Often, there is a buildup of call open interest at a key strike price that is significantly out-of-the-money on a stock or index. Those who sell these calls run the risk that a rally in the underlying stock will result in significant losses, and they often hedge this risk by buying shares in the stock. But of these far-out strike prices, call sellers have little incentive to hedge their risk (which costs money), as the small amount that these "low-delta" options will move relative to the movement in the underlying stock does not pose significant risk (see chapter 3 for a discussion of option delta). However, as the stock or index starts

Exhibit 2.13   **MICRON TECHNOLOGY (MU) WEEKLY CHART, DECEMBER 1994–JANUARY 1997**

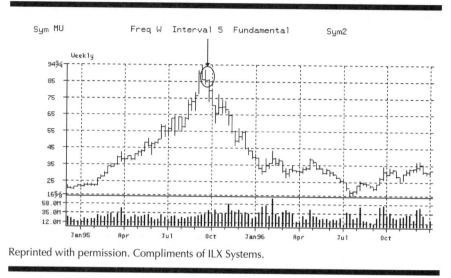

Reprinted with permission. Compliments of ILX Systems.

moving toward the strike, the call sellers need to buy the stock or index in increasing quantities to hedge the risk and remain "delta neutral," as their negative delta increases due to the increasing possibility of these options moving into-the-money. Such a process of hedging more of the underlying as it moves closer to the money is known as *delta hedging*.

It is also important to understand what happens when the strike is reached. At that point, the call sellers will likely be hedged, and they will have plenty of incentive to sell the stock, index, or futures to keep the options they sold from finishing in-the-money. This often creates downward pressure on the stock or index. Thus, artificial buying on the way up is converted to increased selling pressure once the strike is reached. Consequently, a heavy out-of-the-money call buildup can be bullish in the short term, yet bearish in the longer term. For example, call open interest at the February 1997 35 strike on ESS Technology (ESST) climbed from 348 contracts on January 10, 1997, to 1,654 contracts on February 5, 1997. During this time period, as shown in exhibit 2.14, the shares experienced an impressive rally from the 30 area, only to be turned back on two separate occasions around the 35 strike, where call accumulation was steadily building. The 35 level marked an important short-term peak, as the shares plunged from this point over the ensuing three weeks. But if the strike with big call open interest is significantly penetrated due to

Exhibit 2.14 **ESS TECHNOLOGY (ESST) DAILY CHART WITH CALL RESISTANCE, DECEMBER 3, 1996–FEBRUARY 21, 1997**

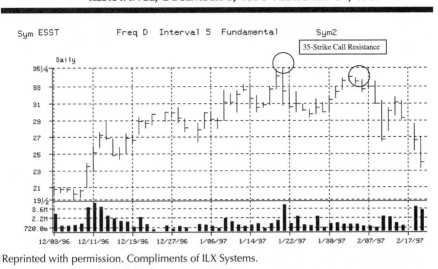

Reprinted with permission. Compliments of ILX Systems.

continued heavy demand for the stock, the delta hedging process will result in further upside impetus as call option sellers scramble to buy even more stock.

This same principle also applies to a large buildup of put open interest on a stock or index. Artificial selling of shares by delta hedgers who are short puts can push the stock or index down to the strike, but often there will be support that emerges at that level. Just as in the case of calls, if a stock or index plunges below the strike with a buildup of put open interest, the stock or index can cascade downward as the remaining unhedged put sellers rush to short the stock. So it pays to be cautious: never assume in advance that an option strike is "impenetrable." It's better to wait for each day's close to see whether the bulls or bears win the battle around the key strike prices, and then take action once the winning side is more clear.

The price action of Coca-Cola (KO) in January 1997 serves as an excellent example of the dynamics of the hedging process. On January 16, KO surged through resistance at the 55 strike, where call open interest of 6,627 contracts outweighed put open interest of 2,553 contracts in the February series. As shown in exhibit 2.15, the shares moved straight up to the 60 area with the help of unhedged call sellers rushing to buy KO stock. Put demand at the 55 strike suddenly materialized, and put open interest at the February 55 strike had climbed to 10,980 contracts by January 28. The surge in put open in-

Exhibit 2.15   **COCA-COLA (KO) DAILY CHART WITH PUT SUPPORT, DECEMBER 6, 1996–FEBRUARY 19, 1997**

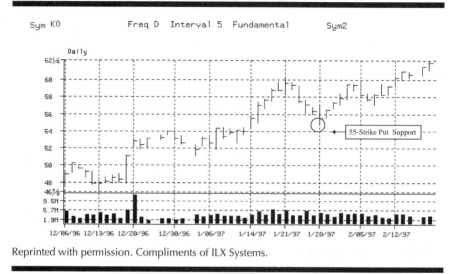

Reprinted with permission. Compliments of ILX Systems.

terest and the resulting increase in hedged short positions contributed to a brief decline, but this downturn came to a halt at the 55 strike, as those traders with heavy unhedged short put positions were incentivized to keep KO above 55.

The pricing of options can also give valuable clues for predicting the future direction of a stock or index. Spikes in an option's implied volatility often precede major moves in the underlying stock and also tend to mark a price bottom. While options that are near-the-money are linked in their pricing by put/call parity (which states that these calls and puts must be appropriately priced or arbitrageurs will create a risk-free profit and thus cause these options to become fairly priced), out-of-the-money calls and puts can be priced at very different volatility levels that can often provide clues on the future direction of the stock.

Frequently, when a stock is plunging (or is expected to plunge), there is a tendency for puts to be priced much more aggressively than calls as option traders rush for protection or speculate on further downside moves. Consequently, as speculators purchase puts in large quantities, the pricing of these puts tends to become richer due to the increased demand.

For example, on July 12, 1996, ValuJet Airlines was at 10⅛ (see exhibit 2.16), and the September 5 strike put on ValuJet shares was trading for about the same premium as the September 15-strike call. Put

Exhibit 2.16   **VALUJET (VJET) WEEKLY CHART, DECEMBER 29, 1995–
OCTOBER 3, 1996**

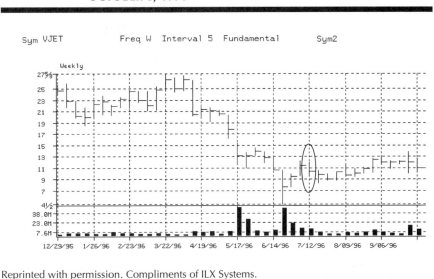

Reprinted with permission. Compliments of ILX Systems.

traders were assuming that ValuJet shares could as easily be zero as 20 by the September expiration. And option traders were giving little weight to the fact that it was theoretically possible for a 15-strike call to trade, say, at 10, if the shares rallied to 25, while the 5-strike put could never be worth more than 5. More technically, the put was trading at an implied volatility of 180 percent, while the upside volatility for ValuJet assumed by call traders was at 90 percent (see chapter 3 for a discussion of implied volatility). This large disparity between the implied volatilities of out-of-the-money puts and calls often develops on a stock that is heavily shorted. In such a case, floor participants can encounter difficulty borrowing the needed shares to short the stock to properly hedge their positions. While the short sellers and put players may well be correct in some cases, the irrational extremes to which they sometimes carry their convictions usually make a strong argument for a bullish scenario emanating from such climactic negative sentiment.

Such heavy demand for puts is often bullish for several reasons. From a contrarian perspective, when option speculators share a view en masse, they tend to be wrong. As a result, floor traders often are happy to sell puts to eager bears driven by crowd psychology. But always keep in mind that floor traders don't like to take risks. So if they are selling puts to the public, the floor traders are essentially long the stock. The floor traders must hedge their positions against the possibility of a weakening in the underlying stock price, which would cause the puts they are short to move into-the-money. To hedge their short put positions floor traders may short the underlying shares. If the underlying security is an index, they will often sell a basket of stocks or short the futures. This activity creates "synthetic" selling pressure—analogous to a compressed spring—when this selling reaches a climax, the unwinding (or short covering) can be quite explosive and lead to huge rallies.

Cover Stories

As discussed at length in chapter 1, media cover stories are a major component of measuring extremes in sentiment that can be very effective contrary indicators. Because magazines are in the business of maximizing sales, the hot trends and topics of the day tend to become the cover stories of major national publications. Major business publications can give excellent contrarian signals that a trend has been fully priced into a stock's valuation simply because the cover story is published. Note that many investors have difficulty following sentiment indicators in general, and magazine covers in particular, because they are concerned that such indicators are too subjective. But a respected colleague, Paul Macrae Montgomery of Legg Mason, has performed quantitative research on magazine covers. He found that in the month after the cover story, the stock could be expected to move in the direction of the story as the last of the public jumps aboard. But one year after the magazine-cover story, 80 percent of the stocks were trading at a price level opposite the cover story's anticipated direction.

For example, the summer of 1995 saw most of the financial press picking up on the technology stock craze of the first seven months of 1995. The volatile Philadelphia Exchange Semiconductor Index (SOX) had gained more than 100 percent over this period (see exhibit 2.17), at which point everyone was abuzz about the potential for Microsoft's new Windows 95 product and the perceived benefits that would ripple throughout the technology sector. At this point, a number of enthusiastic cover stories emerged to "explain" this rally and the technology sector's future upside potential. There were no fewer than three national magazines with optimistic cover stories regarding the promising future of technology stocks. As you can see from the time period over which these cover stories appeared, the uptrend was already ending and the top was forming, and the SOX promptly dropped by 40 percent in just four months.

Exhibit 2.17   **PHILADELPHIA EXCHANGE SEMICONDUCTOR INDEX**
WEEKLY CHART, JANUARY 1995–APRIL 1996

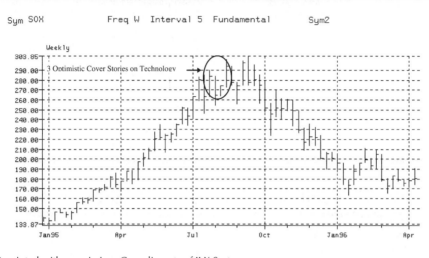

Reprinted with permission. Compliments of ILX Systems.

Sector Mutual Fund Assets

Because of the leverage that industry-specific investments offer compared to general equity funds, sector funds attract a lot of "hot
money"—investors are looking to make a quick buck by switching
into and out of hot sectors. What typically happens, however, is that
the sector players are too reactive. They invest in quantity in the hot
sector only *after* it has run up sharply and the move has been well
publicized. In early 1992, for example, Fidelity sector players piled
into the Fidelity Select Biotechnology fund just as the biotechnology
stocks were near a major peak (see exhibit 2.18). Assets in biotech and
health-related funds reached more than half of all sector assets combined, a historic extreme. In contrast, the automotive sector was out of
favor (see exhibit 2.19). The Fidelity Select Automotive fund held just
$1.5 *million* in assets versus Fidelity Select Biotechnology's $1.2 *billion*
in assets as 1992 began. In other words, sector fund players were almost 1,000 times more bullish on biotechs than they were on autos.
The performance of these two funds over the next twelve months was
dramatically different in a true contrarian sense, despite a moderately
positive broad market in 1992. The auto sector soared 35 percent,
while biotechs fell 20 percent. You can track these asset flows each
month in Fidelity's *Mutual Fund Guide*, which lists the total assets and
top holdings of each Fidelity sector fund.

Exhibit 2.18   **FIDELITY SELECT BIOTECHNOLOGY FUND (FBIOX)**

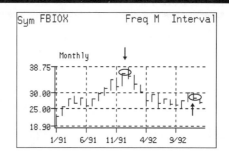

Reprinted with permission. Compliments of ILX Systems.

Exhibit 2.19   **FIDELITY SELECT AUTOMOTIVE FUND (FASVX)**

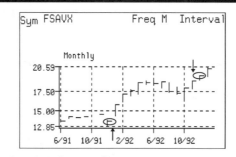

Reprinted with permission. Compliments of ILX Systems.

Sentiment Surveys

Surveys of the bullishness or bearishness of traders, investors, and advisors as a whole make for excellent contrarian readings at extremes. Excessive bullishness means most of the buying has already occurred, so the risk of a negative surprise is heightened. Conversely, if there is pervasive bearishness reflected in these surveys, even bad news will not have much negative impact because most of the selling has already occurred in advance of the news. I monitor three major sentiment polls, published by Investor's Intelligence, Consensus Index of Bullish Market Opinion, and the American Association of Individual Investors (AAII). Investor's Intelligence measures the percentage of bullish and bearish investment advisors; Consensus measures the percentage of professional brokers and advisors who are bullish on the stock indices; and AAII polls individual investors to gauge

Exhibit 2.20   **DOW JONES INDUSTRIAL AVERAGE (DJIA) VERSUS COMPOSITE 5-WEEK BULLISH SENTIMENT**

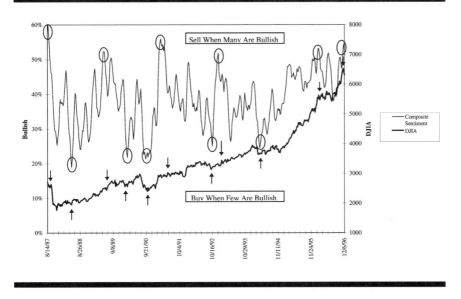

whether they are bullish, bearish, or neutral. We can combine these measures to get a composite reading of the bullish sentiment existing in the market at any point in time. Exhibit 2.20 shows that a composite percentage of bulls above 50 percent is usually a sign that the market is near a short-term peak, whereas a composite percentage of bulls below 25 percent suggests that expectations are unduly low, and the market is near a major bottom.

All three of these polls are available each week in *Barron's*, and *Investor's Business Daily* updates the latest Investor's Intelligence poll each week.

Chapter 5 presents additional sentiment-based indicators to help define the expectational backdrop that can position you for increased effectiveness in predicting major market turns.

TECHNICAL INDICATORS

The technical measures I follow can be classified into two categories: trending and trading range indicators. My focus is primarily on identifying trends, including changes in the overall trend as well as trend continuation signals. Some trading range indicators can be useful as well, although there are some pitfalls to the range-oriented oscillators.

Moving Averages

Moving averages are probably the most widely used technical indicator I follow. Not only do they graphically demonstrate the trend of the security, but they also tend to act as support and resistance levels. These moving average data points create a smoothed representation of a stock's performance trend. It is important when smoothing data to have a moving average period long enough that is doesn't create whipsaw signals, but not so long that it is unresponsive to important changes in trend.

As shown in exhibit 2.21, shares of Eli Lilly (LLY) were in a steady, pronounced uptrend after breaking out above a month-long trading range in early September 1996. The vertical bars show the daily high, low, and close of LLY's share price. The upsloping line under the bars is the 20-day moving average (measuring the average closing price over the last twenty trading sessions). From early September to the end of November, each time the shares pulled back to this 20-day moving average, the decline stopped there. This average thus becomes a support level, and in this case the support level held extremely well. As a result, I would classify LLY as a trending stock, and future pullbacks to this proven support would be likely (although not guaranteed) to provide good risk/reward buying opportunities.

Notice, however, that the more times a moving average is tested, the less likely it is to hold as support, as was the case with LLY in

---

Exhibit 2.21 **ELI LILLY (LLY) DAILY CHART, WITH 20-DAY MOVING AVERAGE, AUGUST 5, 1996–DECEMBER 15, 1996**

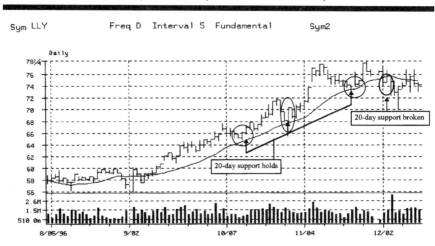

Reprinted with permission. Compliments of ILX Systems.

early December 1996. As this trend becomes common knowledge on Wall Street, the buying power that emerged in previous pullbacks eventually evaporates.

I examine monthly, weekly, daily, and intraday charts with moving averages, and I tend to focus on the 10-unit and 20-unit simple moving average on each chart. You should probably start with a longer-term moving average for your general assessment of price trends and then work your way back to the short-term moving averages to fine-tune your entry and exit parameters on situations that look attractive to you. As an options trader, you must use appropriate moving averages to match the anticipated holding period for your position. If you use a moving average that is relatively slow in responding to changes in daily price action, you will often respond too slowly to changing price trends. Moving averages that are too fast can create too many whipsaw signals. You want to find moving averages that allow you to ride a trend but also accurately signal when to exit a trend that is ending.

Many practitioners will use a moving average crossover system to define buy and sell signals in a trending stock or index. In this type of model, moving averages of different durations are used to generate signals. For instance, when the shorter-term (faster) of the two moving averages crosses above the longer-term (slower) moving average, this is a buy signal. Likewise, when the shorter-term moving average crosses below the longer-term moving average, a sell signal is given. The chart of the Philadelphia Exchange Semiconductor Index (SOX) in exhibit 2.22 shows that moving average crossover signals can be quite powerful and profitable in a trending series (although here, too, we still can see a few whipsaw sell signals). This particular method employs an exponential 5-day/20-day moving average crossover system. Technicians will often use exponential moving averages because they assign a greater weight to the most recent price action, and exponentials consider all the data over time, albeit with diminishing weightings, rather than data for only a finite time period.

Standard Deviation Bands

The standard deviation (SDV) bands on Dell Computer (DELL) shown in exhibit 2.23 provide an excellent example of how I use this technical indicator. Standard deviation bands provide an overbought/oversold indicator based solely on the stock's price action. By drawing a "best-fit" line (line A in exhibit 2.24) through the last 150 trading days, and then applying an upper and lower boundary two standard deviations around this best-fit midpoint, we create a band

Exhibit 2.22   **PHILADELPHIA EXCHANGE SEMICONDUCTOR INDEX DAILY CHART, APRIL 1996–FEBRUARY, 1997**

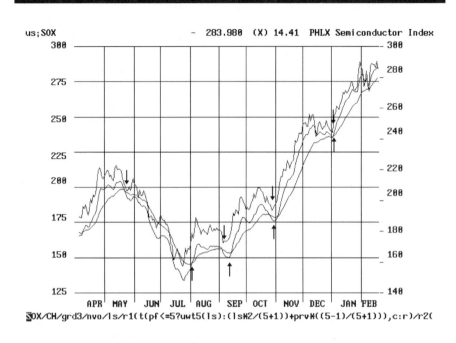

Reprinted with permission. Compliments of Bridge Information Systems.

that contains approximately 95 percent of the stock's price action. As a result, prices near the low end of the SDV band should offer a buying opportunity, whereas traders should consider selling near the top of the SDV bands. In this example, DELL had been trading in the range indicated by line B, and the SDV bands were reliable in containing DELL's rallies and pullbacks. Note the first test of the low end of the SDV bands in late October 1996 at the 50-day moving average (shown as line C, the upsloping trendline near the low end of DELL's SDV bands). During DELL's uptrend, you can see how important lows and highs were marked by the lower and upper extreme of the SDV bands. As with all technical indicators, there are no guarantees—only historical trends and statistical probability—that an indicator will correctly anticipate the future movement of a security.

Regression Channels

The regression channel indicator helps determine a developing trend. A regression channel is formed by drawing a best-fit regression line

Exhibit 2.23   **DELL COMPUTER (DELL) STANDARD DEVIATION BANDS**

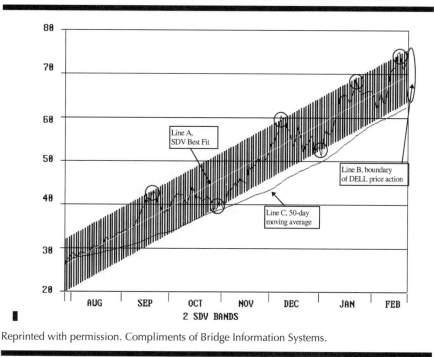

Reprinted with permission. Compliments of Bridge Information Systems.

from an important low to an important high. This approach differs from standard deviation bands in that SDV bands fit a fixed period of days to mark a trend, whereas a regression line is drawn from important highs and lows regardless of the time element. To develop a regression channel, once you have established your regression line (shown as 1R and 2R for two different regression lines in exhibit 2.24), draw parallel channel lines to fit the major highs (lines 1H and 2H) and lows (lines 1L and 2L). Since trending stocks provide the greatest opportunities for winning option trades, this channel is a key indicator. As you can see in the regression channel for Global Marine (GLM, exhibit 2.24), the trend is indeed telling. Many different indicators appear in this one technical picture. Primarily, the high end of a regression channel tends to act as a resistance level, much like a moving average. Similarly, the lower end of the channel acts as support. The first regression channel's high boundary (1H) for GLM provided strong resistance for the shares until the stock finally broke through this level in March 1996. Such a breakthrough is technically significant and provides a bullish entry point for trades, betting on an acceleration of the trend. As you can see from regression channel 2, GLM shares then embarked on a steeper uptrend. The middle line within the channel

Exhibit 2.24   **GLOBAL MARINE (GLM) REGRESSION CHANNELS**

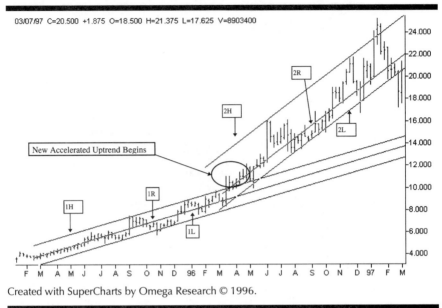

03/07/97 C=20.500 +1.875 O=18.500 H=21.375 L=17.625 V=8903400

Created with SuperCharts by Omega Research © 1996.

also acts as a median, providing a central point to see whether the stock tends to gravitate more toward the lower or the upper end of the channel. Finally, the channel offers a clear picture of the overall trend of the shares, in other words, whether they are in a general uptrend or downtrend, or in a consolidation. This regression channel snapshot provides an excellent method to decipher the direction of a trending stock, as well as the risk/reward ratio, which depends on the stock's location within the channel. Chapter 7 covers regression channel analysis in detail.

Relative Strength Versus the Market

Exhibit 2.25 shows the weekly performance of Merrill Lynch (MER) (top chart) and the performance of MER compared to the S&P 500 Index (SPX) (bottom chart). The traditional focus of the relative strength indicator is a comparison of a stock to an underlying index such as the S&P 500, creating a single line showing relative performance. My preference is to smooth the often jagged points in this relative line in the form of a moving average. By adding a 10-week (heavy line) and 20-week (light line) average of this weekly relative strength line, I can better measure the relative trend. Note the buy (and sell) points when the 10-week relative performance crosses over (and under) the 20-week line, indicated by the arrows on the top chart. A buy signal in

Exhibit 2.25   **MERRILL LYNCH WEEKLY CHART: RELATIVE STRENGTH VERSUS S&P 500 INDEX**

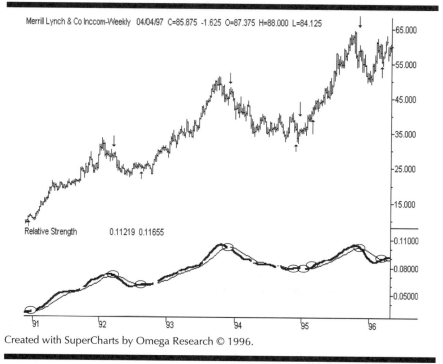

Merrill Lynch & Co Inccom-Weekly 04/04/97 C=85.875 -1.625 O=87.375 H=88.000 L=84.125

Created with SuperCharts by Omega Research © 1996.

December 1990 led to a doubling in MER shares in only three months and a tripling by January 1992. The bearish cross of the 10-week under the 20-week line in April 1992 forecast a consolidation before the next buy signal in August 1992, which led to a doubling in MER shares over the next thirteen months. The December 1993 bearish cross led to a 25 percent decline in MER shares over the next ten months. After a brief fakeout buy signal near the market lows in late 1994, the March 1995 bullish cross provided about a 50 percent gain before the November 1995 bearish cross occurred. After the subsequent consolidation, the March 1996 bullish cross had resulted in a more than 50 percent gain in MER by February 1997.

Support and resistance levels also work well on relative strength charts, as higher highs and higher lows define an uptrend, whereas the break to a new short-term low versus the prior low on the relative strength chart signals potential problems for a stock. For example, using the Merrill Lynch monthly chart versus the S&P 500 Index shown in exhibit 2.26, we start in 1982 at an index of 100. A reading of 200 means MER has performed twice as well as the SPX, and a reading of

Exhibit 2.26   **MERRILL LYNCH MONTHLY CHART: RELATIVE STRENGTH VERSUS S&P 500 INDEX, 1982–1997**

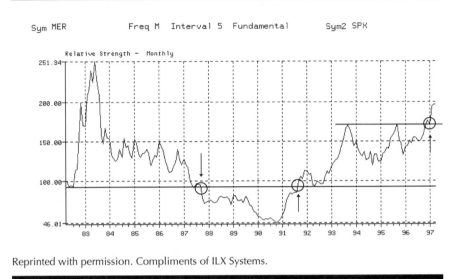

Reprinted with permission. Compliments of ILX Systems.

50 means MER has performed at only half the rate of the SPX. What you can see in exhibit 2.26 is the importance of certain relative performance levels. In this case, just under the 100 base level was key, as the break below this support line in mid-1987 forecast several poor years to come for MER shares (as well as an indication that all was not right with the market before the October 1987 crash). Likewise, when MER shares broke out above the 100 area in relative strength in late 1991 and successfully held this level as support in April 1992, this forecast a new period of outperformance for MER shares. The "double top" that was appearing from the relative highs around the 170 level in late 1993 and 1995 was broken to the upside in late 1996, forecasting another accelerated uptrend in MER shares as well as indicating that the bull market in stocks was not yet near a top.

Oscillators

The behavior of an oscillator is closely related to the concept of the sine wave, similar to that shown in exhibit 2.27. The sine wave moves in regular cycles, and when the wave reaches the low point of the cycle, it then turns up. Likewise, at the high point that equates to prior highs in the cycle, we can expect the wave to turn down.

Technical oscillators measure the movement of a stock's price relative to an assumed cycle of highs and lows. After a rally in a stock, an

Exhibit 2.27 **SINE-TYPE WAVE**

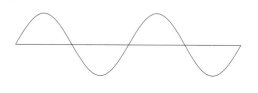

oscillator will signal an overbought condition that implies the stock has reached the top of its cycle and is now turning down. On the other hand, when a stock has declined to a point that an oscillator is classified as oversold, this suggests that buyers will now enter to push the stock off the lows of this cycle.

As traders, we must seek to first identify a potential overbought or oversold condition, but then act only when it is clear that the stock is moving out of that condition. Buying too early into the final leg of a downturn and then having to wait out the turn in the cycle before the wave actually turns up again can be disastrous for options buyers.

Note that the sine wave is a perfect example of a trading range situation, in that the highs and lows each occur at the same level on each subsequent cycle move. However, look at how the sine wave's up and down cycles change when we place the sine wave on a 45-degree upslope, as shown in exhibit 2.28. Note how the rises become more accelerated, and the declines within the wave now become less steep. This paints an accurate picture of the price action that

Exhibit 2.28 **SINE-TYPE WAVE WITH 45-DEGREE UPSLOPE**

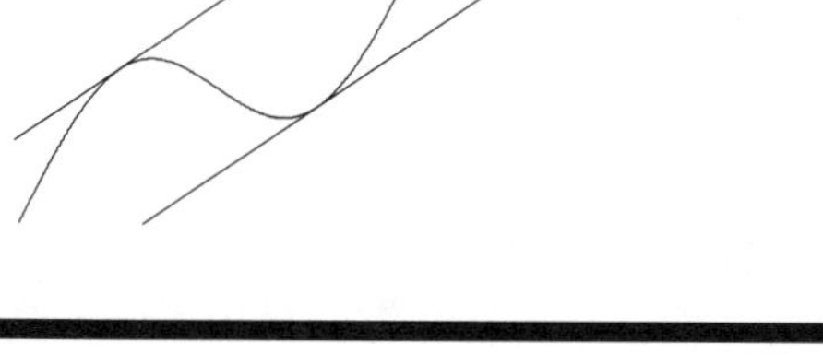

Exhibit 2.29   **SINE-TYPE WAVE WITH 45-DEGREE DOWNSLOPE**

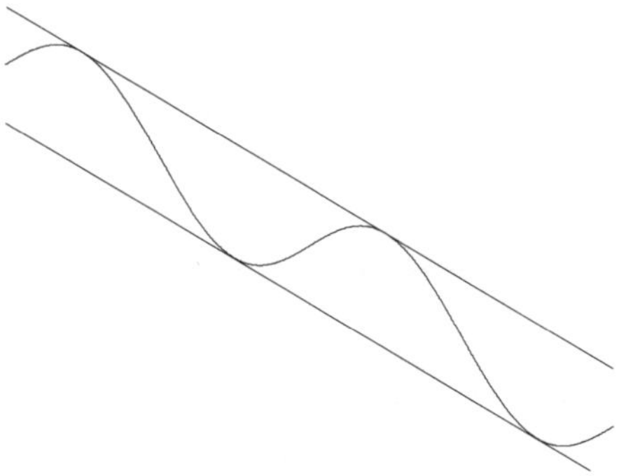

occurs within an uptrend, as rallies are sharp and declines often occur more as sideways consolidations to work off the prior sharp advance. The implication for traders is that to use oscillators effectively, we must first determine the direction and magnitude of the trend. If the trend is up, we only want to use the oversold signals that an oscillator provides as entry points for call positions, because buying puts on the overbought signals will often be a losing battle versus the uptrend.

Similarly, in a downtrend such as the 45-degree downsloped sine wave shown in exhibit 2.29, we want to focus only on buying puts on the overbought signals, which are likely to be successful on the next leg of the downtrend. We do not want to buy calls on the oversold signals in a downtrend, as the rally potential will be minimal relative to the risk of further decline.

With this backdrop on the power of trends to determine which oscillators will be effective, let us examine my favorite oscillators to use within the framework of the trending indicators discussed earlier.

Relative Strength Index

One of the most popular oscillators is Welles Wilder's Relative Strength Index (RSI). This index measures the overbought or oversold nature of a security on a scale from 0 to 100 over a defined past number of trading days.

Relative Strength Index is a deceptive label, and is not to be confused with the relative strength concepts discussed earlier in this chapter; RSI is an oscillator that attempts to determine if the underlying shares are overbought or oversold. As a contrarian, I like to use this oscillator as a sign that a short-term move will soon reverse course, assuming I am not fighting the broader trend. In exhibit 2.30, the 9-day RSI reading on Toys 'R' Us (TOY) is superimposed over the shares' daily chart, providing a perfect example of how this indicator works. The RSI readings above 70 indicate the shares are overbought, and dips below 30 amount to an oversold condition. TOY's most extreme RSI highs occurred in May, August, and November 1996. This means that after a run-up in the shares, the overbought condition now suggested an imminent pullback. As the daily chart shows, the stock experienced short-term declines after such overbought signals, in addition to the longer-term top in November 1996.

The same reasoning applies to oversold readings. An extremely low RSI reading indicates the shares are so oversold that you can soon expect a rally. The most extreme oversold readings for TOY occurred in July and September 1996. The July oversold period took several days to work off the downside momentum, but proved to be near a key turning point. The September oversold reading was more quickly successful as TOY shares had only mildly corrected after a more dramatic rally. Note that RSI buy and sell signals *both* worked for TOY because the stock was not in an uptrend or a downtrend. As exhibit 2.30 shows, TOY shares finished in March 1997 almost exactly where they began in April 1996, showing virtually no net price movement

Exhibit 2.30   TOYS 'R' US (TOY) 9-DAY RELATIVE STRENGTH INDEX

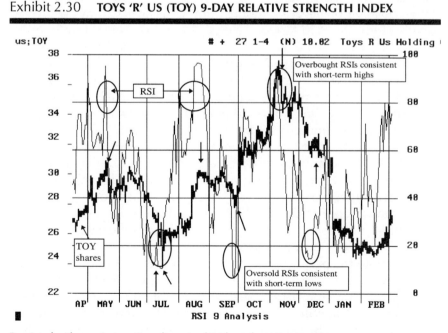

Reprinted with permission. Compliments of Bridge Information Systems.

over this period. One important factor to remember is that uptrends can keep stocks overbought for a long time, and downtrends can prevent oversold stocks from bouncing back. That is why you should monitor trends very closely in relation to RSI analysis. To rely exclusively on oscillators such as RSI during strongly trending markets is a recipe for disaster, as you will be continually buying puts on overbought stocks that continue to rally in a bull market, and buying calls on oversold stocks that continue to decline in a bear market.

Moving Average Convergence Divergence

Gerald Appel developed moving average convergence divergence (MACD). This excellent twist on moving averages measures the difference between a fast exponential moving average and a slow exponential moving average. The MACD traditionally uses a 12-unit fast and 26-unit slow combination. Crossovers of the 12-unit line above the 26-unit line denote buy signals, whereas a 12-unit cross under the 26-unit line is a sell signal. What is exciting about MACD is that it is often a leading indicator of a coming breakout in a stock above or below its key moving averages. The MACD chart (bottom graphs in exhibit 2.31) shows not only the fast 12-unit line (top line on left) and slow 26-unit line (bottom line on left), but also the MACD histogram. The histogram uses a baseline of zero and then plots whether MACD shows positive or negative momentum. Crossovers from positive to negative indicate an MACD sell signal (12-unit crosses below 26-unit), and crosses from below zero to above zero indicate MACD buy signals (12-unit crosses above 26-unit). Note that the oscillator aspect of MACD occurs when the stock has been uptrending and the MACD 12- and 26-unit lines move from positive territory back near the zero point of the histogram. This often indicates an oversold situation, and as soon as the 12-unit crosses back over the 26-unit, I would want to buy, to bet on the next leg of the uptrend then commencing.

Exhibit 2.31 shows these systematized buy and sell signals using MACD on a weekly chart of SunAmerica (SAI) (top graph). Note that when MACD stays on a buy signal for more than four weeks, SAI shares can experience the steady prolonged uptrends, as in 1995 and since mid-1996. Note that in nontrending periods such as early 1996, MACD can give whipsaw signals.

Also note the performance summary of the MACD bullish trades for SAI in table 2.1, created using Omega Research's SuperCharts software. This summary shows MACD to be highly effective for SAI, with 78 percent of bullish trades profitable. The largest closed winner saw a $10 move in SAI shares, and the current open position shows a $16 per-share profit since mid-1996.

Exhibit 2.31 **SUNAMERICA (SAI) WEEKLY CHART WITH MOVING AVERAGE CONVERGENCE DIVERGENCE (MACD)**

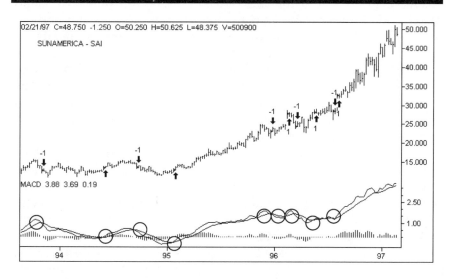

02/21/97 C=48.750 -1.250 O=50.250 H=50.625 L=48.375 V=500900

SUNAMERICA - SAI

MACD 3.88 3.69 0.19

Created with SuperCharts by Omega Research © 1996.

Table 2.1 **SUNAMERICA (SAI) PERFORMANCE SUMMARY WITH MACD SYSTEM**

MACD Sunamerica Inc [3/B]-Weekly 01/05/90 - 02/21/97

Performance Summary: Long Trades

Total net profit	$ 15.67	Open position P/L	$	16.19
Gross profit	$ 19.00	Gross loss	$	-3.33
Total # of trades	9	Percent profitable		78%
Number winning trades	7	Number losing trades		2
Largest winning trade	$ 10.10	Largest losing trade	$	-3.25
Average winning trade	$ 2.71	Average losing trade	$	-1.67
Ratio avg win/avg loss	1.63	Avg trade(win & loss)	$	1.74
Max consec. winners	4	Max consec. losers		1
Avg # bars in winners	23	Avg # bars in losers		6
Max intraday drawdown	$ -5.25			
Profit factor	5.70	Max # contracts held		1
Account size required	$ 5.25	Return on account		298%

Created with SuperCharts by Omega Research © 1996.

FUNDAMENTAL INDICATORS

I have generally found that price-to-earnings (P/E) ratios, dividend yields, and other well-known fundamental indicators are not particularly useful to the options trader. While the fundamentals usually assert themselves over a longer period of time, they are of little use over the short term. However, I do follow one fundamental indicator that is very important for short-term trends: earnings momentum. The magnitude of a stock's quarterly earnings surprise tends to be a short-term catalyst for the stock's performance. The bigger the positive surprise relative to analysts' consensus estimates (assuming a positive market reaction to the news), the more likely a new uptrend will assert itself. Positive market reactions to other fundamental developments can also be very powerful in the short term. These reactions are important because they provide a "driver" for future stock performance—a story that gets investors excited about the stock's future prospects. Additional fundamental drivers are covered in chapter 6.

For example, Medicis Pharmaceutical (MDRX) experienced a technical breakout above the 50 level in January 1997 in conjunction with a much stronger than expected earnings report. The earnings drove the technical price action in the stock, as it surged from 50 to 70. My January 14, 1997, recommendation of the February 1997 50 call at 5⅜ benefited from this quick acceleration in MDRX shares (see exhibit 2.32). I recommended taking profits on half the position when

Exhibit 2.32   **MEDICIS PHARMACEUTICAL (MDRX) DAILY CHART, NOVEMBER 1996–FEBRUARY 1997**

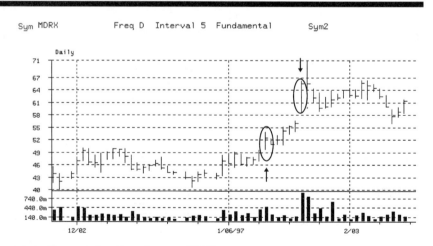

Reprinted with permission. Compliments of ILX Systems.

the stock gapped up on the earnings announcement on January 22. This half position was closed at an average price of $12^{13}/_{16}$ for a 138 percent profit. I sought to ride the other half position for a bigger gain, but when the uptrend failed, I recommended the sale of the remainder of the position at $12^{1}/_{2}$ on the next bounce in MDRX shares, for a 170 percent profit.

THE DANGER OF TOO MANY INDICATORS

As you seek to improve your methods, one of the natural outgrowths is that you create new indicators and then have a decision to make: Do you incorporate these indicators into your existing method, or use them separately? One of the main problems with integrating new ideas into an existing method is that you may end up with a jumble of indicators that give conflicting signals on a stock. This leads to a potential state of confusion—the least desirable position for the trader. It is important to weed out the indicators that duplicate each other or use practically the same method. For example, there are a number of oscillators that tell you if a stock is oversold or overbought. If you have five oscillator indicators, but none of them define the bigger trend within this overbought/oversold condition, you gain no additional perspective.

Another problem is that the trend indicators may be at odds with the oscillator indicators. For example, by the time a stock gives a relative strength buy signal versus the S&P 500 Index, it may have rallied initially to a point where the RSI shows the stock to be in an overbought zone. The best way to determine which indicator may be appropriate is to let price action guide you. If the stock continues to rally from that point, the relative strength signal likely had validity whereas the RSI signal was likely faulty. This is something you see at the beginning of big trends; after a series of whipsaw trades using trending indicators such as relative strength or moving averages, a new buy signal occurs and the stock then quickly moves to an overbought condition. However, it never really corrects and keeps trending. This signals a major trend that you should ride for a broader move.

CONCLUSION

The lesson to be learned from studying indicators is that you must first define the market conditions and then apply the right indicators to the state of the market. If conditions were static, the game would be too easy and everyone would be rich beyond their wildest dreams. The fact that investors seek Holy Grail systems to relieve themselves of the assiduous work that must go into analyzing the markets shows the power of the fantasy of perfect trading. The great traders recognize when they are wrong as well as when they are right. The great traders also develop a trading method that has the flexibility to adjust to changing conditions. They then stick to their plan.

Superimposing sentiment indicators on various technical and fundamental indicators gives the extra edge needed to understand the expectations of market participants. Incorporating such an expectational analysis will allow you a perspective that few enjoy. You will thus avoid many of the "landmine" situations that surprise the crowd, and instead position yourself in the low expectation situations that the crowd has not yet discovered.

Now that we have reviewed the indicators to use to determine the underlying stock's direction, let us look at how to determine which *option* to choose to get the best possible reward relative to the risk incurred.

3

Options Basics:
The Psychology and
Dynamics of Profitable
Options Investing

INTRODUCTION

This chapter first discusses the basic options principles and then moves on to its ultimate goal of helping you to master the psychology and dynamics of profitable options investing. Along the way we explain how you can avoid the pitfalls of the two major misconceptions that entrap most beginning options traders:

1. Options can be traded like stocks.
2. Volatility and directional price movement are synonymous.

OPTIONS BASICS

As discussed in the Preface, a *call* option gives you the right (but not the obligation) to *buy* 100 shares of a stock at a specified price (called the *exercise price* or the *striking price*) until a specified date (called the *expiration date*). Buying call options is a *bullish* strategy initiated when the call buyer believes that the underlying stock will rise substantially in price over the life of the option, with the understanding that any price appreciation in the stock beyond the expiration date of the option is completely irrelevant, as the option will have expired.

The call buyer is essentially renting the price appreciation in the stock over the life of the option, and should the call buyer choose to exercise his contract before it expires and buy the stock at the striking price, he effectively owns the amount by which the price of the stock exceeds the striking price. For example, if you buy a 40-strike call option, the stock is at 45 on expiration day and you exercise your option, the option seller *must* sell you the stock at 40, as he has forfeited any appreciation above 40 by selling you the call option. So you, as the call buyer, own any appreciation in the stock above 40, which in this case was 5 points.

A *put* option gives you the right (but not the obligation) to *sell* 100 shares of a stock at the striking price until the expiration date. Buying put options is a *bearish* strategy that is initiated when the put buyer believes that the underlying stock will decline substantially in price over the life of the option. The put buyer is essentially renting the price decline in the stock over the life of the option, and should the put buyer choose to exercise his contract before it expires by selling the stock at the striking price, he effectively owns the amount by which the striking price exceeds the price of the stock.

CALL OPTIONS PRICING

The price of an option that is listed on one of the four options exchanges is determined by supply and demand in the marketplace. Underlying this *free market price* is a combination of factors that determine the *theoretical price* of that option, and it is rare that the free market price of an option differs markedly from its theoretical price. The theoretical price of an option depends on the following factors:

1. The price of the underlying stock relative to the striking price of the option
2. The amount of time remaining until the option expires
3. The volatility of the underlying stock
4. The level of the risk-free interest rate
5. The dividend paid by the underlying stock

The most important factor in determining the price of an option is the price of the underlying stock relative to the option's striking price. The price of a call option prior to expiration will increase at an accelerating percentage of the increase in the stock price. When the stock price is below the striking price, a call option is said to be *out-of-the-*

money, whereas a call is *on-the-money* when the stock price is equal to the striking price.

A call is *in-the-money* when the stock price exceeds the striking price. In-the-money call options have what is known as *intrinsic value*, which is the amount by which the stock price exceeds the striking price. On-the-money or out-of-the-money options have no intrinsic value, and their entire price consists of what is known as *time premium*. The price of an in-the-money option consists of a combination of intrinsic value and time premium.

Exhibit 3.1 shows the profit and loss characteristics of an on-the-money call option purchased with sixty days until expiration (see dotted line) at various prices for the stock above and below the striking price, as well as the profit and loss characteristics of this same call option at expiration (see solid line). Note from the dotted line that an instant move by the stock well above the striking price results in an accelerated increase in the profit from buying the call option, whereas an instant move by the stock well below the striking price results in an increasingly muted rate of increase in the loss from buying the call. This characteristic of the option profit and loss curve is called convexity, and it relates to the fact that the option buyer benefits more from immediate large moves in the right direction than he loses from immediate large moves in the wrong direction.

Exhibit 3.1   **CALL OPTIONS PROFIT AND LOSS: AT EXPIRATION AND SIXTY-DAYS PRIOR**

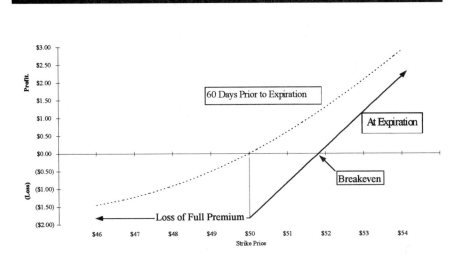

Now let us examine the solid line in exhibit 3.1, which represents the profit and loss profile of the option at expiration. Note that the entire call premium is lost if the stock finishes at or below the striking price, and then the loss is reduced as the stock price increases above the striking price to a level where the intrinsic value of the call equals the initial call premium. At that point the call buyer breaks even, and as the stock increases further in price the call buyer begins to profit. In fact, every additional point of appreciation in the stock price translates directly into a point increase in the call buyer's profit.

The call buyer's profit is theoretically unlimited as the stock moves higher (note the arrow pointing higher at the top of the upsloping solid line), while the call buyer's loss is limited to the initial premium paid for the option no matter how low the stock price finishes at expiration (see the arrow pointing sideways to the left of the flat solid line). This concept is known as *truncated risk,* and it is the expiration day equivalent of the convexity concept previously discussed.

To summarize the call option concepts depicted on exhibit 3.1:

1. Prior to expiration, call options behave in a convex manner. A call will increase in price on a large, instantaneous increase in the stock price at a greater rate than it will decrease in price on an identical decrease in the stock price.

2. At expiration, the call buyer loses his entire investment if the stock finishes at or below the striking price and loses part of his investment if the stock finishes above the striking price but below the point at which the option's intrinsic value equals the premium the buyer paid for the call (which is the break-even level for the call buyer). As the stock price increases beyond this break-even level, the call buyer profits on a point-for-point basis.

3. The risk for the call buyer is truncated, as his maximum loss is limited to the premium he paid for the option, whereas his profit level is theoretically unlimited.

PUT OPTIONS PRICING

The price of a put option depends upon the same five characteristics as were enumerated for a call option, although, as we shall see later, the level of interest rates and dividends has an impact on put prices opposite to that of call prices.

Exhibit 3.2 **PUT OPTIONS PROFIT AND LOSS: AT EXPIRATION AND SIXTY-DAYS PRIOR**

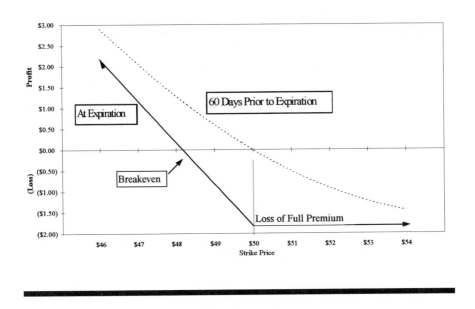

As with a call option, the most important factor in determining the price of a put is the price of the stock relative to the option's striking price. The price of a put option prior to expiration will increase at an accelerating percentage of the decrease in the stock price. When the stock price is *above* the striking price, a put option is said to be *out-of-the-money*, whereas a put is *on-the-money* when the stock price is equal to the striking price.

A put is *in-the-money* when the striking price exceeds the stock price. The *intrinsic value* of a put option is the amount by which the striking price exceeds the stock price.

Exhibit 3.2 for a put option is analogous to exhibit 3.1 for a call option, as it displays the profit and loss characteristics of an on-the-money put option purchased with sixty days until expiration (see dotted line) at various prices of the stock above and below the striking price, as well as the profit and loss characteristics of this same put option at expiration (see solid line).

Note that profits are achieved by the put buyer as the stock declines below the striking price, and losses occur as the stock advances above the striking price.

To summarize the put option concepts depicted on exhibit 3.2:

1. Prior to expiration, put options behave in a convex manner. A put will increase in price on a large, instantaneous decrease in the stock price at a greater rate than it will decrease in price on an identical increase in the stock price.

2. At expiration, the put buyer loses his entire investment if the stock finishes at or above the striking price and loses part of his investment if the stock finishes below the striking price but above the point at which the option's intrinsic value equals the premium the buyer paid for the put (which is the break-even point for the put buyer). As the stock price decreases below this break-even level, the put buyer profits on a point-for-point basis.

3. The risk for the put buyer is truncated, as his maximum loss is limited to the premium he paid for the option, whereas his profit level is theoretically unlimited (but is in reality limited to the difference between the striking price and the initial put premium, as a stock cannot be priced below zero).

TIME AND ITS IMPACT ON OPTIONS PRICING

The above discussion of put and call options pricing gave little consideration to the continuous impact of the passage of time other than to examine the specific profit and loss characteristics at a point prior to option expiration and then at option expiration. As discussed in some detail later in this chapter, *time is the enemy of the options buyer.* The price of an on-the-money or out-of-the-money option will decrease at an accelerating rate as time passes until it expires worthless at expiration. An in-the-money option will deteriorate at a lesser rate, as the passage of time impacts only the time premium portion of its price and has no impact on the option's intrinsic value.

The passage of time can more than offset the advantages of the convexity feature for the options buyer, and truncated risk can become a moot point if an options buyer consistently loses his entire investment because his options fail to finish in-the-money. (Later in this chapter we discuss the steps the options buyer must take to limit the negative impact of the passage of time.)

Exhibit 3.3 graphically illustrates the negative impact of the passage of time on an on-the-money call option purchased sixty days prior to expiration with the stock price held constant throughout this

Exhibit 3.3   TIME DECAY FOR AN ON-THE-MONEY OPTION

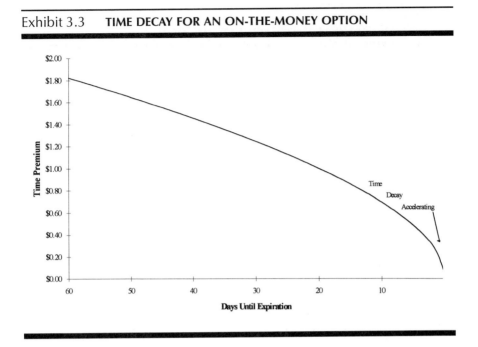

period. Note in particular the accelerating deterioration of the option premium as we move closer to option expiration, until it becomes worthless on expiration day. As you can see, the deterioration as depicted on exhibit 3.3 is not linear as time passes, as it is initially relatively modest and then becomes quite pronounced near expiration. Given a constant stock price, an on-the-money call option deteriorates in proportion to the square root of the amount of time that has elapsed relative to the time remaining until expiration. On-the-money put option premiums deteriorate analogously, but at slightly lesser rates due to the fact that the premium levels for put options tend to be lower than those for call options.

The time premium that an on-the-money option buyer pays increases as the time remaining until expiration increases, and increases or decreases in proportion to the anticipated volatility of the underlying stock (the next section discusses the impact of volatility on options premiums). An options seller requires a higher premium when an options buyer desires to buy more time, or, if the underlying stock is considered to be highly volatile, as the probability of an option finishing substantially in-the-money increases as the time remaining until expiration or the volatility of the underlying stock increases.

Exhibit 3.4   **TIME PREMIUM OF A 30-DAY OPTION AS IT GOES FROM
IN-THE-MONEY TO OUT-OF-THE-MONEY**

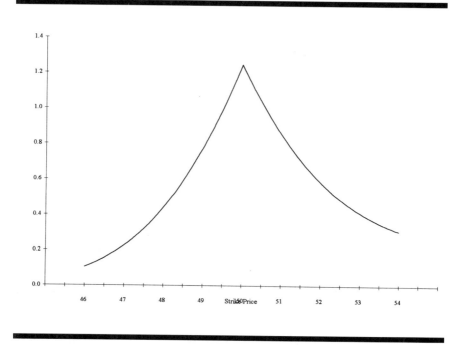

At any point in time the absolute amount of time premium is greatest for on-the-money options, and it declines in magnitude as options move out-of-the-money or in-the-money. As mentioned earlier in this chapter, the prices of all on-the-money and out-of-the-money options consist entirely of time premium, whereas the price of an in-the-money option consists partly of time premium and partly of intrinsic value. Exhibit 3.4 illustrates the impact of time premium as options move from in-the-money to out-of-the-money.

Note in table 3.1 that the deep in-the-money April 55 call on Coca-Cola (KO) holds only 14 percent of its total premium as time value and 86 percent as intrinsic value. The slightly in-the-money April 60 call has ½-point of intrinsic value (17 percent of its total premium) and 83 percent of its total premium consisting of time value. And 100 percent of the premium of the out-of-the-money April 65 call consists of time value. Also note that as we buy more time with the August expiration options on KO, the intrinsic value of the 55-strike and 60-strike in-the-money options does not change, but since more time value is purchased due to the longer holding period, the percentage of the total premium that is derived from intrinsic value decreases.

Table 3.1   **COCA-COLA CALL OPTIONS: INTRINSIC VALUE VERSUS TIME VALUE**

	Closing Stock Price	Closing Options Price	Intrinsic Value	% of Premium	Time Value	% of Premium
April Series						
55 Strike	$60\frac{1}{2}$	$6\frac{3}{8}$	$5\frac{1}{2}$	86	$\frac{7}{8}$	14
60 Strike	$60\frac{1}{2}$	3	$\frac{1}{2}$	17	$2\frac{1}{2}$	83
65 Strike	$60\frac{1}{2}$	$\frac{13}{16}$	0	0	$\frac{13}{16}$	100
August Series						
55 Strike	$60\frac{1}{2}$	$8\frac{1}{4}$	$5\frac{1}{2}$	67	$2\frac{3}{4}$	33
60 Strike	$60\frac{1}{2}$	$5\frac{1}{4}$	$\frac{1}{2}$	10	$4\frac{3}{4}$	90
65 Strike	$60\frac{1}{2}$	$2\frac{7}{8}$	0	0	$2\frac{7}{8}$	100

Note: Figures are based on 3/7/97 closing asked prices.

VOLATILITY AND ITS IMPACT ON OPTIONS PRICING

Overview of Volatility

As mentioned in the previous section, options buyers must pay increasingly higher time premiums as the volatility assumption for the underlying stock increases, due to the fact that the higher the volatility the greater the assumed probability that the stock will undergo major price fluctuations and that an option on that stock will finish substantially in-the-money.

Volatility can be defined as *the propensity of the underlying security's market price to change in either direction.* Often, volatility is measured by the daily standard deviation of the stock's price, which is then annualized.

Historical volatility is based on the past trading patterns of the stock. The theoretical or fair value of an option is based on a calculation of the underlying stock's historical volatility and provides a frame of reference when viewing stocks over the long term.

Future volatility is simply that which the options trader believes will prevail over the life of the option. The future volatility expected by the trader must be compared to the market's implied volatility assessment (see below), to determine if the option may be underpriced or overpriced.

Implied volatility is the market's best guess of future volatility, and it is obtained by plugging the current option price into option pricing models on an iterative basis. Volatility is the only unknown factor in the standard interpretation of traditional option pricing models such as the Black-Scholes model and must be estimated. Implied volatility is calculated by asking: "Given the known factors of time until expiration, interest rates, dividends, stock price, and striking price, what implied volatility must be inserted into the model to result in the current option price?"

Volatility in the Real World

Volatility is a measure of the actual and potential fluctuation of a stock on which an option trades. Simply put, stocks whose price ranges are large are said to have a high volatility; those whose ranges are small are said to have a low volatility.

The following procedure is a way to approximate the annual volatility of a stock: Look in the newspaper and note the price range for the stock for the last fifty-two weeks. Take the difference between the high and low price of the year. Then take the midpoint of the high and low price. Divide the high/low difference by the midpoint to get an estimate of the stock's volatility.

For example, suppose XYZ Corp. has a range of $53 to $75 for the past year. The difference is $75 − $53 = $22. The midpoint is ($75 + $53)/2 = $64. Dividing the difference by the midpoint, we get $22/$64 = 0.34, or 34 percent as an estimate of the volatility of XYZ Corp.'s stock.

What can we do with this number? First, it can be used to estimate the price range for the stock over the next year. For example, if XYZ Corp. stock is now selling for $60, it is reasonable to expect that the stock will sell for no more than approximately $80 [$60 + (0.34 × $60)] and no less than approximately $40 [$60 − (0.34 × $60)], 68 percent of the time. Those of you familiar with statistics will recognize 68 percent as the area under the normal curve that encompasses one standard deviation from the mean of a sample. Indeed, one way to interpret volatility is that it is the standard deviation of the stock's price for the period analyzed, in this case one year. This form of volatility is commonly called the historical volatility.

But suppose an investor is interested in the price range for the stock for only the next ninety days—the life of the option he is thinking of buying. Volatilities depend upon the square root of the time until expiration. Ninety days is one-quarter of a year, and the square root of 0.25 is 0.5. In our example, multiplying the 34 percent annual volatility by 0.5 converts the annual volatility to a ninety-day volatility of 17 percent. For the next ninety days you would therefore expect there to be a 68 percent probability that the price of XYZ Corp. stock remains between approximately $70 [$60 + (0.17 × $60)] and $50 [$60 − (0.17 × $60)].

There is another way to arrive at volatility, and that is through the options that trade on XYZ Corp.'s stock. The formula used to forecast the price of an option, usually some variant of the Black-Scholes formula, has a term in it called "volatility." This formula can be solved for the volatility if you input the current price of the stock, the current price of the option, the time until expiration, the dividend, and the risk-free interest rate into the formula. The volatility obtained this way is called the implied volatility.

Returning to our example, suppose the market has priced the options on XYZ Corp.'s stock so that they have an implied volatility of 25 percent for the next ninety days. We have previously calculated the stock's historical volatility for that amount of time at only 17 percent. A comparison of those two numbers could lead investors to believe that the market has overpriced XYZ's options (because a higher volatility assumption results in higher option prices) and might induce investors to become sellers of those options. However, this is a potentially dangerous approach, as there might be very good reasons for the market to overprice the stock's options. For example, a much-anticipated earnings report might be expected, or a takeover may be in the works. A seller of XYZ options would hope that the market would reprice the options so their implied volatility is closer to the stock's historical volatility, thus permitting the seller to quickly buy the options back for less than the prices for which they were sold. In other words, the seller would hope that the future volatility of the stock for the next ninety days is closer to its historical lower levels than to the implied volatility.

Conversely, if the market were to price these options with a 10 percent volatility, investors might be tempted to be options buyers, knowing the options are trading at a volatility assumption substantially below their historical level and hoping that the stock behaves over the next ninety days in a manner consistent with its historical higher volatility.

For on-the-money options on non–dividend-paying stocks, options premiums are directly proportional to the expected volatility of the underlying stock. So if we have two stocks that are each trading at 100, and the expected volatility of stock #1 is 25 percent and the expected volatility of stock #2 is 50 percent, on-the-money options for stock #2 will trade at twice the premium of on-the-money options on stock #1 (assuming identical expiration dates).

INTEREST RATES AND DIVIDENDS

Interest rates and dividends are the final two, and the least important, of the five major factors that affect option prices. Rising interest rates result in higher call premiums, as higher interest rates increase the *forward price* of the underlying stock. The forward price is equal to the current stock price increased by the risk-free interest rate over the life of the option, and is the price at which the stock is assumed to trade at option expiration in the option pricing models. For this same reason, rising interest rates result in lower put premiums.

Larger dividends result in lower call prices and higher put prices, because as dividends increase, the advantage of buying calls and holding cash instead of holding stock decreases. It then becomes more attractive to buy puts and hold cash instead of shorting stock, as the short-seller must pay out any dividends on the stock.

"THE GREEKS"

We have already discussed the three most important factors affecting option pricing: the stock price relative to the striking price, time until expiration, and volatility. Let us now review the "shorthand" that is utilized by options traders to describe the changes in option prices that result from changes in these three factors, which are known as "the Greeks."

Delta

Delta is a measure of the price sensitivity of an option at any given moment. Technically, delta is the expected dollar change in the price of an option for a $1 move in the underlying stock. For example, an option with a delta of 50 implies that a $1 change in the underlying stock will result in a $0.50 change in the option. Table 3.2 illustrates the relationship between the price of call and put options and the underlying stock or index. Note that with all other factors the same, call premiums tend to be slightly higher than put premiums.

The absolute value of delta can also be viewed as the probability that the option will finish in-the-money at expiration. Calls have positive deltas that range in value from 0 to 100, whereas puts have negative deltas that take values between 0 and −100. As an out-of-the-money option gets closer to the money, the delta of that option will rise. Remember, however, that delta is a dynamic measure whose value will change as the price of the underlying stock, its volatility,

Table 3.2   CALL AND PUT OPTIONS VERSUS UNDERLYING STOCK

Stock Prices	Call Prices	Put Prices
54	2½	3¼
54½	2¾	3
55	3	2¾
55½	3¼	2½
56	3½	2¼

and the time until expiration changes. At expiration, delta will approach 100 if an option is in-the-money, and it will approach zero if it is out-of-the-money.

Gamma

Gamma is the unit change in the delta of an option for each $1 change in the price of the underlying stock or index. For example, assume XYZ Corp.'s stock is at 60, and its 55-strike call option has a gamma of 0.05 and a delta of 75. If the stock moves to 61, the new delta will be 80, for an increase of five "deltas." Gammas are highest when an option is at-the-money. Gamma has limited value to nonprofessional options traders, particularly those who confine their activities to options buying. Gamma is used mostly by professional traders who have large positions and are attempting to maintain portfolios that are indifferent to market direction at various price levels of the underlying stocks.

Gamma is always a positive number if you are a buyer of option premium (i.e., you are "long" option premium). In other words, if you buy calls or buy puts, your gamma is positive.

Vega

Vega is the change in an option's price based on the change in its implied volatility expressed in dollar terms. For example, suppose XYZ stock has an option with a vega of 0.25. The option's price will change by $0.25 for each percentage point change in the option's implied volatility. It is worth noting that volatility changes have less impact on the premium of longer-term options (LEAPS), on far out-of-the-money or deep in-the-money options, and on options with little time until expiration.

Theta

Theta represents the loss in value an option will experience due to the passage of time. It is usually expressed on a per day basis. For example, an option with a theta of –0.25 will lose about $0.25 a day, provided the underlying stock price and volatility hold constant. A long option position will always have a negative theta, whereas a short option position will always have a positive theta.

As we have discussed, time decay is not linear, as the rate of decay accelerates as an option approaches expiration (see exhibit 3.5). The rate of decay is proportional to the square root of the time remaining until expiration. For example, consider an on-the-money longer-term option with nine months until expiration and a shorter-term option with three months until expiration. If you take the square root of the time remaining on the longer-term option (3) and divide it into the square root of time remaining on the shorter-term option (1.73), your ratio will be 1.73/3.00 or 0.577. Subtracting that ratio from 1.00 leads to the conclusion that a three-month option loses its value 42.3 percent faster than that of a nine-month option. During the first half of an on-the-money option's life, it loses roughly one-third of its time value.

Theta, like the other factors mentioned above, is dynamic and constantly changing. An at-the-money option will have a higher theta, or lose more value as time passes, than an out-of-the-money option

Exhibit 3.5   **THETA FOR 60-DAY AT-THE-MONEY OPTION**

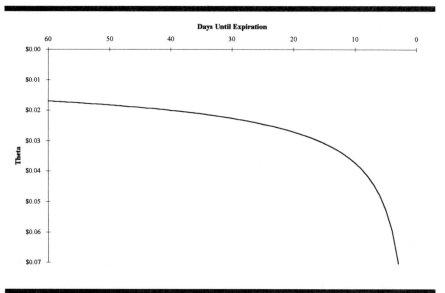

Exhibit 3.6   **THETA: AT-THE-MONEY VERSUS OUT-OF-THE-MONEY OPTIONS**

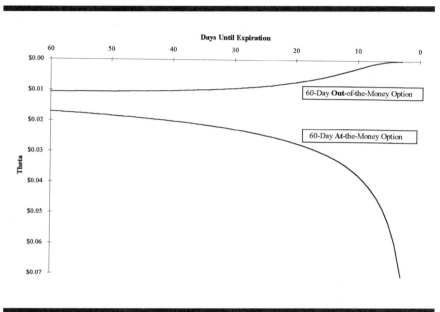

(see exhibit 3.6). But note that the percentage loss in value for the out-of-the-money option may be higher with the passage of time.

Now that we have covered the basic options concepts, let us move on to understanding the options dynamics and psychology that are critical to successful options trading.

OPTIONS TRADING VERSUS STOCK TRADING

Many investors have turned to options trading after they have successfully traded stocks, often concluding that they could have made even *more* money if they had instead leveraged their gains by buying options. Unfortunately, their stock-investing experience generally leads to one of the greatest mistakes made by new option traders—trying to trade options as if they were stocks.

Although an equity option does represent the right to buy or sell 100 shares of the underlying equity, as an option holder you are a *renter*, not an *owner*, of the price movement in the underlying stock. As the lessee of this price movement, you must be much more nimble than you would be as the owner. Your "lease" will "expire" in a matter of days, weeks, or months, whereas stock owners can hold their positions in perpetuity. Stock owners will tend to profit as long as a company remains a going concern, as the long-term upward trend in the market works in their favor. We now examine the critical differences between successful options trading and stock trading.

THE IMPORTANCE OF SPEED OF MOVEMENT

"If [a trader] purchases options, not only must he be right about market direction, he must also be right about market speed. Only if he is right on both counts can he expect to make a profit."[1] This principle, as expressed by Sheldon Natenberg in his book *Options Volatility and Pricing,* must be thoroughly understood before you can hope to develop a profitable options trading approach.

If you are a beginning options trader, you must always keep in mind that "options expire." Unlike stocks, options have a limited life. If a price move does not occur as expected, a stock investor can say, "I'll give it another month," or even "I'll wait another year." This is *not* true with options trading. Each option has a set expiration date, beyond which the option will cease to exist. At expiration, a call option is worth the difference between the stock price and its striking price or, if the stock is below the striking price, the call option is worthless and the option buyer loses 100 percent of his investment.

Your objective as an options buyer is not to hold a position passively until expiration. Rather your mission must be to purchase options in situations where you can expect speed of movement in the underlying security over the projected holding period of your option trade. As an options buyer, you have an edge when the underlying security's speed of movement is of a greater magnitude than the market expects. Without this greater-than-expected speed of movement, your edge as an options buyer is eliminated.

Speed of movement is *critical* to the options trader, whereas a stock investor is not as apt to care how fast a stock moves over the short term as long as the stock achieves a satisfactory longer-term rate of return. But if you, as an options buyer, are not getting the desired speed of movement in the underlying stock, you must close out your position and move on to the next opportunity. An options buyer needs the underlying stock to move FAR—Fast, Aggressively, and in the Right direction—to be successful.

The impact of time is the most significant line of demarcation between options and stock trading. For the stock investor, time is an

---

1. Sheldon Natenberg, *Option Volatility and Pricing* (Chicago: Probus Publishing, 1994), 36.

ally; the longer your time horizon, the more predictable your rate of return on quality stock investments. In contrast, the options buyer does *not* want to stretch out his time horizon, as the value of his option position will deteriorate with each passing day by an increasing amount, absent a significant price move in the predicted direction. Time is the enemy, so the options buyer must accurately define his time horizon. He wants to participate only in those sharper and faster-than-expected directional moves in the underlying security that are conducive to profitable options trading. And when such favorable periods end, and the noisy, directionless periods begin, the options buyer seeks to move on to new situations where big moves are unfolding.

There are several critical success factors to keep in mind when dealing with the finite life of options. As stated in chapters 1 and 2, you must understand that the success of your options trading depends on your ability to correctly predict both the direction and the timing of a move in the underlying stock. The first factor, correctly predicting the direction, is easily understood, and a number of effective directional forecasting tools were presented in chapter 2. We all know that if we expect the stock price to go up and instead it goes down, we lose money trading stocks in line with that overstated, oversimplified stock-trading maxim: "Buy low, sell high."

But a new motto holds for *options* traders: "Buy high, sell higher." The stock trader can afford to wait for his stock to slowly climb out of the basement, but the options trader doesn't have the luxury to buy low and wait out a developing positive move. Buying high and selling higher is not an irrational method, but a logical one, based on trend-driven indicators to predict direction and based on the fact that options buyers need speed of movement. As mentioned in chapter 2, "the trend is your friend" is a key general trading principle. But for you as an options buyer, the trend is your *savior*, as trends provide you with the directional bias that is critical to achieving the speed of movement that you need to trade profitably.

OPTION TIME DECAY VERSUS OPTION LEVERAGE

The options buyer's need for speed of movement is easily understood from the perspective that options expire on a preset date, and if the underlying stock does not exceed the striking price on that expiration day the call option buyer loses his entire investment. But it must also be understood in terms of the fact that when you buy an option, you are paying a time premium over and above the option's intrinsic value, and that this time premium will decay at a steadily increasing rate throughout the life of the option.

You can view the option buying game as a constant battle between the leverage that options provide (the "good guys") and the time decay that will inevitably occur (the "bad guys"). You can "beat time decay" *only* if the underlying stock moves quickly in the right direction. In other words, speed of movement allows the leverage of the options you buy to overwhelm the time decay that they experience, and that's the foundation for a profitable options buying program.

For example, let us assume that you purchase an on-the-money four-month (120-day) call option with a striking price of 100 on non–dividend-paying XYZ shares. If the shares remain at 100 throughout the life of the option, you would see the following situation as time passed:

	Days Until Expiration				
	120	*60*	*30*	*15*	*0*
XYZ shares	100	100	100	100	100
100-strike call	6	4¼	2¾	2	0

Note that the six points that you would have paid for this option with 120 days of life remaining consisted entirely of time premium, and note the steady deterioration of this time premium, and consequently of the price of your option, as time passes. (Each column beyond the first represents a halving of the amount of time until expiration, which results in a loss of approximately 30 percent of the value of an on-the-money option due to the "square-root" nature of option time decay.)

Next, let us assume that XYZ shares did move higher, but at the slow rate of one point per month:

	Days Until Expiration				
	120	*60*	*30*	*15*	*0*
XYZ shares	100	102	103	103.5	104
100-strike call	6	5½	4⅝	4	4

In this example, the investor in XYZ stock achieved slow, steady gains over the 120-day period, culminating in a profit of 4 percent by option expiration day. But the buyer of the 100-strike call was never in a profitable position, and ultimately lost two points on an investment of six points for a 33 percent loss despite the fact that the underlying stock moved in the right direction.

If we were to stop at this example, we would have painted a very grim portrait of option buying and the impact of time decay. But it would be a very incomplete portrait, as we would not have demonstrated how speed of movement can more than overcome time decay, and how this allows the leverage of options to create very large profits on relatively modest moves in the underlying stock.

Let us now assume that the *same* four-point move in XYZ shares that previously occurred over four months occurs in two weeks:

	Days Until Expiration	
	120	*106*
XYZ shares	100	104
100-strike call	6	8½

With the four-point move occurring very quickly, we now move into a very favorably leveraged situation. XYZ shares gained 4 percent over this two-week period, but the 100-strike call gained approximately 40 percent, for a leverage factor of 10 to 1 [(40 precent)/(4 percent = 10].

Let us further assume that the speed of movement of XYZ shares begins to accelerate, so that the shares gain six points over the next two-week period, and then another eight points over the following two weeks:

	Days Until Expiration			
	120	*106*	*92*	*78*
XYZ shares	100	104	110	118
100-strike call	6	8½	12¾	18¾

In this final example in which XYZ shares move fast, aggressively and in the right direction (FAR), the profits for the options buyer explode, and the leverage further expands to about 12 to 1 as the option gains 213 percent (more than triple the purchase price) on just an 18 percent gain in the shares [(213 percent)/(18 percent) = 11.8].

You must realize that this final very happy scenario for the options buyer occurs very infrequently, as an 18 percent move in three weeks is well outside the expected range of possibilities for all but the most extremely volatile stocks, and on such stocks you would pay more for call options than is assumed in the above examples. Later in this chapter we discuss some ways for you to maximize your chances for achieving such quick and sharp moves from stocks that are *not* considered to be very volatile. But for now, let us summarize the interaction of option leverage with option time decay with respect to on-the-money options as follows:

1. Unless the underlying stock moves in the right direction, an option will lose value throughout its life at an accelerating rate until it expires worthless. In this instance, the option time decay factor totally dominates the result.

2. If the underlying stock moves *slowly* in the right direction, the options buyer will generally lose a portion of his investment, as once again time decay dominates the result.

3. If the underlying stock moves *rapidly* in the right direction, the options buyer will begin to achieve larger percentage profits than those achieved by the stock buyer as the leverage factor begins to dominate the results. Note that time decay is still at work under these circumstances but it no longer dominates.

4. If the underlying stock moves *fast and aggressively* in the right direction (FAR), the options buyer begins to achieve huge percentage returns as the impact of the leverage factor further increases and the impact of the time decay factor further recedes.

The above four points specifically relate to on-the-money options. For out-of-the-money options these points apply even more strongly, as time decay becomes an even bigger factor and leverage kicks in as the dominant factor only after the underlying stock moves even further than what is required for on-the-money options. But note that once leverage does begin to dominate for an out-of-the-money option, the profits and the leverage for the options buyer are greater than those for on-the-money options. For example, the profit from buying out-of-the money options on stock XYZ on a three-week move from 100 to 118 would have been in the 250 percent to 400 percent range compared to the 213 percent profit for the on-the-money option in the above example. This comes as no surprise, as it is a fact in the investment world that greater rewards accompany greater risks.

In the case of in-the-money options, time decay is less of a factor because a portion of the option premium consists of intrinsic value. For example, a "flat" scenario for the underlying stock through option expiration day would not result in a total loss of the premium for an in-the-money option. But the profits that would be achieved on the "big, fast move" in the underlying stock would be more muted for the in-the-money option buyer, as lower potential rewards accompany the lower risk.

CHOOSING THE RIGHT OPTION
AFTER CHOOSING THE RIGHT STOCK

Once you understand the interaction between option leverage and option time decay, choosing the right option to buy becomes a fairly straightforward process that involves determining three criteria:

1. An underlying stock that appears to be poised for a major move by utilizing the techniques discussed in chapter 2.

2. Your expectations for the magnitude of the move in the stock and the time frame in which this move will occur.

3. An option whose profit and loss characteristics are consistent with your expectations in criterion 2 above and consistent with your tolerance for risk.

Assume, for example, that you expect XYZ stock to move from 100 to 110 over the next thirty days. You could therefore rule out buying the following options on XYZ:

1. Any put option, because you are expecting XYZ to rally.

2. A 110 (or higher)-strike call that expires in thirty days, because even if the stock moved exactly as you had expected, this option would still expire worthless (although you could theoretically profit from a much quicker rally than you were expecting).

3. A 100-strike call that expires in thirty days that is selling for a premium of 10. Although it would be possible for you to profit with this option on an immediate move by XYZ to 110, you would merely break even on this trade if the stock moved to 110 in thirty days, as you had expected. The market is clearly pricing the 100-strike call for a potentially much larger move than you were anticipating, and you should therefore avoid this option.

4. A 130-strike call that expires in a year. The delta on such a long-term, far out-of-the-money option on the 10-point move you were expecting would be insufficient to justify the risk of

this trade unless you were expecting significant further gains well beyond your 30-day time horizon.

Which options on XYZ should you consider buying?

1. A 100-strike call that expires in thirty days with a premium of 5. You would thus double your money with XYZ at 110 at expiration.

2. A 105-strike call that expires in thirty days with a premium of 2. You would achieve a 150 percent profit with XYZ at 110 at expiration, as this option would sell for 5. But you would be assuming additional risk relative to the 100-strike call, as the 105-strike call would expire worthless with XYZ between 100 and 105 at expiration.

3. A 105-strike call with a premium of 3 that expires in sixty days. Your profit potential should XYZ move as expected is lower than that for the 30-day, 105-strike call (about 100 percent compared to 150 percent). But your risk is also lower, as you would be able to sell this option and recover some of your original cost should the stock not reach 105 in thirty days.

4. A 110-strike call that expires in ninety days with a premium of 2½. The risk/reward characteristics of this option over a 30-day holding period are similar to those for the option in (3) above but with slightly less reward and slightly less risk. However, if XYZ were to rally substantially beyond a 30- or 60-day holding period, this 90-day option would offer the best potential gains.

Clearly, the decision on which option to buy is affected by your expectations for the underlying stock as well as your tolerance for risk. The riskiest option of all those listed above is the 30-day, 105-strike call, but if you could tolerate the heightened possibility of incurring a total loss you would be rewarded with the highest potential return. Chapter 4 discusses in great detail the principles of risk/reward management in your options trading, which will help you to further clarify the characteristics of the options that would be most suitable for you.

VOLATILITY VERSUS DIRECTIONAL PRICE MOVEMENT

For two identically priced stocks and with the same time remaining until option expiration, the higher volatility stock will have richer option premiums, and if the options are on-the-money, their premiums will be directly proportional to the volatility of a non–dividend-paying stock. This is due to the simple fact that a higher volatility suggests a greater probability that an option will finish significantly in-the-money. But don't confuse volatility with price direction, as they are entirely different concepts.

Earlier, this chapter indicated that for an option buyer requiring speed of movement, "the trend is your savior." And although many traders long for the action of trading, or feel they need to be busy trading to justify the time spent following the markets, this line of thinking is not conducive to making money in options trading. Simply put, if there is no clear price trend, don't trade. The impact of this point becomes more pronounced when you consider that tradable trends occur only about 15 percent of the time.

So why are price trends important enough that we need to be so selective in our option trading? Because options pricing already reflects the anticipated volatility of the underlying stock. Certainly if there is much buying interest in a certain option and few natural sellers, the option price will rise due to demand outpacing supply. But the anchor for determining the option price you pay is the price calculated by one of the popular options pricing models. In these models, the higher the volatility of the stock, the higher the theoretical price of the option.

Intuitively, we can expect that a volatile stock such as U.S. Robotics (USRX) will have richer-priced options than a much less volatile stock such as Coca-Cola (KO). USRX rose more than fifteenfold in the period from August 1994 until May 1996 and then subsequently plunged, so it has a tendency for sharp moves. Meanwhile, KO is a steady mover, so its options tend to be priced more cheaply within the context of the lower-volatility ongoing uptrend in the stock (see table 3.3).

Table 3.3   **COMPARISON OF COCA-COLA AND U.S. ROBOTICS ON-THE-MONEY OPTION PREMIUMS**

Option	Coca-Cola (KO)	U.S. Robotics (USRX)
March 60 call*	$1\frac{5}{16}$	$2\frac{11}{16}$
April 60 call*	$2\frac{3}{8}$	$4\frac{7}{8}$

* Asked prices on March 5, with KO trading at $59\frac{1}{2}$ and USRX trading at $59\frac{1}{4}$.

Options Pricing Models

The traditional options pricing models (such as the well-known Black-Scholes model) make two major assumptions:

1. Stock price movement is random.
2. Stock price returns are distributed in a bell-shaped pattern, known as a lognormal distribution.

These option pricing assumptions are important when viewed in conjunction with the following principle that many options traders never fully understand: *Volatility and directional price movement are two entirely different concepts.* You can have loads of volatility with little or no net price movement over time. Buying an option on a volatile stock that isn't trending is a recipe for disaster. And sometimes the least volatile stocks have the strongest price trends. Returning to our U.S. Robotics/Coca-Cola example, is it worth paying twice as much for USRX's options as you would for KO's options? Clearly not, if USRX remains stuck in the nontrending mode it had been in since mid-1996 (see exhibit 3.7) and if KO continues its steady uptrend (see exhibit 3.8).

Meanwhile KO's steady uptrend has not caused a subsequent surge in options pricing. In fact, the steadier a stock's uptrend, the

---

Exhibit 3.7   **U.S. ROBOTICS (USRX) WEEKLY CHART, JANUARY 1995 TO SEPTEMBER 1996**

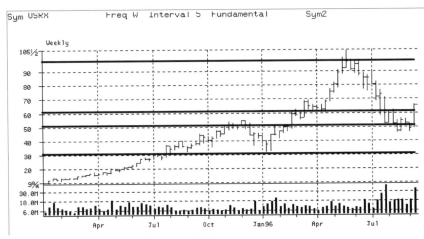

Reprinted with permission. Compliments of ILX Systems.

Exhibit 3.8   COCA-COLA (KO) WEEKLY CHART, JULY 1994 TO MARCH 1997

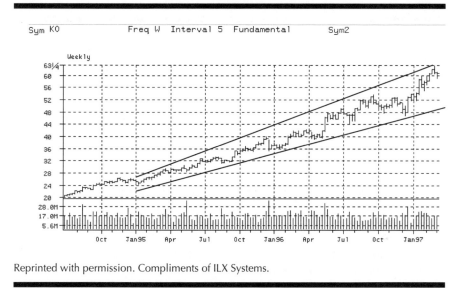

Reprinted with permission. Compliments of ILX Systems.

more likely the implied volatility will actually drop, which results in cheaper options.

Let us take the most extreme possible example. Assume that a stock goes up by exactly 1 percent per week, week in and week out. What will its volatility be in such a situation? *Zero.* There is zero volatility because the stock moves by the same amount each and every week, with no deviations. Those options priced at 0 percent volatility would be an incredible bargain, and clearly no one is going to sell you an option "for nothing." But you *can* pick up options bargains when you focus on stocks in steady trends with low volatility. By finding sustainable price trends where the percentage move in the stock will be greater than that anticipated by the implied volatility of the options, you obtain a substantial edge over how the options pricing model prices the options you are considering buying. The wider the gap between a trending stock's actual return and the expected return priced into the options market, the bigger your edge.

While volatility is a very important factor in options pricing, too many investors get caught up in the mistaken notion that making money in options is as simple as buying "low" volatility and selling "high" volatility. Always remember that the future direction of the underlying security is far more important to the success of options buyers and options sellers than the impact of normal volatility fluc-

Exhibit 3.9   **BELL-SHAPED CURVE FOR THE STANDARD PROBABILITY
                DISTRIBUTION**

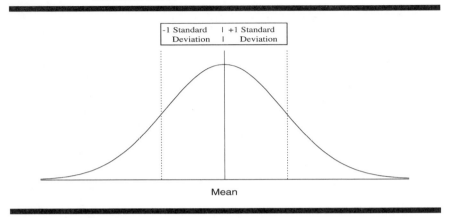

tuations, and that forecasting price direction is often a much less daunting task than forecasting future volatility.

The real key to trading options successfully is understanding that stocks have strong directional trends roughly 15 percent of the time, yet most of the options pricing models assume that the movement of a stock is random and distributed in a bell-shaped curve, known as the standard probability distribution (see exhibit 3.9). These models assume that a stock has roughly as much chance of going up as going down (with a slight bias to the upside). And the use of standard deviation as a measure of dispersion, which is critical to the accuracy of an options pricing model, is valid *only* if the underlying system is random.

Now, let us look at a chart of Safeway (exhibit 3.10). Clearly, based only on the strong uptrend apparent in this chart, you would assume Safeway stock has a high probability of continuing to rise in price. This is because day-to-day stock price movement is often *not* random, but the result of a feedback process that creates directional price trends.

Directional Price Movement Versus the Efficient Market Theory

Efficient market theory holds that market prices reflect the full knowledge and expectations of investors. Under this theory there are no trending stocks, and market timing is impossible. Any new information is instantaneously incorporated into a stock's price, and therefore it is impossible to beat the market. Consequently, throwing a dart at the stock page to select equities has as much chance of outperforming the market as professional stock selection. This hypothesis also main-

Exhibit 3.10   **SAFEWAY (SWY) WEEKLY CHART**

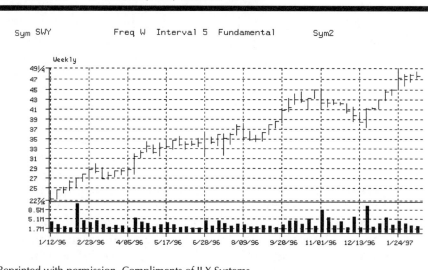

Reprinted with permission. Compliments of ILX Systems.

tains it is impossible to use technical, fundamental, or expectational analysis to beat the market, and that future price changes cannot be predicted from past price changes.

I strongly disagree with this interpretation of market behavior. As was aptly stated by William O'Neil in Jack Schwager's book, *Market Wizards*, "The stock market is neither efficient nor random. It is not efficient because there are too many poorly conceived opinions; it is not random because strong investor emotions can create trends."[2]

Profiting From Chaos by Tonis Vaga and *Chaos and Order in the Capital Markets* by Edgar Peters each argue that there is an underlying nonlinear structure in the capital markets that promotes a trending bias in the markets. Rather than price levels being random and the price of a stock on day number two having no dependence on its price on day number one, chaos theory postulates a feedback process (or trend), whereby prices are dependent on each other over time.

Typically, you must assume more risk to achieve higher returns. However, chaos theory suggests there are periods when the normal risk/reward relationship no longer holds. In fact, above-average returns with below-average risks are possible. This theory claims there are times when the market is *not* efficient. Investors tend to extremes, as this is the nature of crowd behavior. So periods of undervaluation or overvaluation are created and can create profit opportunities. Any-

---

2. Jack D. Schwager, *Market Wizards* (New York: New York Institute of Finance, 1989), 235.

one who has followed the market has seen situations when a fundamentally strong company falls temporarily out of favor with Wall Street, and a buying opportunity is created as the stock pulls back to a key moving average support line. Above-average returns can be generated, for example, by purchasing fundamentally strong, "low-expectation" stocks that have pulled back to an uptrending support line. This is in sharp contrast to the efficient market theory, which postulates the only way to achieve higher returns is to assume more risk.

Note from exhibit 3.11 that Safeway has been trending strongly along its 100-day moving average. But during these trending periods, the pricing of Safeway options tends to drop to very low levels relative to the stock's historical volatility. Also note on exhibit 3.12 the low implied volatility of Safeway options in the 20 percent to 35 percent range, with the exception of two spikes in March and July. This compares with actual annualized volatility in SWY shares of more than 50 percent in both 1995 and 1996. This is one way you can beat the options pricing model—by buying options on trending stocks that traditional pricing models, which assume random price movement, price cheaply.

This is truly a remarkable situation, whereby options on the stocks that have the highest probability of moving strongly in a particular direction are actually priced cheaply by the options pricing

Exhibit 3.11 **SAFEWAY (SWY) WEEKLY CHART WITH 100-DAY MOVING AVERAGE**

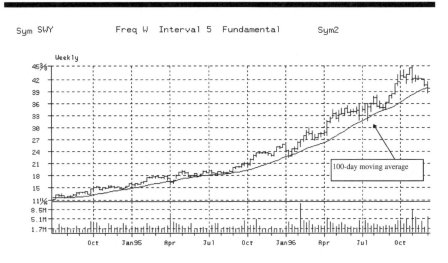

Reprinted with permission. Compliments of ILX Systems.

Exhibit 3.12   SAFEWAY (SWY) DAILY CHART WITH IMPLIED VOLATILITY

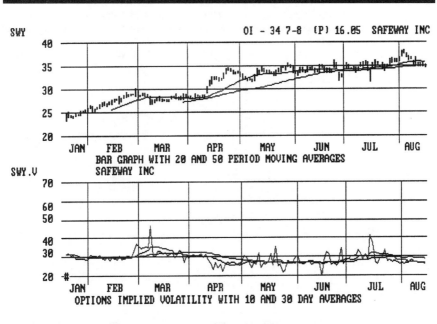

Reprinted with permission. Compliments of Bridge Information Systems.

models because these stocks are in non-volatile price trends. And this is a powerful reminder that low volatility and big price moves often occur hand in hand, which provides the options buyer with cheap options and a big trading edge, as these cheap options have a higher-than-normal probability of finishing significantly in-the-money.

THE PITFALLS OF VOLATILITY TRADING

Volatility traders (those who sell options premiums in an attempt to profit from divergences between future volatility and implied volatility) often say, "Directional trading is risky; you may hit on some big gainers but you can also have some heavy losses. Volatility trading offers consistency by shooting for singles instead of home runs." Volatility traders are generally looking to profit from implied volatility levels that are "high" or "low" relative to historical volatility. Their methodology would be sound if you can assume that volatility always "reverts to the mean," that is, that high volatility and low vola-

Exhibit 3.13   **PICTURETEL CORP. (PCTL) DAILY CHART WITH IMPLIED VOLATILITY: THE RISKS OF SELLING "HIGH" PUT VOLATILITY, AUGUST 1996 TO MARCH 1997**

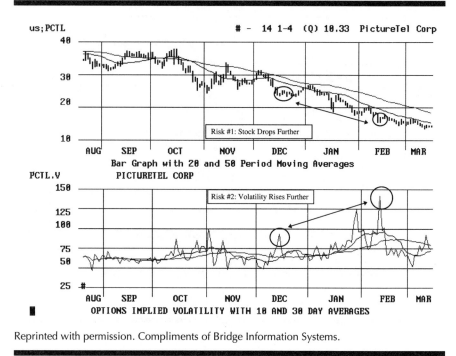

Reprinted with permission. Compliments of Bridge Information Systems.

tility are both temporary phenomena that will move toward the historical average. But this theory often fails in real-time trading, particularly when volatility begins to trend. And the impact of major price movements on options prices can overwhelm the impact of changes in volatility.

Indeed, volatility is often in an uptrend among stocks whose price is in an increasingly severe downtrend. A perfect example of this situation occurred with Picturetel Corp. (PCTL) in late 1996 (exhibit 3.13). The stock had already declined from 40 to 25, and the implied volatility of PCTL options had surged from 60 percent to 90 percent. Volatility traders were salivating at the prospects of selling PCTL options, given the high implied volatility relative to the "norm." But put sellers were devastated when the stock plummeted even further from the 25 zone to the 15 area and implied volatility surged from a high 96 percent to a much higher 140 percent. Not only did put sellers get hurt by the drop in the stock, but they had to buy back losing positions at even higher premiums on an implied volatility basis. Such is the power of trends, whether they be in stock prices or in volatilities.

VOLATILITY IMPLOSION

Although selling unusually high implied volatility options can be dangerous, it is also generally wise to avoid buying such options. You may have purchased an option on a volatile stock and had the stock move in your predicted direction by several points, only to find that you did not profit from your option purchase due to a volatility implosion. The market simply repriced the option at a much lower implied volatility than the unusually high implied volatility that existed at the time of your purchase. Therefore, the stock moved but your option didn't. These situations are very frustrating for beginning options traders and often lead them to conclude that the options market is unfairly structured, when in reality it is a simple matter of "buying too dear and selling too cheap" on volatility. Let us look at some actual examples.

On July 17, 1996, Sun Microsystems was trading at $55 with earnings due to be released after the close on July 18. The August 55 puts were trading at 4 and had an implied volatility of 64.7 percent, substantially above the historical volatility for the stock of about 50 percent. The next day, with the stock slightly higher at $55\frac{1}{4}$, the August 55 put was trading at 3 with an implied volatility of 52.1 percent. The August 55 put holders lost 25 percent of their investment overnight despite virtually no change in the stock price. Once the major uncertainty associated with the earnings report had passed, the implied volatility of the options simply collapsed, leaving their owners sadder but (perhaps) wiser.

Another good example of a volatility implosion occurred in Iomega. On June 12, 1996, with Iomega trading at $41\frac{3}{8}$, the July 35 put was offered at $3\frac{1}{2}$. Six days later, on June 18, with the stock $5\frac{3}{8}$ points lower at 36, the July 35 put was offered at $4\frac{1}{4}$, a mere $\frac{3}{4}$ point higher than it was trading before the stock's collapse.

These two examples underscore the importance of understanding volatility and the pitfalls of buying options with unusually high implied volatilities relative to historical levels. Investors must also understand that highly volatile stocks generally have richly priced options, thus substantially reducing the leverage of these options. The best option trades are on trending stocks whose options are priced cheaply by the options pricing model relative to their true potential.

CONCLUSION

It is important to understand the factors that determine the price of an option: stock price, option striking price, time until expiration, risk-free interest rate, dividends, and volatility of the underlying stock. But it is equally important to understand why options cannot be traded like stocks, due to the all-important requirement of speed of movement in options trading. In addition, inherent in the options pricing models upon which options prices are based are the flawed assumptions that stock price movement is random and that volatility determines the fair value of an option with no consideration of directional price trends. With this foundation, let us now learn in chapter 4 how to best manage our trading capital to maximize the chances that our options trading program will be profitable over time.

4

Managing Your Options Portfolio to Maximize Reward and Minimize Risk

THE IMPORTANCE OF SOUND MONEY MANAGEMENT

Sound money management and intelligent risk reduction principles must be at the heart of every options trading strategy. Your long-term success as an options trader is determined by your ability to profit from tradable trends in the security while withstanding the inevitable fluctuations within those trends. The money management and risk reduction principles you follow are the keys to surviving these fluctuations as well as those situations in which you are flat-out wrong.

As an options trader, you will have losing trades. Although this is not a pleasant thought, it is a very important concept to understand before you begin trading because such an understanding will allow you to create a plan to manage losses as well as gains. And it is also a very logical concept when you consider the three conditions that are necessary as an options buyer to achieve a profitable options trade:

1. The underlying stock must move in the predicted direction.
2. That move must be of sufficient magnitude to overcome the time premium that you pay for the privilege of the leverage that you receive from the option.
3. This big move in the predicted direction must occur quickly so that the option does not expire before the move unfolds.

Of course, the rewards for success in achieving these three conditions in an options trade can be huge, but the probability of this occurring for a particular trade is significantly lower than a coin flip, even for the best of traders. Options buyers attempt to preserve as much of their capital as possible over the course of their losing trades so that these losses can be more than offset by their occasional big winners. Options sellers, on the other hand, attempt to minimize their losses in those occasional situations where the options they sell increase substantially in price so that these losses can be more than offset by the small, steady profits they achieve in the majority of their trades.

Although successful options buyers almost always have more losing trades than profitable ones, they can still achieve substantial bottom-line gains. They accomplish this because their winning trades yield far more dollars per trade than are lost in their losing trades. As Victor Sperandeo said when referring to great traders, using a baseball analogy in *Trader Vic—Methods of a Wall Street Master*, "The best players only get hits 30 to 40% of the time."[1] Remember that options trading is a probability game. You win this game by diversifying your positions, using only a fraction of your total capital on any one trade, and winning big on your profitable trades.

Let us examine the results of trader 1 and trader 2 in table 4.1, and note what stands out in the comparison of the two performances. Trader 2's winning percentage was only 30 percent, whereas trader 1 posted a 70 percent winning percentage. Yet the bottom-line performance was significantly better for trader 2 than for trader 1. This can all be traced to the size of their winners versus the size of their losers.

Trader 1 may be pleased with a 70 percent winning percentage, but the 30 percent of trades that are losses average $1,267, 48 percent larger than the $857 average gain. Put another way, trader 1's "average win/average loss" ratio is 0.68. Any time this ratio is less than 1.00, your losers are eating into your profits too heavily and you will be in trouble unless you have an unusually high winning percentage. And 70 percent winners is unrealistic to achieve in options buying over the long haul. Ideally, you should seek an average win/average loss ratio of 2.00 or more. In the case of trader 2, although only 30 percent of the trades were winners, they were big winners—on average gaining 150 percent. The average win/average loss ratio is 4.12, which is very strong.

The other benefit of trader 2's success profile is that it is much better suited for trading options. Too many big losers can seriously deplete an option trader's capital, particularly if these losers are consecutive. So trader 2's style of keeping losses modest will better allow

---

1. Victor Sperandeo, *Trader Vic—Methods of a Wall Street Master*, with T. Sullivan Brown (New York: John Wiley & Sons, 1993), 25.

Table 4.1   **TWO DIFFERENT PATHS TO OPTIONS PROFITS**

	Trader 1				Trader 2		
Com-pany	% Gain/ Loss	$ Invested	$ Profit	Com-pany	% Gain/ Loss	$ Invested	$ Profit
AAA	+30%	$2,000	$600	MMM	−30%	2,000	$−600
BBB	−50%	2,000	−1,000	NNN	−40%	2,000	−800
CCC	+40%	2,000	800	OOO	+200%	2,000	4,000
DDD	+15%	2,000	300	PPP	−50%	2,000	−1,000
EEE	−40%	2,000	−800	QQQ	−20%	2,000	−400
FFF	+60%	2,000	1,200	RRR	+100%	2,000	2,000
GGG	+100%	2,000	2,000	SSS	−25%	2,000	−500
HHH	−100%	2,000	−2,000	TTT	−50%	2,000	−1,000
III	+25%	2,000	500	UUU	+150%	2,000	3,000
JJJ	+30%	2,000	600	VVV	−40%	2,000	−800
Total profit			$2,200	Total profit			$3,900
Average gainer		6,000/7	857	Average gainer		9,000/3	3,000
Average loser		3,800/3	1,267	Average loser		5,100/7	729

him to "stay in the game" to achieve the big winners, whereas trader 1 will be very badly hurt on any decline in his winning percentage if his losers remain big.

The winning percentage and the average win/average loss ratio when examined together give a quick evaluation of a trading method's potential viability. Multiplying the percentage of successful trades times the ratio of the average win to the average loss results in what is known as the "robustness factor." As an example, consider the case in which a trader achieves a 50 percent win rate, with his average win equal to his average loss. These are "flip of the coin" results, and the robustness factor is just 0.50 (50 percent wins × 1.00 = 0.50). To gain an edge over the markets, with commissions and slippage taken into account, you need to achieve a robustness factor of at least 1.00 if you expect to make significant profits.

In our trader 1 example, the 70 percent winners times the 0.68 average win/loss ratio produces a robustness factor of only 0.48, slightly worse than flipping a coin. In the trader 2 example, the 30 percent winning percentage times the 4.12 average win/loss ratio results in a 1.24 robustness reading, two-and-a-half times better than that of trader 1 and the coin flip. So clearly trader 2 has a major edge versus the markets, even with his low winning percentage.

Remember that the impact of commissions must also be considered. In the above examples, if $125 is spent in commissions on each trade, the net profit of trader 1 is reduced from $2,200 to $950, dropping his return from 11 percent to 4.75 percent of invested capital. Trader 2's net profit would drop from $3,900 to $2,650, dropping his return from 19.5 percent to 13.25 percent. The good news is that the commission rates available to options traders have been declining steadily over the years, particularly in the 1990s, with the rapid growth of deep-discount brokers, Internet trading, and brokers who specialize in options trading. See chapter 10 for further information on brokers and commission rates.

THE TWO MAJOR "PROFIT ROBBERS"

Why do many options traders unwittingly embrace a losing strategy? Usually, this happens for reasons related to emotion rather than logic. After all, people do generally buy options in the hope of achieving substantial profits. But human nature frequently interferes, often in the forms of fear and greed, as elaborated below.

At one end of the emotional spectrum is fear. Purchasing an option involves the risk of a total loss of the initial investment. However, in exchange for the assumption of this risk, the options investor has the opportunity to realize profits that are many times this investment. Many investors bail out of a position when it first moves against them, fearing a total loss. Unfortunately, they are robbing themselves of the potential for huge gains, and negating their reason for buying options in the first place.

At the other end of the emotional spectrum is greed. The options investor will accept the possibility of a total loss as the price to pay for achieving large gains, which is fine. So where does the greedy investor go wrong? The answer is both simple and financially tragic: No profit level is enough for this individual. If he doubles his money, he wants to triple it. If he achieves a hat trick, why not shoot for a quadruple? The process never ends. The result? Some very healthy "paper profits" (unrealized gains) become tiny realized gains when the direction of the underlying stock reverses. In fact, many paper gains become actual losses.

What will cure these very human, very common, yet very financially damaging afflictions?

HOW TO ELIMINATE THE NEGATIVE IMPACT OF FEAR

Many investors are attracted to options trading by the unique opportunity to achieve profits of many times their original investment. Unfortunately, a basic tenet of options trading is often ignored or forgotten: To be in a position to realize the rewards of the options market, you must be financially and emotionally capable of withstanding the ups and downs of the options marketplace. Even the most profitable trades often show "paper losses" at some point. Very few options go straight up, simply because very few stocks go straight up or straight down. If you panic out of a position with every downward blip in price, you will ultimately lose in options trading.

Use Only Your Trading Capital for Options Trading

Never buy puts or calls with money needed to pay bills or meet potential emergencies, nor should you borrow money for the express purpose of trading options. Intelligent trading decisions are rarely made when "scared" money is involved. You should restrict your options commitments to funds you can lose without undue financial hardship. Aggressive traders can invest 20 percent or less of their trading capital in an options buying program (i.e., in long premium options positions), whereas conservative traders should limit themselves to no more than 10 percent of their trading capital.

Once you determine the limited percentage of your total trading capital that you will commit to an options buying program, you must also limit the percentage of that capital that is committed to an individual trade. Table 4.2 dramatically demonstrates the potential negative impact of committing 50 percent of your options trading capital to each trade. In this example, commitments of 10 percent and 20 percent resulted in bottom-line profits of about 13 percent and 0.2 percent, respectively, whereas a commitment of 50 percent of capital to each trade produced a loss of about 75 percent, with the identical trade-by-trade track record.

This huge contrast in results based upon the percentage of capital committed may seem surprising, but it is merely a logical outgrowth of the mathematics involved when you are investing in a vehicle that has the potential to produce very large losses on individual outcomes. Surely you would not consider risking 100 percent of the money you have earmarked for gambling at a casino on each hand of blackjack, because you understand that it is almost certain that you will encounter a losing hand that will wipe you out. Yet it is surprising how many options traders, perhaps "inoculated" from the possibility of a major

Table 4.2   **BOTTOM-LINE IMPACT: PERCENTAGE OF CAPITAL ALLOCATED PER TRADE**

Trade Result (%)	10% Invested	Initial $10,000	20% Invested	Initial $10,000	50% Invested	Initial $10,000
−74.63	$1,000.00	$9,253.73	$2,000.00	$8,507.46	$5,000.00	$6,268.66
−61.90	925.37	8,680.88	1,701.49	7,454.16	3,134.33	4,328.36
400.00	868.09	12,153.23	1,490.83	13,417.48	2,164.18	12,985.07
−62.96	1,215.32	11,388.03	2,683.50	11,727.87	6,492.54	8,897.18
−48.48	1,138.80	10,835.88	2,345.57	10,590.63	4,448.59	6,740.29
−80.77	1,083.59	9,960.68	2,118.13	8,879.83	3,370.14	4,018.25
−73.91	996.07	9,224.45	1,775.97	7,567.16	2,009.12	2,533.24
100.00	461.22	9,685.68	756.72	8,323.88	633.31	3,166.55
120.00	461.22	10,239.14	756.72	9,231.94	633.31	3,926.53
−100.00	1,023.91	9,215.23	1,846.39	7,385.55	1,963.26	1,963.26
−17.50	921.52	9,053.96	1,477.11	7,127.06	981.63	1,791.48
56.41	905.40	9,564.70	1,425.41	7,931.13	895.74	2,296.77
−56.10	956.47	9,028.14	1,586.23	7,041.30	1,148.38	1,652.55
−57.14	902.81	8,512.25	1,408.26	6,236.58	826.28	1,180.39
−81.11	851.22	7,821.81	1,247.32	5,224.87	590.20	701.68
−25.81	782.18	7,619.96	1,044.97	4,955.20	350.84	611.14
50.00	762.00	8,000.96	991.04	5,450.72	305.57	763.92
106.25	400.05	8,426.01	545.07	6,029.86	190.98	966.84
400.00	400.05	10,026.20	545.07	8,210.14	190.98	1,730.77
56.41	1,002.62	10,591.78	1,642.03	9,136.41	865.38	2,218.93
−45.00	1,059.18	10,115.15	1,827.28	8,314.14	1,109.47	1,719.67
129.27	505.76	10,768.93	831.41	9,388.89	429.92	2,275.42
114.63	505.76	11,348.70	831.41	10,341.98	429.92	2,768.25
−41.38	1,134.87	10,879.10	2,068.40	9,486.09	1,384.13	2,195.51
133.33	543.96	11,604.37	948.61	10,750.90	548.88	2,927.35
−14.29	543.96	11,526.67	948.61	10,615.38	548.88	2,848.94
16.22	1,152.67	11,713.59	2,123.08	10,959.67	1,424.47	3,079.93
−32.61	1,171.36	11,331.62	2,191.93	10,244.91	1,539.97	2,577.77
−2.82	1,133.16	(11,299.70)	2,048.98	(10,187.19)	1,288.88	(2,541.46)

or total loss on a trade from their stock-investing experience, will invest a major portion of their capital at risk on a single trade. Table 4.3 offers some eye-opening insight into the exponentially greater gains that are required to offset individual losses as they increase in magnitude. Managing your trading capital and individual trade commit-

Table 4.3   **LOSS/RECOVERY**

Loss	Subsequent Gain Needed to Recover to Break Even
–10%	+11%
–20%	+25%
–33%	+50%
–50%	+100%
–75%	+300%
–90%	+1,000%

ments is the key to allowing you to stay in the options game over the long term and profit from the big winners when they come along.

It is preferable to maintain a cash reserve that can be devoted to new opportunities as they develop, as well as provide a cushion of protection. As a rule, your entire trading capital should never be at risk at any one time in the options market, regardless of how attractive the current situation appears. There will always be losing trades, so by compounding your capital after some profitable trades, you are exposing yourself to some potentially painful dollar losses.

OVERCOMING GREED BY USING TARGET EXIT POINTS

The trading rules just discussed will maximize your chances of having several very profitable option positions at any given time. The following question is extremely important, because it will ultimately determine your bottom-line profitability: *When do you sell?*

1. *Set a target exit point for each trade.* A *target exit point* is an option price that would result in a substantial, yet attainable, profit. Set your profit objectives in advance and determine your target exit point before you trade or at the time you make your option purchase. By doing so, you avoid the consequences of one of the major stumbling blocks to achieving trading profits—greed. It is virtually impossible for most investors to set reasonable profit goals once an option has advanced substantially in price. That extra point or extra half-point becomes a moving target with each advance in the option's price. Therefore, it is not surprising that a reasonable profit is not achieved when the investor is forced to bail out because of tumbling prices.

You might view the above discussion of target exit points as perhaps conflicting with the old trading maxim of "cut your losses short and let your profits run." Although setting profit goals in advance may seem simplistic and not the most flexible approach to options trading, and by so doing you will likely miss out on the 1,000 percent profits that are the stuff of many options traders' dreams, the target exit point approach to taking profits is a necessary compromise for the nonprofessional options trader who has neither the savvy nor the emotional control to know "when to hold 'em and know when to fold 'em" in the heat of battle, and who is also unable to stay tuned to the markets throughout the trading day. Note that the profit objective should be *substantial*, meaning at least 100 percent, or double your initial investment, so you will not be walking away with meager profits by using this approach. With this approach, you will miss out on those 1,000 percent gains that are the options equivalent of (and have comparable probability to) hitting the lottery jackpot, but much more important, you will minimize the instances of solid profits becoming painful losses and you will regularly be taking respectable gains off the table. As fellow Market Technician's Association member Linda Bradford-Raschke has said, successful trading is about "staying in the game long enough to be lucky," and the discipline provided by the target exit point approach is designed to keep you in the options game.

Once you have entered the heat of battle, the tendency will be to base your decisions upon emotion, and therefore your decisions will tend to be incorrect. To avoid this pitfall, set a *closeout date* based on the amount of time you expect the option needs to reach its target exit point. If that profit level has not been reached by the closeout date, exit the position on that date. Closeout dates should be set so that there is still enough time until expiration to salvage some time value from the option if the underlying stock has failed to move.

Resist the temptation to sell at a small loss prior to your closeout date. You will be yielding to fear, robbing yourself of some potential gains. Also resist the temptation to raise your profit objective as the price of the option nears your target exit point. You will be yielding to greed, and your profits will slip away.

2. *Do not take profits haphazardly.* Taking profits haphazardly encompasses a multitude of sins. It includes having no specific profit objective (the greed syndrome) as well as setting illogical and insufficient profit objectives (such as a 10 percent gain) or emotional profit objectives ("This will be my lucky week. I just know I will make 1,000 percent on those XYZ calls.")

The next question is equally important: *When you should* not *sell?*

You should not sell a position the instant it moves against you. Many options traders will purchase an option at 3 and then, out of fear, sell it the same day should it decline to 2½. There is never a need to engage in panic selling if it is assumed that the following conditions hold:

- Your market outlook and your outlook for the stock on which you own options has not changed.
- You are not committing an excess amount of trading capital.
- You are purchasing options within your risk threshold.
- You are sufficiently diversified in calls and puts, relative to the current market condition.

An option is purchased for its huge profit potential, which can be fully realized only by allowing positions to remain open for a reasonable period of time.

OVERCOMING GREED BY USING A MAXIMUM ENTRY PRICE

One of the most common reasons options traders suffer losses is that the prices they pay for their options are too high relative to the profit that can be achieved on a reasonable move in the underlying stock. When analyzing an option opportunity, you should calculate the maximum price that you are willing to pay to enter the option (refer to chapter 3 for details on how to measure an option's price relative to its theoretical value). Frequently, traders get excited by rising prices and end up paying too much for an option because they don't want to miss out on an opportunity.

To illustrate this pitfall, let us take a look at a full-year track record for one of my electronically delivered services. For this example, let us assume that $2,500 was invested in each recommendation. Table 4.4 lists my maximum entry price (MEP) for each of these recommendations and the profit or loss achieved based upon purchasing each position at the MEP compared to the result of "chasing" each recommendation and paying ⅛-point *more* than the MEP.

As you can see from table 4.4, the investor who paid ⅛ point more for each position cut his total profits by almost 120 percentage points relative to the investor who followed the maximum entry price guidelines. Clearly, chasing the market and paying even an extra ⅛ point can drastically reduce your profit potential and increase your risk/reward ratio.

Table 4.4   **TRACK RECORD**

	Actual			MEP ⅛ Higher		
Date	Maximum Entry Price	Sale Price	Percentage Profit (Loss)	MEP Plus ⅛ Point	Sale Price	Percentage Profit (Loss)
01/31	2.938	5.875	100	3.063	5.875	92
01/31	2.625	0.000	(100)	2.750	0.000	(100)
03/07	2.875	2.875	0	3.000	2.875	(4)
04/25	1.938	3.250	84*	2.063	3.250	73*
05/15	1.719	1.813	5	1.844	1.813	(2)
06/01	3.063	2.000	(35)	3.188	2.000	(37)
07/12	1.906	0.000	(100)	2.031	0.000	(100)
08/09	1.688	3.500	107	1.813	3.500	93
09/14	2.906	4.500	55	3.031	4.500	48
09/20	1.719	3.063	78	1.844	3.063	66
09/20	2.625	10.500	200*	2.750	10.500	191*
09/21	2.438	1.875	(23)	2.563	1.875	(27)
10/18	2.063	4.188	103	2.188	4.188	91
10/23	2.375	3.188	67*	2.500	3.188	64*
11/29	1.813	1.125	(38)	1.938	1.125	(42)
12/01	1.875	2.375	63*	2.000	2.375	59*
12/18	1.563	0.813	(48)	1.688	0.813	(52)
12/27	1.438	2.500	74	1.563	2.500	60
Cumulative profit			592			473

*Indicates a double (100 percent profit) taken on half the position.

HOW TO CONTROL YOUR TRADING LOSSES

None of us likes to lose. Yet in options trading, taking losses along the way is part of being a successful trader. You must realize that losses occur and incorporate them into your game plan. If you don't take the necessary steps to contain risk, your losses will grow in magnitude until you eventually deplete most or possibly all of your trading capital.

One of the challenges of successful trading is to develop a mind-set that loss-taking must occur as a disciplined part of the trading process. Part of the nature of your methods must be to know when to cut a loser as painlessly as possible. The exponentially greater gains required to make up for each larger loss, as previously shown in table 4.3, really enlightens options traders on the need to have loss control levels predefined before initiating a trade. This behavior serves to keep losses contained and to instill the discipline to follow your trading method, while still not forcing you to panic out of a position on the first tick against you.

The discussion so far has outlined a way for you to set profit objectives and instructed you to always use a closeout date for option positions not developing as expected, but this is merely *theory*. What you are going to do in your account is *real life*. Not all objectives will be reached. Some will be reached and you will exit your trade as planned only to see the price of the option triple from where you took your profits. That's life. In other cases you will abandon a position on your closeout date only to see the market turn and the options sold as planned rise to very attractive profit levels. Again, that's life.

Do not think the market is singling you out for special punishment—it happens to every trader. If you don't think you can handle such situations, you shouldn't be trading options. The plan presented here will allow you to earn consistent profits year after year without spending many hours second-guessing what might have been. Use the plan and leave the second-guessing to the amateurs.

DISCRETIONARY VERSUS SYSTEMATIZED TRADING

One of the regular debates among traders relates to which approach will produce the best results over time: those methods that are rigidly applied via mechanical trading systems, or those methods that depend upon the discretion of the trader. Here we summarize the views of each side, and then I will give you my opinion.

The systems trader has the advantage of taking the emotion out of trading, primarily by consistently implementing mechanical buy and sell signals, and also by keeping the size of each new position constant as a percentage of the portfolio. This eliminates the impact of personal judgment as to which positions will work best, which allows the system to exploit its edge consistently over time while minimizing the impact that one position can have on the portfolio. Invariably, there will be bad periods with any method, and a system allows you to stick with the process through the bad as well as the good. Both discretionary and particularly system traders now use computers to screen large numbers of stocks, seeking out those that seem exploitable by their strategies. It is therefore almost imperative for serious options traders to use computers or have access to computer-generated information, if only to keep pace with their trading competitors.

The discretionary trader's critique of system trading relates to the fact that conditions change. Due to today's accelerating pace of change in the markets, a system based on a fixed set of parameters is not likely to succeed indefinitely. The discretionary trader focuses on achieving the big trade, which is the "monster move" that can earn a portfolio's annual return in one fell swoop. By having the ability to vary bet size based on the expected size of the profit and the perceived risk, the discretionary trader can be in a position to hit a home run on that big trade. In return for this flexibility, discretion will lead to more volatility in the portfolio, as the trader must be willing to stay with the big ideas despite bumps in the road. At the same time, risk control measures must be in place on every trade so that capital will always be available for the next big opportunity.

So which approach is best? The answer depends on the individual. I've followed the options market since its inception, and I believe it is in discretionary trading that I offer the most value to my subscribers. While I research the market based on thoroughly tested methods, the fact that I have seen a number of cycles and can sense where the "big trades" are likely to surface leads me down this discretionary path.

However, if you are a new trader and prefer not to depend upon someone else's expert advice, you might feel more comfortable developing a system for trading. But you must be aware of the trap into which nearly all new system designers fall at least once in their lives: "data mining." That is, a neophyte system designer takes a data set and develops a system that trades the past nearly perfectly. It looks great on paper. But there is absolutely no reason to believe that it would actually earn a profit in future trading. That is because in markets, as in life, the past rarely repeats its performance in exactly the same way, so the system fails.

The only viable way to have confidence that a system will work is if you first formulate your intuitive reasoning into a model that you believe will lead to success. You then apply that model to a set of data that you have not looked at before and study the results. If the preliminary results look good, additional testing is called for on so-called "out-of-sample" data until you are confident that your model produces profitable results without benefit of hindsight. Then and only then should you consider trying a system in the market with real money.

As you can see in the chart of Dell Computer in exhibit 4.1, systems traders could catch the two "out of bands" uptrends that occurred from August 22 to September 25 and from November 19 to December 12, 1996. The discretionary trader, however, could have jumped on these uptrends even more quickly, right after Dell reported

Exhibit 4.1   **DELL COMPUTER (DELL) DAILY CHART WITH 20-DAY VOLATILITY BANDS**

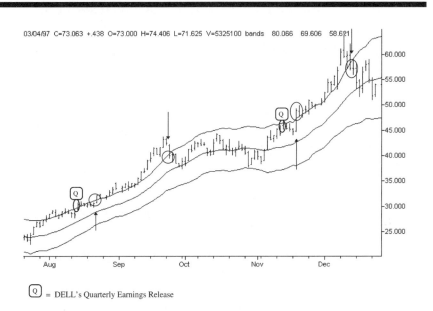

03/04/97 C=73.063 +.438 O=73.000 H=74.406 L=71.625 V=5325100 bands 80.066 69.606 58.621

Q = DELL's Quarterly Earnings Release

Reprinted with permission. Compliments of Bridge Information Systems.

quarterly earnings surprises on August 13 and November 12, shown by the "Q" in exhibit 4.1, which denotes the reaction after each release of Dell's quarterly earnings report. These earnings-driven news releases ultimately fueled the technical trends and gave discretionary traders a big edge.

THE TOP 10 RATIONALIZATIONS MADE BY THE AVERAGE OPTIONS TRADER

10. My broker doesn't know the meaning of the phrase "good fill."

9. If it weren't for commissions, I'd be in positive territory.

8. If I had only invested less in that one big loser.

7. If I can only break even on this options trade, I'll get out.

6. Other people lost money on this same bet, so I don't feel so badly.

5. If only I hadn't let that loss get out of control.

4. My stock was stronger than its group, but the sector went bad on me.

3. If I could trade full time, I'd have caught that ideal tick for entry/exit.

2. That money I lost was the equivalent of a brand-new car, motorcycle, vacation.

1. If I only had more time on my option.

Each of the above examples has one common thread: The options trader is trying to shift responsibilities that are his to someone or something else—his broker, the stock, the sector, the part-time nature of his trading, and so on. Rationalizations might temporarily make you feel better but they will do nothing to help you become a profitable options trader. As you will see from the comments below that relate to each of these rationalizations, you must take personal responsibility for your actions and your plan if you expect to be successful.

10. You cannot consistently blame your broker (find a new broker if you need to, but if you find you are constantly switching brokers, take a hard look at yourself and your trading method).

9. Commissions are a fact of life, and any trading plan must take them into account.

8. You must control the percentage of your account that goes into any one trade so as not to be overexposed on any one position.

7. The market doesn't care whether you as a trader are at a breakeven. This break-even mentality has cost traders countless millions, not only through holding underperforming positions, but also by draining energies and capital away from potentially better opportunities.

6. If others lose money on their trades, this should not offer you consolation. There is an excessive benchmarking culture in the investment world, when what you *should* be focusing on is making steady absolute returns without the risks inherent in running with the herd.

5. You must plan for loss control.

4. An awareness of sector performance should be part of your analysis, as it is better to buy a lesser stock in a strong sector than a quality stock in a weak sector.

3. If you are not trading full time, you are at a disadvantage, unless you create a method that is intermediate to longer-term in

nature. Alternatively, you could have someone else, such as your broker, watch the markets for you.

2. The gains or losses in trading must not be equated with material possessions, as that will distort your objective analysis of the markets. Try to keep the desire for dollars to a minimum and just concentrate on taking your entry and exit signals. If you do this properly, the dollars will then take care of themselves.

1. And finally, although it is frustrating to be wrong in the short term and then see a stock move as expected after your options have expired, that is sometimes part of the options game. One good antidote is to buy more time than you otherwise would, to give yourself more of a cushion for events developing less rapidly than you initially expected. You may also want to buy a strike that is closer to the current stock price, as often it is not the time factor that hurts as much as the fact that the stock moved, but not far enough to turn your trade into a winner.

STAGES OF THOUGHT FOR OPTIONS TRADERS

1. *Easy money*—The most damaging possible circumstance occurs when you, as a beginning options trader, immediately win big. These early profits lull you into a false sense of security and confidence, particularly if you had experienced some success with stocks. The result is an overcommitment of capital to future trades. Shortly after that overcommitment the invariable losers occur, potentially transforming you into a self-doubting, disillusioned loser.

2. *Paranoia*—Once you get into a cycle of frustration and self-doubt regarding your trading, you are likely to stay mired in a mindset that gives power away to others and leaves you clinging to very little other than ill-founded hope. Only when this stage ends and you proactively take control and responsibility for your trading wins and losses are you ready for the next stage, hard work.

3. *Hard work*—This is what is required to develop the consistent game plan that is necessary for success in options trading. One of the most important transformations at this stage is that the rationalizations of external sources of blame disappear, and you recognize that responsibility for trading results lies within yourself. With this recognition comes a great deal of searching for the right method that fits your style as far as risk, winning percentage, and the ratio of the size of the average win to average loss. Once such a method is found, you are ready for the never-ending final stage of thought.

4. *Disciplined follow-up for continuous improvement*—Personal accountability for trading results means that you, as an options trader, must constantly seek to improve existing methods. One of the best ways to achieve continuous improvement is to keep track of your trades with a trading journal. The trading journal will give you an objective source of information about why each trade was entered and exited, which is necessary for a successful follow-up process. As we have all experienced, the mind can be selective in what it remembers, often recalling only the events it wants to recall. With a trading journal, you can identify patterns and strategies that either worked and should be repeated, or didn't work and should be abandoned.

ADDITIONAL RISKS

After you have taken the steps to minimize the pitfalls of greed and fear, you should then work to reduce other forms of risk. The total options trading risk you face can be viewed from the standpoint of the following components:

1. *Systematic risk* (also called undiversifiable risk) is risk that cannot be eliminated because it arises from factors that cause the market as a whole to move up or down. It is not diversifiable because it affects all securities. Examples of systematic risk are political or sociological changes, such as a presidential election. However, the most common forms of systematic risk are those caused by changes in interest rates or inflation. The expectational analysis concepts discussed throughout this book will help you measure how much complacency or fear exists ahead of key systematic events, and is in fact part of my method for determining the risk/reward ratio of any situation. Options traders have a unique advantage in their approach to reducing systematic risk, as they can easily purchase puts as well as calls to help neutralize their exposure to major market moves.

2. *Unsystematic risk* (also called diversifiable risk) is the portion of risk that is unique to a particular company. Examples of unsystematic risk include labor strikes, a shortage of raw materials, weather or seasonal changes, a company's financial structure, or earnings surprises in either direction. Since unsystematic risk affects a single company or industry, you can minimize it by diversifying investments in many companies across a broad range of industries.

3. *Truncated risk* (where your loss is limited to your initial invest-ment yet your profit is theoretically unlimited) is a major advantage of purchasing options. Diversification allows you to use truncated risk to its maximum advantage. Even though some of your positions will inevitably be unprofitable, each profitable position can offset sev-eral unprofitable trades. Also, because options can be purchased for a mere fraction of the price of a comparable purchase of the underlying stock, they are ideally suited for diversification. In fact, many inves-tors who cannot afford sufficient diversification in their stock invest-ments are able to broadly diversify using options. Options diversifica-tion should be two-dimensional, which is accomplished by buying both calls and puts on a variety of companies. You are then somewhat insulated from the impact of overall market movements (systematic risk). The key to achieving profits in options trading is to maximize your chances to realize very large percentage gains. This requires the financial and emotional staying power provided by controlling fear and greed to assure that you will be around to achieve these huge profits. The finishing touch involves the risk-reducing and profit-maximizing technique of diversification. By always carrying several different option positions, you will maximize your chances to achieve huge winners and minimize your chances of incurring large losses within your options portfolio. The strategies that the prudent options trader uses to minimize risk are outlined below.

a. *Invest in options in a variety of companies.* Establish option posi-tions in several underlying stocks in unrelated industries.

b. *Invest in both calls and puts.* Always invest in puts as well as in calls, so that you will be in a position to profit regardless of overall market conditions, and so that guessing wrong on the overall market does not severely deplete your trading capital. Many investors believe the only way to make money in the market is to take a bullish position on an advancing stock. With the ability to purchase puts on thousands of stocks, it is now just as easy to take a bearish position as a bullish posi-tion. And the limited risk of put purchasing offers a less dicey method of speculating on a down move than the alternative of selling stock short.

PROFILES OF OPTIONS TRADING OFFENSES: "WANTED" FOR BAD MONEY MANAGEMENT PRACTICES

It is clear that the fearful investor sharply limits his profit opportuni-ties, and the greedy investor lets his profits slip away. Variations of these traits are evident in the profiles below. Perhaps you'll even recognize someone you know all too well.

The Trigger-Happy Investor

The trigger-happy investor is often new to options trading, although the same trading practices can occasionally be found in veteran investors. As this type of investor uncovers a potentially profitable opportunity, he becomes extremely excited. In his excitement, the investor loses track of trading guidelines and plows all of his trading capital into the investment. As other opportunities arise, the investor is caught holding an empty gun and cannot participate. Because of a lack of cash, the trigger-happy investor is required to sell open positions to invest in the potentially better opportunity. Under the best of circumstances, this trading style results in high commission costs and poor exits from potentially profitable positions. Under the worst of circumstances, this trading style ends in a complete loss of the investor's capital when a "sure-fire" investment goes sour or the market makes a quick turn. If you know a trigger-happy investor, you should convince him to allocate only a small percentage of trading capital to each individual trading opportunity. By not risking everything on one investment, there is a much better chance of staying afloat through volatile periods in the market and of having the ability to make additional investments when opportunities arise.

The Living-on-the-Brink Investor

The living-on-the-brink investor is often highly confident—indeed too confident—in his trading ability. This confidence level leads him to invest capital that will be needed for noninvestment purposes in the future. Whether this investor's optimism comes from a very successful trading record or from other reasons, this trading style will ultimately end in disaster. Eventually, an investment will not perform as expected, and the investor will be under pressure to sell, which may result in a premature exit of a potentially profitable position and the wasting of commissions. If this trader encounters a string of losing trades, he could be forced to use high-interest or credit-card loans to meet regular living expenses. If you know a living-on-the-brink investor, immediately stress the importance of trading with capital that will *not* be needed for other obligations.

The One-Dimensional Investor

The one-dimensional investor is often considered overly cautious. This individual will not invest in unfamiliar situations. Even though not investing blindly is a desirable trait, this individual's portfolio is usually not diversified, resulting in needless risk. Often, the entire portfolio is represented by only one type of investment, or worse yet, an investment in only one company. For example, if the investor is familiar with stocks, his portfolio contains only stock investments, because he does not feel comfortable with other vehicles. In the case of an options investor, his portfolio may contain only calls with no put positions, endangering the entire portfolio in the event of a downturn in the market. If you know a one-dimensional investor, immediately stress the importance and rewards of diversification. In the long run, exposure to good call and put ideas will lead to a balanced portfolio less subject to systematic risk.

The Read-It-on-the-Street Investor

The read-it-on-the-street investor is often very excited about a stock after hearing about the company or its products in the news, or after reading about the company in a business newspaper or magazine. This investor is often disappointed and confused when the investment does not perform according to his expectations. Unfortunately, this investor often pays inflated prices for his options because he buys during the tail end of a success story, when market optimism is high. Although companies that are positively mentioned in the media can continue their strong performance, it is important to remember that high expectations and the possibility of upcoming good news have often already been incorporated into a company's stock and option prices, as it takes only minutes for the market to adjust to such news. It is often better for an investor to stand aside and wait for more favorable prices than to rush in and buy at bloated prices, which drastically reduces profit potential. If you know a person who is a read-it-on-the-street investor, stress the importance of investing before most of the crowd piles into a well-publicized situation.

The Indecisive Investor

The indecisive investor often begins with a solid investing strategy. However, as time passes and the value of his investments change, so do his expectations. For example, this type of investor will purchase a stock with the expectation that it will quickly move from $25 to $30 per share, where he plans to sell it for a 20 percent profit. However, as the stock approaches the $30 mark, he is not satisfied with just a 20 percent return and holds for even bigger gains. In many cases, he holds the stock much longer than originally planned, and often never realizes the increased profit objective. Likewise, this type of investor frequently continues to hold losing trades in the expectation that prices will reverse and the trade will become profitable. Although a reversal is possible, the investor is risking further losses. If you know an indecisive investor, suggest setting target exit points for profits and closeout dates when positions that have not reached their targets should be closed.

The Gung-Ho Investor

The gung-ho investor is known for paying too much for his positions. This individual will risk his entire investment capital for a small profit. Since most options traders have more losing trades than they do profitable ones, this is a doomed strategy. Because of the high risks associated with at-the-money and out-of-the-money options, individuals who purchase these investments should never risk more than they expect to profit. Due to the high volatility of options trading, the minimum objective for this type of an investment should be a two-to-one reward-to-risk ratio, with a much higher reward preferred relative to the risk taken. For example, an individual should not invest $2,000 in an out-of-the-money option trade unless he stands to gain at least $4,000 if the stock performs as expected. If you know a gung-ho investor, convince him to invest only in opportunities with a favorable reward-to-risk ratio.

SUMMARY—THE KEYS TO SUCCESSFUL TRADING

The two most important factors for successful options trading are:

1. *A reasonable percentage of successful trades that achieve big profits.* No trading approach is perfect, and there will always be trades that are unprofitable. Because of the huge profit potential and limited risk in options trading, you can achieve highly profitable results with a success ratio on individual trades of under 50 percent. For example, with a 300 percent profit target, you will break even if the profit target is achieved in only one-quarter (one out of four) of your trades. This assumes that you invest equal units of capital in each trade and that all trades that do not achieve their targets become total losses. In many cases, of course, your trades will include partial losses and profits lower then the targeted amount. If you assume a 300 percent target profit and a total loss on all trades that do not achieve their targets, a success rate of 40 percent will result in an average gain of 30 percent per trade. (All of these returns are before commissions.)

2. *An intelligent money management system that preserves capital.* The first step toward intelligent money management is to trade only with that portion of your capital that can comfortably be devoted to speculation, as trading options is a speculative activity. This will permit you to act rationally and to sleep soundly, neither of which is possible when your nest egg is at risk. Once you have determined your trading capital, there is one final important rule: *Never* risk your entire trading capital on a single trade. This rule holds regardless of how successful you have previously been and regardless of how attractive the next trade appears. There will always be losing trades. By compounding your capital after a few profitable trades, you are exposing yourself to some potentially very painful dollar losses once that loser comes along. *Always* keep a large portion of your trading capital in reserve. By doing this, you will have the staying power to ride out the losers so you can ultimately profit from the winners, including those winners that show paper losses early, but are eventually closed out for gains. Commit no more than 10 percent of your total trading capital to any one position. The latter aspect of this trading strategy prevents you from overcommitting capital to any one trade; the former aspect insures that you have sufficient capital in reserve to let you take advantage of opportunities when they come along.

By applying all of the above techniques, you will have effectively managed the trading process in such a way to reduce your risk and increase your profit potential. Let us review how this is accomplished.

1. *Manage your risk.* You are trading only with speculative capital. Your positions are diversified using the principle of *two-dimensional diversification*, and your capital is protected from accelerated time decay by your predetermined closeout dates.

2. *Manage your rewards.* Because you have managed your risk, you will never bail out too early and thus rob yourself of profit opportunities. You are targeting substantial yet achievable profits using predetermined *target exit points*. With this strategy, you will stand to profit more at your target exit point than you stand to lose. Your targeted risk/reward ratio is in your favor.

CONCLUSION

Applying the principles of risk/reward management discussed in this chapter will allow you to profit despite the inevitable losses that will occur on specific options trades. In fact, just one large gain could more than wipe out several losses, and result in a healthy bottom-line profit. For example, $1,000 invested in an option that achieves a 200 percent profit target (three times the original purchase price) will yield a profit of $2,000. If two other $1,000 positions each result in losses of 50 percent, the bottom-line profit would be $1,000 ($2,000 gain less $1,000 loss), which is a 33 percent precommission gain on a $3,000 total investment. And this could be achieved in a matter of weeks. It is likely that during some weeks and months you will experience no profits but, instead, will encounter a string of losses that will eat into, but not wipe out, your trading capital. The strategies detailed here will allow you to continue to initiate more trades, which will help return your account to profitability.

A steadfast application of these principles of risk/reward management will substantially improve your chances for success in options trading and give you the staying power to achieve the big winning trades that ultimately define success in the options market.

One final thought is in order: Although you must realistically expect to have losing trades in your options trading mix, you cannot afford to *think* like a loser. Every trade, winner or loser, adds to your options trading education and must be treated with the respect its lessons impart. Don't allow yourself to get caught in a mire of self-pity or self-congratulation and miss the next opportunity. Learn your lessons and apply them to future trades. In that way, you will become a much more accomplished options trader.

5

Market Timing Indicators and Techniques

INTRODUCTION

To trade options successfully you must first and foremost know how to choose the right stock and the right option on that stock. But you must also know the impact of the broad market on your investments.

The Greek poet Hesiod wrote in 700 B.C., "Observe due measure, for timing is in all things the most important factor." Expanding on this observation, the shorter term your perspective, the more critical timing the market becomes; I call this "time-critical investing." As a short-term options trader, you must have an arsenal of time-critical market indicators to keep you generally positioned on the right side of the market.

Not only will these indicators help you determine which calls and puts you expect to do well under certain market conditions, they will also dictate the proportion of calls you hold relative to puts, or your "net exposure." By aligning your net exposure on call and put positions as closely as possible with your market view, results can be maximized by correctly determining the expectations for the market.

Some of the most useful market-timing indicators are based on investor sentiment. Significant changes in market direction are usually preceded by extremes in investor optimism or pessimism. The consistency of the market boom over the past fifteen years has been fueled by pessimistic sentiment, especially since the 1987 crash. Brief periods of excessive investor optimism have been cooled by healthy corrections within the ongoing bull trend. An analysis of sentiment from a contrarian perspective is often a large part of the market-timing picture. Extreme bearishness often precedes huge market advances, and high levels of optimism can forecast an impending decline. So many investors have so much trouble with their market timing because they lack a perspective on measuring and interpreting sentiment.

But sentiment cannot be analyzed in a vacuum. The student of sentiment must have accurate ways to gauge not only the best indicators of investor attitudes, but also the technical and fundamental factors that define the nature of the market. Only when sentiment flies in the face of the fundamental and technical facts (or is off the charts relative to past extremes) is it an especially useful contrarian indicator.

SENTIMENT INDICATORS FOR THE MARKET

Why must you look at sentiment indicators in relation to prevailing fundamental and technical trends, and not just on an absolute basis? Because pessimistic sentiment should be expected if fundamentals are negative and the technical trend is down. But when overly pessimistic sentiment appears at unexpected times, as has been the case during the market rally since the 1987 crash on most every minor pullback, that's meaningful and tradable information. In contrast to such bearish sentiment in the 1990s amid many technical and fundamental positives, pre-crash 1987 was marked by a bullish sentiment that the market couldn't shake. At that time put selling was considered the "safe" play, as opposed to put buying, which, ever since the crash, has been considered the "safe" approach. And these complacent put sellers were hurt most in the 1987 crash, just as the put buyers have been badly hurt in the 1990s. There is a big difference between "safe and popular" and "correct" in the investment world.

Often, so-called "contrarians" will jump at the opportunity to buy when the market has lost a great deal of value and has very few remaining bullish proponents. That is like trying to catch a falling knife—it can hurt you badly if you don't catch it just right. Only when sentiment reaches an "off-the-charts" extreme can you be confident enough to bet that the negative fundamentals and technicals are fully incorporated into the market's pricing. Late 1990 is a case in point: Following a poor year for stocks and after the final downleg low in October 1990, the equity put/call ratio of options traded on the Chicago Board Options Exchange (CBOE) soared to its highest levels in more than two years (see exhibit 5.1). This off-the-charts negative sentiment reading suggested the damage was done and that there was more reward than risk, and in fact this proved to be a major market bottom.

Exhibit 5.1   **S&P 100 INDEX WITH EQUITY PUT/CALL RATIO, 1990–1991**

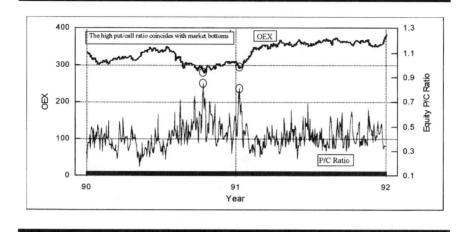

The CBOE Market Volatility Index

Along the same lines as put/call ratio analysis, extreme readings in the CBOE Market Volatility Index (VIX) are a great contrarian resource for gauging future market direction. The VIX is a combination of the implied volatilities of eight S&P 100 Index (OEX) options to give a reading of expected market volatility over the next thirty calendar days.[1] Put/call ratios typically surge higher when the OEX declines, and the VIX also tends to spike up during declines, as nervous investors bid up the price of index puts to either hedge their portfolios or speculate on further downside potential. In other words, not only is put *volume* heavier during these OEX pullbacks, but investors are willing to *pay* more for these puts.

Extremely high and low readings of the VIX normally give good contrarian signals, but it actually doesn't matter where the reading lies on an absolute basis if it is extremely high or low relative to its recent readings. We can measure this by plotting Bollinger bands around the daily VIX reading, as shown in exhibit 5.2.

Bollinger bands were developed by John Bollinger. The top band equates to two standard deviations above the 21-day moving average; the bottom band is two standard deviations below the 21-day moving average. Whenever the price moves outside the lines it can be consid-

---

1. For further information on the technical issues related to the calculation of the CBOE Market Volatility Index, contact the CBOE and ask for the document entitled "The Risk Management Series."

Exhibit 5.2   CBOE MARKET VOLATILITY INDEX WITH BOLLINGER BANDS

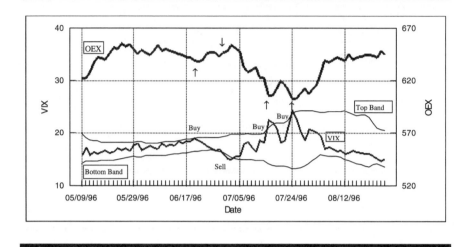

ered to be significantly high (or low) relative to its recent price trends and to its normal volatility. *Buy* signals occur as soon as the VIX moves back below its upper band after it has closed above of this boundary. *Sell* signals occur after the VIX closes back above its lower band after it has closed below this boundary.

Since the beginning of 1986, if the VIX advances by 20 percent over ten days, the OEX has *fallen* by 2.66 percent on average, compared to an average gain of 0.48 percent. This illustrates the inverse correlation between the OEX and VIX. But the speculative rush to buy puts, which forces the VIX higher, has often provided support for the falling OEX at VIX extremes.

When you want to buy the OEX following a sharp decline, it is best to do so *after* the top in the VIX has occurred. Another means of determining this VIX top has been a move above 20.00 and then back below 20.00. As you can see in exhibit 5.3, after the VIX closes back below 20.00, the OEX rallies by nearly two and a half times more than is typical.

You can see the importance of VIX spikes above 20.00 since 1994 in exhibit 5.4. These sharp jumps above 20.00 tend to correspond to major market lows, as fear causes a rush to buy puts from portfolio hedgers and speculators. This increased demand pumps up the implied volatilities for the puts, which results in an extreme VIX reading. Note that such spikes have corresponded with major market lows in November 1994, as well as in March, July, and December 1996.

Exhibit 5.3   **S&P 100 INDEX PERFORMANCE AFTER A VIX CLOSE BACK BELOW 20.00**

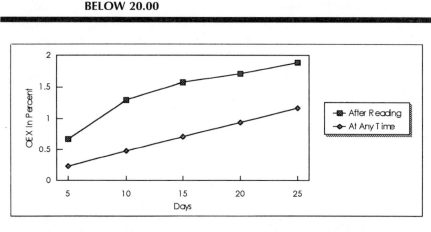

Money Market Sector Fund Assets

Future market direction can also be predicted by tracking mutual fund money flows in the Fidelity Select Money Market fund assets as a percentage of all Fidelity Select sector fund assets. Exhibit 5.5 shows that extremely high levels of cash held by these mutual fund speculators signal excessive fear that usually marks major market lows, whereas extremely low cash levels show these players to be heavily invested, implying market weakness since buying power is depleted

Exhibit 5.4   **S&P 100 INDEX AND VIX SPIKE ABOVE 20.00**

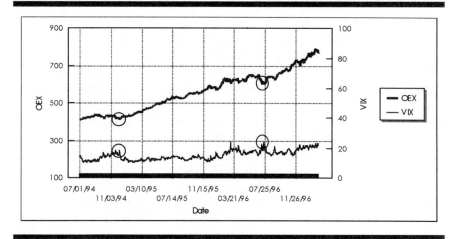

Exhibit 5.5   **S&P 100 INDEX RELATIVE TO FIDELITY SELECT MONEY MARKET ASSETS**

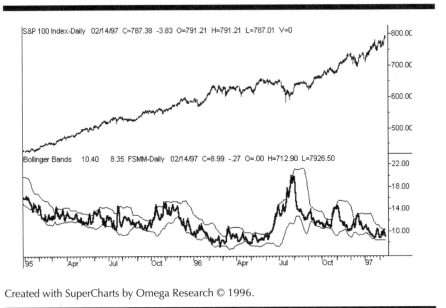

Created with SuperCharts by Omega Research © 1996.

and also since speculators are invariably incorrect when they agree en masse. The relative extremes are measured by applying the 21-day Bollinger band to the money market data. High cash levels at the upper Bollinger band suggest relative fear, whereas low cash levels suggest fully invested speculators near short-term tops.

Open Interest Analysis

Analyzing the *open interest* in OEX options can also provide keys to future market volatility and direction. As already mentioned, the VIX often spikes higher during market declines based upon the fear of speculators who rush to buy puts. You will also see these apprehensions materialize when you notice increasing put open interest in the OEX options. A certain amount of fear is healthy for the market, and that is why demand is greater for OEX put options relative to calls during sustained bull markets. The best way to gauge this sentiment picture is to measure the magnitude of the open interest in out-of-the-money OEX calls and puts in the front-month options that will soon expire. These are the preferred options of speculators, and we want to determine when speculator fear or greed is at an extreme. One such example occurred on November 25, 1996, as we approached a market bottom, and I noted to my daily fax clients that fourteen out-of-the-money OEX December put strikes carried open interest of more than 10,000 contracts, whereas none of the out-of-the-money OEX December call strikes had open interest of 10,000 or more.

Large amounts of put open interest provide support for the market for three primary reasons:

1. They typically define points of extreme market pessimism, which usually coincides with the depletion of selling strength. Once selling strength becomes less than buying power, the market will rally.

2. Those who sold these put options to bearish speculators may short the OEX synthetically or short index futures to offset the bullish position they acquired by selling the puts. These short positions initiated as a hedge will ultimately be bought back once the put players unwind their positions or see these options expire, thus providing a boost to the OEX.

3. Unhedged put sellers often attempt to support the market as it declines toward the strike at which they sold their puts so as to avoid substantial losses on their options.

Similar to the discussion of open interest in chapter 2 relating to individual stocks, analyzing the open interest on the most actively traded OEX options can provide insight into future market direction over the near term. Only when the OEX open interest for calls is greater than that for puts should there be cause for major concern for the bulls.

My peak open interest indicator measures the largest amount of open interest in the front-month OEX call and put options. These options are nearest to their expiration, and thus attract the speculative crowd due to their lower absolute cost and higher leverage. After determining the amount of the peak open interest for the biggest front-month index call, compare that amount to the peak open interest for the largest front-month index put.

The peak put open interest normally exceeds the peak call open interest during bull market phases, and the market has more reward than risk, according to my contrarian analysis, as long as the put peak exceeds the call peak. This shows up in exhibit 5.6 as periods where the peak put/call open interest ratio is greater than 1.00. Note that major buying opportunities have occurred when the peak put/call open interest ratio has been significantly above 1.00. Likewise, in the few instances where this ratio has been below 1.00 since 1993, the market has run into trouble in the near term. Most notable are the February 1994 reading below 1.00 and the January 1996 reading below 1.00. Such periods of optimism occurred after strong

Exhibit 5.6   **BULL MARKETS AS DEFINED BY PUT/CALL OPEN INTEREST RATIO GREATER THAN 1.00**

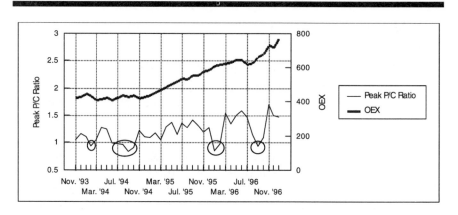

price uptrends, and led to corrections once these option traders swung too far to the bullish side.

Open Interest and Options Pricing

Options pricing is another factor that needs to be considered in conjunction with open interest. Excessive optimism is normally found very near market tops, but there have been occasions when this optimism was reflected, surprisingly, in the form of large amounts of *put* open interest. Although heavy put open interest is generally a bullish contrarian indicator, a look at the comparative pricing of equally distant out-of-the-money puts and calls can give us further clues about which players and strategies are predominant, and thus reveal the true sentiment picture.

For example, prior to the 1987 crash the index put open interest was higher than the call open interest. By itself, this heavy put activity might suggest that the market should have continued on its upward course. But the index put open interest in 1987 resulted from naked put selling (see chapter 9) on a massive scale. Most investors were convinced that the market would not go down, so they wrote puts in huge quantities. Many considered selling naked puts the equivalent of a "homegrown money machine," and seminars on naked put selling were very popular. In addition, prior to the 1987 crash, far out-of-the-money puts and calls were comparably priced, whereas in the 1990s put premiums have been running about twice that of call premiums. So in pre-crash 1987 the large amounts of put open interest represented excessive optimism, not excessive pessimism. Those who worry about a market crash should consider the fact that speculators throughout the 1990s have been willing to pay considerably higher premiums for index puts than for index calls. Such pessimistic behavior has *never* occurred at major market tops.

See chapter 2 for additional sentiment indicators such as put/call ratios, cover stories, sector fund assets, and sentiment surveys.

EXPECTATIONAL ANALYSIS IN THE BROAD MARKET

There are two primary factors that support the conclusions of expectational analysis when applied to the market as a whole: psychology and mechanics, as elaborated below.

1. *Psychology.* When investors are exhibiting an extreme in sentiment in one direction or another, the trend that has been in place is most likely near an end. This is a simple fact of investment psychology: The markets are driven by the fear and greed inherent in human nature, which tend to reach extreme levels at market bottoms and tops, respectively.

2. *Mechanics.* Index option activity directly affects the underlying market. When there is heavy index put activity, and put prices are very high due to rampant investor fear, that put activity directly translates into short positions in the futures market as put sellers hedge their positions. When the market rallies and thus defies those negative expectations, these short positions get covered, and such short covering provides even more buying power for the rally to continue.

THE IMPLICATIONS OF EXTREMES IN EXPECTATIONS

If prior to significant events there is an extreme in sentiment (with heavy call activity indicating bullish sentiment and heavy put activity indicating bearish sentiment), the resolution is usually *opposite* to the direction of the speculative activity. If bullish sentiment reaches an extreme, a very strong positive event must occur if the market is to go up, because most of that bullish sentiment is already priced into the index via the heavy call option activity prior to the event. And it takes only a very minor negative surprise (a slightly less-than-favorable event) in this situation to prompt a very negative reaction.

For example, sentiment on both stocks and bonds became overly optimistic heading into 1994. The gains in these markets in 1993 caused investors, the media, and speculators to have very high hopes for a bull market year in 1994. However, even after the Federal Reserve raised interest rates in February 1994, speculators viewed this initial decline as a buying opportunity, as OEX call open interest exceeded put open interest at the largest front-month strike price (a rare occurrence). This indicated to contrarians that the market had not yet bottomed, and the market plunged another 6 percent in March.

Similarly, an extreme in *bearish* sentiment ahead of an event has *bullish* postevent implications. After the 1990 bear market lows sparked by worries over a prolonged war in the Gulf, investors were fully expecting the Dow Industrials to drop sharply once fighting broke out after the mid-January deadline. Despite all the reports of the dangers from "battle-hardened" Iraqi troops, the Dow shot up 115 points, or 4 percent, on January 17, and rallied another 15 percent over the subsequent month.

This expectation-based methodology has also proven valuable in timing the overall market on an intermediate and longer-term basis. For example, index option traders have been betting against the rally in stocks, almost without interruption, since the 1987 crash. This pessimism has persisted despite the powerful technical uptrend and the strong fundamentals as evidenced by sixteen consecutive quarters of positive earnings surprises exceeding negative earnings surprises. Such doubt in the face of strong technicals and strong fundamentals has driven my belief that this low-expectation bull market offers solid reward potential with below-average risk.

You can easily get sidetracked when trying to gauge expectations because very often the sentiment is simply consistent with the movement in the market. You expect bullish sentiment when the market is going up and you expect bearish sentiment when stocks are going down. That is just normal human behavior (what I call "dog bites man"), and it is very difficult to draw conclusions from it. However, if the market has been consistently going up, yet sentiment is negative as speculators attempt to call a top, that's a "man bites dog" situation on sentiment, as it isn't the reaction you would normally expect. If instead of going with the trend, speculators are betting against the trend, this has historically had powerful contrarian implications.

It is also important to monitor sentiment on pullbacks in a bull market. During the 10 percent OEX decline from a high on July 1, 1996, to an intraday low on July 16, 1996, sentiment reached a climactic peak in bearishness, as the equity put/call ratio was higher on July 16 than at any time since the end of 1989. Confirmation came from the intraday VIX high on July 24, which was higher than any reading since January 1991. This indicated that the bull market was still alive, and the ensuing market rally ratified this conclusion. But when a pullback is greeted with complacency and a "no fear" attitude (as was the case in 1987 from the mid-August top until the crash in October), then the market can be expected to have further difficulty. (Note that on an October 2, 1987, *Timer Digest* hotline, *all* of the "top ten timers" were bullish on stocks, even though the market had pulled back from its August highs.[2]) But as long as negative sentiment continues to flow into the market after even small declines, a bull market is very likely to resume its upward course.

TRENDS AND TRADING RANGES IN THE MARKET

Another important consideration that needs to be a part of your analysis is the trend (or lack of trend) in the market. Just as chapter 2 discussed the impact of trends and trading ranges on individual stocks, so too must we understand when the market is in a trend or a range. The OEX experiences some trending periods in which it moves in steady steps, continuing in the same direction for some time. The 1995 period is a good example of a steady uptrend. In other instances, a trading range defines resistance at the top end and support at the bottom end of the range. The choppiness of 1994 displays such a range very clearly (see exhibit 5.7).

It is always more desirable to take long positions in options on a low-volatility trending market than in a high-volatility trading range market. The reason is that volatility in the market helps define the price of the underlying option, so options in high volatility markets will be more expensive. Understanding that all options will be devoid of volatility premium when the option expires, you can appreciate the fact that options priced higher due to higher volatility may decline in price at a faster rate, especially in directionless markets. Therefore, you should endeavor to search out those opportunities where you expect the OEX to move more than the implied volatility suggests; this often occurs in trending situations.

For example, if OEX options have an implied volatility of 20 percent, they are priced based upon the expectation that two-thirds of the time the OEX will move higher or lower by 20 percent over the coming year. From here, we need to define our expectations for the OEX in comparison to the implied volatility, adjusted for a shorter time frame. Using the square root to adjust the annualized 20 percent vola-

---

2. *Timer Digest* hotline, October 2, 1987. *Timer Digest* is published by Jim Schmidt, who monitors the bullish, bearish, and neutral advice of more than 100 market timers. For more information, write Timer Digest, P.O. Box 1688, Greenwich, CT 06836–1688.

Exhibit 5.7   **S&P 100 INDEX WEEKLY CHART: TRADING RANGE VERSUS TREND**

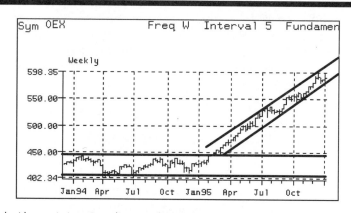

Reprinted with permission. Compliments of ILX Systems.

tility assumption to a three-month (0.25 year) time frame, we get an implied 90-day volatility of 10 percent ($\sqrt{0.25} \times 20\% = 0.5 \times 20\% = 10\%$). If we have a strong directional outlook for the OEX over the next ninety days, and in particular if we expect that directional price move to be in excess of 10 percent, we will profit significantly from buying OEX options. For example, if we expect the OEX to rally by 15 percent or more over the next ninety days, OEX call options, which are priced based on a nondirectional 10 percent volatility assumption, would be a very strong buy. The opposite is also true. When OEX options carry very high implied volatilities relative to where the OEX is likely to go directionally, selling OEX options and allowing time decay to work in your favor is likely to prove very profitable.

The stage of a trend is also a key component in your options decision-making process. The best time to buy options is when the trend is already established. In other words, buy options in the heart of the trend, not at the beginning. Being a "hero" in options investing will get you killed. Here's why: It might be tempting to look at a chart of the OEX and fantasize about how much money you could have made by buying a call option at the very bottom of a pullback. This can be frustrating, but it is also unrealistic. By searching out methods to pick reversals, you often stack the deck against yourself in terms of options pricing. The options pricing model assumes random movements of the underlying security. Buying options in trending markets is an advantage, so trying to "bottom fish" and catch the reversal point will put you at a disadvantage over time.

The fact that the VIX spikes higher in conjunction with OEX declines indicates that option prices become more expensive due to increased volatility assumptions. Time decay will hurt more expensive options by a greater percentage relative to less expensive options. So why take the risk of buying options on reversals when you can be much more sure that you will be correct in trending situations? Trends have been proven to be more likely to continue in the same direction than to reverse. Trends also tend to persist much longer than most market participants would expect. Now let us look at some ways to help determine specifically if the broad market is in a trend.

METHODS TO DEFINE MARKET TRENDS

It is not uncommon to hear that the market has gone up so far for so long that it has to correct itself at some point. This may be true eventually, but an upward trend in the market at any random point in time is more likely to continue than to reverse. There are many ways to define whether a trend exists. Here we will discuss upward trends, but downward trends are also tradable. The fact that stock market indices have advanced over long periods of time leads us to concentrate more on upward trends than on downward trends. By allowing the "trend to be your friend," you will be more likely to buy less expensive options on stocks or indices that will probably keep going in the same direction.

Moving Averages on the OEX

Simple moving averages are probably among the best methods to define trends. If the OEX is above its 20-day moving average, its 20-day is above its 50-day, and its 50-day is above its 200-day, the market is in a clear upward trend. This is the best-case scenario for the market, because these upward trends are likely to continue for two main reasons: First, there is likely a good reason why the OEX is above its moving averages. Perhaps the OEX is benefiting from a good fundamental backdrop, a low interest rate environment, or strong earnings prospects for its underlying 100 large-capitalization component stocks. Regardless, the market doesn't often find itself in this environment of "moving average perfection" if fundamental conditions are not bullish.

The second reason involves moving averages as support points. Pullbacks occur in every uptrending market, and these declines often bottom out at their moving averages, especially if the moving aver-

Exhibit 5.8   **S&P 100 INDEX WITH 10-WEEK AND 20-WEEK MOVING AVERAGES**

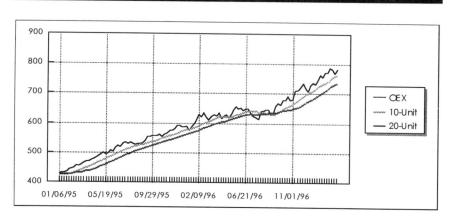

ages are upward-trending. Notice the graph of the OEX with its 10-week and 20-week moving averages on exhibit 5.8. The OEX has consistently found support at these key moving averages.

There are many reasons why moving averages provide support, but one of the most meaningful is the fact that investors often allocate additional funds to stocks that have pulled back to an important trendline. As Edgar Peters pointed out in his insightful book, *Chaos and Order in the Capital Markets*, "Real feedback systems involve long-term correlations and trends, because memories of long-past events can still affect the decisions made in the present."[3] Since the "feedback" aspect of chaos theory supports the evidence of trends, you can see how moving averages can provide support or resistance. As more investors become aware of the trend along a moving average, more money is then allocated to the stock as it pulls back to a key moving average. Mr. Peters's belief rings true that many investors are generally slow to react to a trend and also tend to adhere to their current outlook or belief until there is overwhelming evidence or confirming information. This explains why many contrarians are often premature in their analysis and do not ride the trend to its full extent.

Despite the strong price action of the OEX in 1995–1997, investors have been slow to abandon the consensus thinking that the market is overvalued. Therefore, with more recent events having greater im-

---

3. Edgar E. Peters, *Chaos and Order in the Capital Markets* (New York: John Wiley & Sons, 1991), 6.

pact, the trend feeds on itself. Not until the investment herd totally capitulates—often signaled by a parabolic surge in the market followed by a subsequent break below the key moving average—is the uptrend likely to be finished. Moving averages have been used by market technicians for many years and are fairly well known. In this sense, moving averages can become a self-fulfilling prophecy when acted upon by enough traders and investors.

The Number of Days Below a Moving Average

Another means of analysis associated with the 50-day moving average can help determine if the market is in a trending environment. There are relatively few days that a stock market index will close below its 50-day moving average if it is in the midst of a strong upward trend. Specifically, if the OEX closes below its 50-day moving average less than five days out of the prior fifty, we define the OEX as being in an upward trend. The OEX tends to decline or move sideways on average after posting more than five days out of the prior fifty below the 50-day moving average (see exhibit 5.9). Put buyers at that point will get the double benefit of a decline in the underlying OEX and a corresponding increase in volatility.

One aspect of trading ranges is the fact that the market is kept from trending higher by overhead resistance. There are often several peaks at the same level that define the top of the trading range. Upward trending markets, on the other hand, have little or no such

Exhibit 5.9   **S&P 100 INDEX AFTER MORE THAN FIVE DAYS OUT OF THE LAST FIFTY HAVE BEEN BELOW THE 50-DAY MOVING AVERAGE**

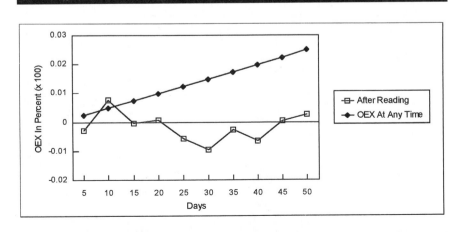

upside resistance. A market that is consistently making new all-time highs is likely to continue moving up, due in part to the lack of such overhead resistance.

Percent of Daily Range

Another factor that can help define an upward trend is the point within the daily range at which the index closes. Did it close near the high of the day or near the low of the day? This is the basis for the "percent of daily range" indicator. This indicator is calculated by taking the 10-day moving average of the closing point as a percentage of the daily range.

For example, if the high on a particular day on the OEX is 660, the low is 650, and the close is at 655, the percent of daily range would be 50 percent [(655 close − 650 low)/(660 high − 650 low)]. A close at the exact high would return a reading of 100 percent, and a close at the low would be 0 percent. When this daily indicator is smoothed by a 10-day moving average, specific readings can be seen as especially relevant as a market momentum indicator. Many analysts might view a high reading in this indicator as an overbought situation that is destined to precede a market decline. This is occasionally true, but not in a bull market. A study of this indicator for OEX data back to the beginning of 1985 supports this assertion. Exhibit 5.10 shows that a reading of greater than 75 percent on the percent of daily range indicator precedes a period of at least 25 days that is 48 percent stronger

Exhibit 5.10   **S&P 100 INDEX AFTER 10-DAY PERCENT OF DAILY RANGE IS GREATER THAN 75%**

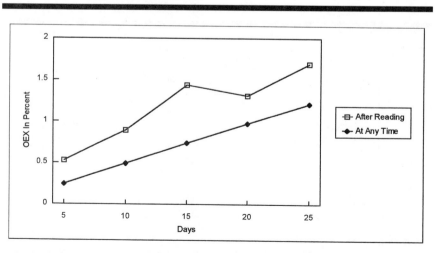

on average than what the market would normally return for the same period. Further, the average advance after 25 days is more than twice the normal average. This study shows that when the OEX consistently pushes to the high end of its daily trading range at the close of the day, it is *not* the harbinger of market calamity that some may expect; rather, it almost certainly defines a bullish trend that is much more likely to continue than reverse.

CONCLUSION

There are many fine publications that deal with either technical analysis, fundamental analysis, or both. Some of my most effective means of understanding and predicting the market are derived from a combination of these traditional indicators with sentiment-based research. Sentiment analysis measures the opinions and expectations of the investing community. I seek to quantify expectations where possible and compare to historical levels in search of significant extremes.

Technical analysis of historical data and fundamental analysis certainly play a role in market activity, but you must understand that people—not machines—ultimately buy and sell stocks. Therefore, the analysis of the emotions and expectations of market participants increases the accuracy of your predictions.

"A chain is only as strong as its weakest link." This popular phrase illustrates the fact that an isolated methodology in stock market analysis may be more useful when incorporated with other effective indicators. You can profit with greater confidence if the chain of research ideas contains a number of strong links, including not only traditional forms of analysis but also expectational forms of analysis. This gives you a well-rounded perspective on the important facts that influence market valuations at any point in time.

Now it's time to put all of this information to good use. The next chapter begins a discussion and demonstration of specific trading strategies showing how you can use the indicators we have discussed to profit with options.

Part II

Applications

6

Aggressive Option
Trading Strategies

INTRODUCTION

"It never was my thinking that made the big money for me. It was always my sitting."[1] Legendary trader Jesse Livermore's philosophy on profits might seem out of place when focusing on options trading. Options usually conjure an image of a quick entry and quick exit, scalping the market with very short holding periods. However, intraday market scalping is very difficult for the off-the-floor options trader, particularly the average individual trader. *Slippage* (when off-floor traders buy at the asked price and sell at the bid price) and commission costs make consistent profits from scalping very difficult, if not impossible. Beyond that, the floor trader tends to have better information about what may move the underlying stock hour-by-hour throughout the day.

However, you can give yourself an edge by taking a broader view—the position trader's view—of price direction. Floor traders are not in the business of divining where a stock will be in subsequent days, weeks, or months. Also, riding big trends for gains of 100 percent or more renders commissions and slippage much more manageable compared to the absolute profit earned. The more significant the trend, the greater the edge you can gain as a position trader in the options market.

So Livermore's trading philosophy does come into play if you expect to gain this edge. But what is required to fight the temptation to scalp and take a quick profit? How can you register gains that are truly market-beating?

---

1. Edwin LeFèvre, *Reminiscences of a Stock Operator* (New York: John Wiley & Sons, 1994), 68.

The following four rules are necessary for success. You need to:

1. *Control fear.* As discussed in chapter 4, fear of every adverse price tick against you can panic you out of an otherwise sound position. A trading method must be established to prevent fear from taking root, by following a disciplined and objective approach that will let you know precisely when to stay with a position and when to cut and run.

2. *Conquer greed.* Chapter 4 also discussed the importance of keeping greed in check by targeting an ambitious yet attainable profit to allow you to exit at a healthy gain while preventing you from overstaying a position once your initial expectations have been realized.

3. *Cultivate patience.* For a highly leveraged instrument such as options, patience can be one of the most valuable skills you possess. While many market participants are reactive to the invariable intraday blips in a security's price, the position trader must have the patience to see past fleeting price movements and stay with the position's ultimate trend over the anticipated holding period. This is the true lesson of the Livermore quote.

4. *Cut noise to maintain focus.* Many traders will enter a position trade and then use inappropriate indicators that confuse their original perspective. For example, a weekly chart watcher would not want to focus on intraday indicators as the driver for exiting trades. By matching the appropriate indicators to your personality and anticipated holding period, your focus will improve, as only the important indicators are monitored for significant changes.

THE "OPTION PROFIT" STRATEGY

With these guidelines in mind, I have developed a six-point approach—the "Option Profit" approach—for position trading with options. This method calls for concentrating on intermediate-term moves, usually over a two- to three-month period.

1. *Buy longer-dated options to ride multimonth trends.* By owning options with several months of life, you obtain the flexibility to free yourself from worrying about the temporary blips in price, and instead benefit from the broader trend in the underlying security.

2. *Target a 200 percent profit on the trade.* Assuming the steady trend plays itself out as expected, a 200 percent profit on an option with several months until expiration usually amounts to a move in the underlying stock of approximately 20 percent. At this point the stock is often overextended and it is time to take your money off the table.

3. *Take a 100 percent profit in a week or less if you get a quick windfall move.* Experience has shown that when a stock moves in an anticipated direction too quickly, you are usually better off taking this windfall profit and re-evaluating the trend on the next retracement in the security.

4. *Identify when your analysis loses validity and exit the position.* Just as you want to let profits ride, you also must have a pre-defined closeout level at a point where your initial analysis is proven incorrect. This trigger point can be based on a violation of a stock price level, an indicator reversal, or a point in time by which the position must be profitable. When this trigger point is reached, you must take action to exit the position.

5. *Work with a mental "time stop" to close your position if nothing significant is happening.* For positions that are not moving significantly in either direction, you must have an exit strategy when you are an options buyer. Otherwise, time decay will steadily erode the value of your position. Define a date in the near future when you will close a position if it has not reached a certain level. For example, on a two-month option you may want to exit if the position is not profitable after five trading days. This strategy keeps capital committed to the best opportunities while minimizing the "slow burn" in the option premium in nontrending situations.

6. *Follow the longer-term trend.* This is the key to the Option Profit approach. The shorter-term your focus on the market becomes, the more potential exists for noise to move the security opposite to its ultimate direction. Such noise is a factor out of any trader's control, and you should minimize this noise to the greatest extent possible. The primary way to accomplish this is to focus on the broader trend first, and then always seek to stay on the right side of this trend. Typically, company fundamentals will help drive these longer-term trends, so it pays to stay aware of changes in the underlying outlook. In the next section, we see how to identify the drivers for such long-term trends.

AN EXAMPLE OF A LONG-TERM UPTREND

Successful traders employing technical methods tend to agree on one thing: Don't fight the trend, or the size of your losing trades will inevitably dwarf the size of your winning trades, and eventually knock you out of the game. As discussed in chapter 2, your chances of success are greatly enhanced by jumping on board the trend.

To illustrate how riding the trend and taking advantage of countertrend pullbacks makes the difference in profitability, let us take a look at the case of America Online (AOL) in 1996. When AT&T announced it was entering the Internet access market in mid-February 1996, investors panicked and began selling their Internet-related stocks, and AOL shares fell from an all-time high of 57 to 45¾ in one week. However, AOL had proven to be a strong player and its membership numbers continued to grow. Revenues were up threefold from the previous year, and 1996 revenues were expected to top the $1 billion mark.

I made a recommendation on February 28, 1996, for the AOL April 50 call, which was closed on March 13 for a profit of 223 percent. I issued this recommendation after AOL shares hit support near 45 and stabilized. Relative strength versus the S&P 500 Index had recently hit a new high and was still in a clear uptrend. Other indicators were also flashing a buy signal, as seen in exhibit 6.1. A successful test of the 50-day moving average was doubly bolstered by the longer-term support just below at the 100-day moving average. Tests of the 100-day moving average had proven exceptional support areas from the time this uptrend began in November 1994. Moving average convergence divergence (MACD) was also back in an uptrend, showing favorable upside momentum. Also, options speculators were busy buying *puts* into the pullback to support, showing undue skepticism at that juncture, and providing a contrarian buy signal. As stock buyers shrugged off the doom and gloom of the media, AOL shares rallied, more than tripling the option from its recommended price of 3¼ to 10½ over ten trading days.

Although the bottom had dropped out of the stock briefly, the strong long-term uptrend of AOL stock was soon re-established. But note in exhibit 6.1 that the uptrend in AOL shares finally ended in May 1996, in classic fashion according to expectational analysis. Options speculators, who had been so pessimistic on AOL during the 1995 and early 1996 uptrend, converted to nearly unanimous bullishness in front of AOL's quarterly earnings report. The high expectations for AOL's earnings led to a sharp rally in AOL shares before the

Exhibit 6.1   **AMERICA ONLINE (AOL) WEEKLY CHART**

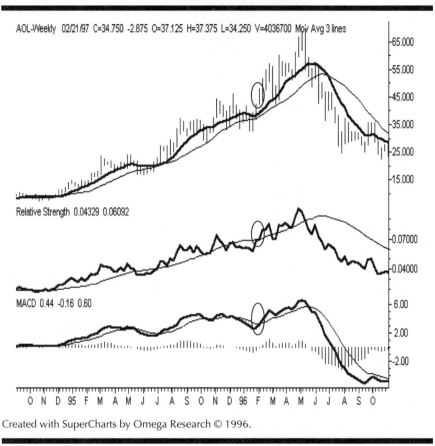

Created with SuperCharts by Omega Research © 1996.

earnings were released. Despite reporting earnings well above Wall Street's consensus estimates, AOL shares experienced a major negative reaction, which soon led to the breakdown in the technical trend.

REASONABLE LOSS CONTROL WITH THE OPTION PROFIT APPROACH

Loss control presents the options trader with a potential dilemma. Should the trade be driven by a stop-loss on the option (i.e., "at a 50 percent loss on the option, close my position")? Or should it be driven by what's happening with the stock (i.e., "if the stock trades below support at 57, close my call option")? My strong belief is that the price action of the underlying stock and the passage of time should be the focal points driving the entry and exit of your option trades, rather than an arbitrary loss level on your option position. If the stock is going nowhere, your option has no directional impetus and will simply erode due to time decay. As a result, you need a mental time stop to enforce the discipline of avoiding nondirectional situations in addition to your other criteria for closing positions.

EVENTS THAT CAUSE NEW TRENDS

Trends occur in part because investors gradually recognize the impact of new information on a stock's price. Efficient market theory would postulate otherwise, suggesting that any public news would be immediately discounted by an omniscient group of investors. This assumption doesn't hold water, as demonstrated by the consistency of such trend-based indicators as channels and moving averages, which can successfully identify trends that predict future price action.

The most powerful trends that can drive big profits using the Option Profit approach develop from important underlying fundamental changes in a firm's prospects, which can take many forms, as discussed below.

Earnings Acceleration or Deceleration

Quarterly earnings reports are among the most powerful of the underlying factors that drive stock prices. Most significant is the magnitude of the quarterly earnings per share relative to the consensus estimate and to investor expectations. For example, in an October 21, 1996, article titled "Remarks by IBM Executive Often Affect Entire Market," the *Wall Street Journal* chronicled the influence of IBM's chief financial officer, who invited industry analysts for a slide show and question-and-answer session each quarter. IBM's stock price promptly responded and sometimes took the entire market with it. The CFO's downbeat comments in April 1996 sent IBM stock down $9\frac{3}{4}$ points, leading to a 70-point drop in the Dow. Then his optimistic remarks three months later sent IBM stock up to $11\frac{7}{8}$, accounting for more than half of a 67-point Dow gain that marked a turning point for the entire market. These optimistic CFO remarks coupled with a stronger-than-expected earnings report in July 1996 led to a 60 percent gain in IBM shares in less than six months. The lesson here is that you want to go *with* the earnings momentum, not against it.

Exhibit 6.2   **INTERNATIONAL BUSINESS MACHINES (IBM) MONTHLY CHART, 1992–1996**

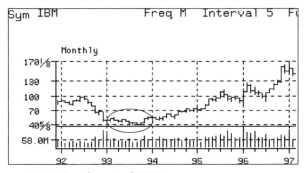

Reprinted with permission. Compliments of ILX Systems.

Corporate Restructuring

Corporate restructuring gained much notoriety in the early 1990s, primarily due to the downsizing trend that impacted a large number of Fortune 500 firms, including IBM, a one-time bastion of "lifetime employment." While the media has much preferred to expound on the woes that result with leaner firms—the angry laid-off employees, the low morale among remaining workers, the negative effects on the surrounding community—Wall Street often sees this leaner and meaner structure as very positive for profits. Note from exhibit 6.2 that when IBM announced its restructuring in 1993, the stock had already made its bottom and was an excellent buy even *after* the initial positive reaction to the news.

What accounts for this positive market reaction to restructurings that make negative headlines? Perhaps, as noted by Albert Dunlap, the turnaround specialist who revived Scott Paper beginning in 1994 in a high-profile restructuring, "If I hadn't saved the company, *everyone* would have been out of work, not just a percentage of people."[2]

As can be seen on the weekly chart of Scott Paper (exhibit 6.3), the turnaround's initial positive market reaction was just the beginning of a doubling in the share's price over the next twelve months. One of the common denominators is that the initial reaction of the stock price to the restructuring news must be very positive to establish that Wall Street believes in the leaner company's improved prospects.

---

2. Albert J. Dunlap, *Mean Business* (New York: Times Business, 1996), 21.

Exhibit 6.3   **SCOTT PAPER (SPP) WEEKLY CHART**

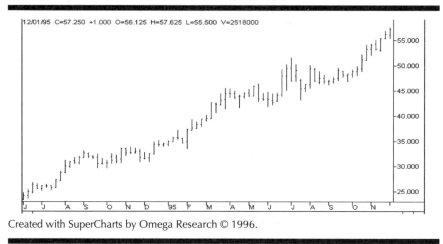

12/01/95 C=57.250 +1.000 O=56.125 H=57.625 L=55.500 V=2518000

Created with SuperCharts by Omega Research © 1996.

Once you determine that restructuring news is being viewed favorably by the Street, you can check your own technical and sentiment indicators to make sure the stock has a high probability of maintaining this price action in the form of a new uptrend. As long as the expectations for the turnaround are not particularly high, you can expect to find reasonably priced call options with excellent potential for leveraged returns.

New Products

Iomega's Zip disk drive was launched in early 1995 and quickly became a hit with computer gurus. Buyers were attracted to the drive's portability, cheap price, and fivefold increase in traditional memory capacity, and the company couldn't produce them fast enough. Before the Zip drive came to market, there was not much to excite investors about Iomega (IOM), but with this product investors had a solid fundamental story to buy. As a result, investors bid the shares higher, and IOM embarked on a monster trend from a low of just over 1 in January 1995 to a peak of $55\frac{1}{8}$ in May 1996. The trend was also fueled by skepticism from speculators, as IOM became a favorite of short sellers who were continually forced to cover their positions by buying back stock (see exhibit 6.4). In addition, options speculators placed bets on the downside throughout the climbing trend, as shown by the put/call open interest chart in chapter 1 (exhibit 1.4). This negative mentality in the face of strong fundamentals and strong technicals signaled to me, as a contrarian, that IOM was a low-expectation stock

Exhibit 6.4   **IOMEGA (IOM) MONTHLY CHART WITH SHORT INTEREST**

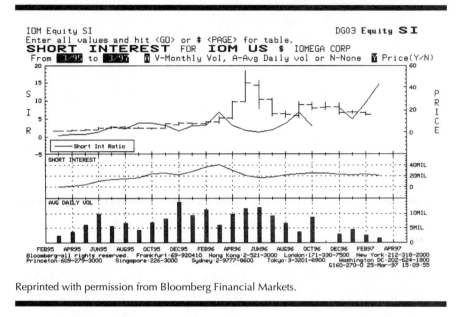

with plenty of future upside potential. It was not until there was a shift in sentiment, where the shorts covered in great quantity and where the options crowd converted from bearish to bullish, that the uptrend in IOM became history. I took advantage of the long-term uptrend in IOM by buying the April 17½ calls on March 1, 1996, at an average price of $1^{31}\!/_{32}$, and in less than three weeks took profits of 122 percent at an average exit price of $4^{3}\!/_{8}$ on March 18.

New CEOs

Eastman Kodak (EK) stock had been static in the mid-30 range for several years when George M.C. Fisher took over as CEO in December 1993. According to *Business Week*, Kodak had "seemed trapped in the slow-growth photography industry, hobbled by huge debts, a dysfunctional management culture, and a dispirited workforce."[3] Fisher's first order of business was to sell off recently acquired health-care businesses and reduce a massive debt load of $7.5 billion.

   Much anxiety surrounded Fisher's move from Motorola to Kodak. But by refocusing the company on the core photography business, spinning off the Eastman Chemical business, and moving for-

---

3. Mark Maremont, "Kodak's New Focus," *Business Week*, January 30, 1995.

Exhibit 6.5   EASTMAN KODAK (EK) MONTHLY CHART

Reprinted with permission. Compliments of ILX Systems.

ward in digital technology, Fisher overhauled Kodak's balance sheet and corporate management culture. As exhibit 6.5 shows, over the course of 1993 and 1994 EK stock uptrended to the mid-40 to mid-50 range with several minor setbacks. Since early 1995, the stock has been on a steady upswing, and by early 1997 EK was trading above 90.

The lesson in new CEO situations is that you want to see two conditions in place before you can realistically expect a longer-term uptrend. First, the new CEO must have a record of success with other firms. Second, and more important, the expectations of the investment community should not be too high, or the initiatives of the new CEO may be set up for disappointment. There are plenty of examples of the initial luster being quickly tarnished amid such high hopes. The great turnarounds, as in the case of Kodak, or IBM when Louis Gerstner took over in 1993, occurred in the face of plenty of doubters on Wall Street.

Stock Buybacks

The value of a stock buyback plan is in the perception that a company is willing to spend its own money to repurchase outstanding shares. In general, a stock buyback of 6 percent to 8 percent of the outstanding shares makes investors take notice, and 10 percent or more is often a screaming buy. But you need to be cautious in interpreting the impact of buyback plans. Buybacks can be viewed as either good news or bad news, depending upon the circumstances. Some skeptics say that if a company doesn't have anything better to do with its excess cash, it may be plagued with unimaginative management. Sometimes buybacks mean that management believes that the stock is a strong buy at current prices and therefore you should follow in management's footsteps. However, you must watch the percentage of shares bought back, not the absolute dollar amount.

Hospitality Franchise Systems, Inc., a hotel, real estate, and car rental management company, announced plans in July 1996 to buy back $50 million in stock. On further analysis, however, this $50 million investment actually represented less than 1 percent of the market value of the 100 million shares outstanding. I interpreted this conclusion bearishly and recommended a put. Once the Street recognized the disappointing nature of the buyback plan, the stock price dropped from 56 to 50 in short order, and the put recommendation was closed for a quick 29 percent profit in one week. The lesson here is to not accept any "positive" news on the surface without further investigation. Many investors would take *any* stock buyback as a positive sign, but if the company isn't committing to repurchase of a meaningful amount of stock, it can come across as only a short-term effort to bolster the share price. Make sure you heed Humphrey Neill's advice and "think things through" before reacting to the initial news headlines.

Takeovers

A stock will invariably jump significantly higher when the company is a takeover target. But you must be careful in purchasing call options on mere rumors of a takeover. By the time the rumor is circulated, the stock has most likely rallied substantially. You might therefore be buying into a short-term top, which is anathema to call options buyers.

Because of the rumors, high expectations become built into the stock. As a result of the high expectations, you risk a "sell on the news" reaction even if the rumors are true. And if delays arise in the takeover process for any number of reasons, the stock could be hit by a serious decline.

There is an extra disadvantage for options traders who attempt to play the takeover game. Options market makers and floor specialists tend to quickly pump up the implied volatilities of the rumored takeover target's options in response to initial public demand, as the options are priced for an anticipated increase in the underlying stock's volatility. Therefore, you are often forced to pay hefty option premiums to play this game. However, these volatilities will quickly implode (as will the premium on the option you are holding) should the rumor be invalidated. A trader who is in a call position before the takeover rumors surface should consider the hearsay as a potential opportunity to *close* this option position. In this instance, he has al-

Exhibit 6.6   **NOVELL (NOVL) WEEKLY CHART**

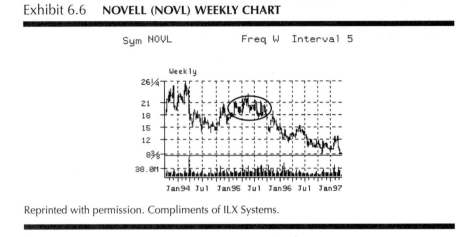

Reprinted with permission. Compliments of ILX Systems.

ready benefited from the stock's move and is selling the option at a rich implied volatility.

Novell (exhibit 6.6) presents a classic example. For more than a year, it was mentioned as a possible takeover target by cash-rich companies such as IBM. In 1995, with the stock trading below 20 for several months and the shares in a downtrend due to negative earnings momentum, options speculators were accumulating out-of-the-money calls at rich premiums in anticipation of the rumor becoming reality. However, month after month, these calls expired worthless, resulting in heavy losses for those buying into the takeover rumors.

Once a takeover is announced, look for opportunities in the near future to buy calls on the *acquiring* firm. Such stocks are usually beat up initially by Wall Street, as fears run rampant about earnings dilution or that the company is overpaying for the firm it is acquiring. For example, NationsBank (NB) shares had a huge run in 1995 and the first half of 1996, gaining nearly 100 percent over this 18-month period. NationsBank has been a leading acquirer of regional banks and grew into a superregional powerhouse. When the company announced plans to take over Boatmen's Bancshares in late August 1996 in a $9.5 billion transaction, more than half of which was financed with stock, NB shares were hit hard and fell about 15 percent in a matter of days. Yet this pullback was held in check at the longer-term 100-day moving average, showing an uptrend that was still intact. As the shares firmed up and began to work their way higher, I spotted an opportunity in November 1996 when the stock pulled back to its 20-day moving average (see exhibit 6.7). On November 14, I recommended purchase of the January 47½ call (prices adjusted for 2-for-1

Exhibit 6.7   **NATIONSBANK (NB) DAILY CHART WITH 20-DAY MOVING AVERAGE**

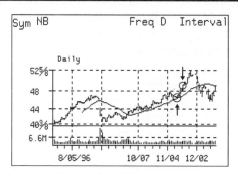

Reprinted with permission. Compliments of ILX Systems.

split), targeting a 200 percent profit on the trade. However, on November 20 the position had reached a double, triggering my rule to take a 100 percent profit if achieved in one week or less. Watching for acquiring stocks that are beaten down by the Street and then picking one's spot for a speedy uptrend to occur can lead to a quick, healthy profit.

There are even more profitable ways to score big profits in trading options. The next section presents one such game plan.

THE BASEBALL STRATEGY

The home run and the grand slam in baseball are rare occurrences that generate massive excitement and enthusiasm. These events add another dimension to the game and attract crowds to the ballpark. With only one swing of the bat, the course of the game can change completely.

The electricity of a clean sweep hit can also be achieved in the options game. Your most memorable moments will come from the trades that score huge returns—profits of 300 percent and more. Who wouldn't want the satisfaction of investing $2,500 in a trade and, within a month or two, selling the position for $10,000?

The thrill of these big gains lures traders to the options market. Of course, like the home run and the grand slam, these lavish profits will not be common in your everyday trading world. It is a very challenging undertaking, but the opportunity is real nonetheless. And the potential for the "four-bagger" exists in bull *or* in bear markets.

Of course, the maxim that "the greater the potential return, the bigger the risk" could not apply more than to home-run trading strategies. Before considering the most aggressive end of the options spectrum, you should be well aware that the "baseball" strategy is the riskiest options strategy of all I recommend. If you do not have the trading capital or the mental discipline to accept and ride out the total losses on individual trades that will inevitably be a part of such a strategy, this "swing for the fences" approach is not for you. Although options traders in general are aggressive investors, targeting profits of 300 percent and more is an approach that should be reserved for only the most aggressive speculators who can handle the associated higher risk.

In his illustrious career, Babe Ruth slammed 714 home runs, a record that held for many years. It is significant, though, that Babe Ruth was also the strikeout leader in his day. Nevertheless, the Babe is in baseball's Hall of Fame, as his home runs and key hits had a much greater positive impact than the negatives associated with his strikeouts. You can expect a similar profile with a successful baseball options strategy. Strikeouts—or the complete loss of capital dedicated to one trade—will be a part of the game. However, by letting profits run on winning positions, you can score substantial returns with only one swing of the bat. In the long run, you can be a hall-of-fame trader, as one grand slam trade (+300 percent) and two strikeouts (–200 percent) result in a +33 percent gross return, assuming equal capital invested in each trade.

LET PROFITS RUN, CUT LOSSES SHORT

A common rule for successful trading is to let profits run and cut losses short. Unfortunately, options traders have a tendency to take profits too quickly on winners, while hanging on to losers for far too long. Fear of losing the quick profit causes an early closeout, while hope of recovery to a break-even position inhibits taking a loss when required. In fact, my research has shown that quick winners often go on to even bigger gains, *if* there is an underlying driving force in addition to the favorable price action. At the same time, hanging on to positions that are under water for extended periods is a loser's game in options trading, where the time decay will destroy your investment. As discussed in chapter 4, the psychology of options trading must be quite different from the mind-set of the stock investor, who can afford to wait for a losing position to turn around.

"Let profits run, cut losses short" is also a theme for the aggressive baseball trading strategy. However, keep in mind that losing trades are inevitable, and therefore, the same amount of energy that was used to initiate the trade must be used in the management of the position. In other words, contain your losses as best you can while realizing there will be strikeouts inevitably mixed in with those losses you can control, and allow the winners to ride to greater profits if you continue to see a favorable outlook. But you should be aware from the outset that in many of your attempts to clear the outfield wall, you will see some significant winners turn into break-even or losing positions as the underlying stock fails to extend its trend before reversing in the other direction.

OPTIONS TO BUY WHEN SWINGING FOR THE FENCES

Because of the aggressive profit goals in the baseball strategy, the options you purchase must be highly leveraged. In other words, you want to buy an option that will achieve a substantial percentage gain relative to the expected percentage move in the underlying stock.

I do not recommend far out-of-the-money options for this strategy because they are typically extraordinarily low leveraged for most expected price fluctuations in the underlying stock. The return on the option's value compared to the return on the expected move in the stock is just not great enough to justify the added risk that such a low-delta option will expire worthless. You want to be able to achieve big profits on reasonable moves in the underlying stock, rather than looking for low-probability "off the charts" moves to drive your option profits.

If you purchase a call option and the underlying stock moves higher by 5 percent while the option's value increases by only 15 percent, your leverage is only three to one. Because options are risky and time will erode their value, you need a greater ratio of the option's return relative to the underlying stock's return to justify the trade. Options that carry potential leverage of five to one or ten to one on an achievable quick move in the underlying stock are usually worth the risk.

IMPLEMENTING THE BASEBALL STRATEGY

Two types of options with expiration dates one to two months out are most suitable for use in the baseball strategy.

The first type is out-of-the-money options (usually one-strike from the money). This strategy requires a correct call on a strong di-

Exhibit 6.8   **COMPAQ COMPUTER (CPQ) WEEKLY CHART**

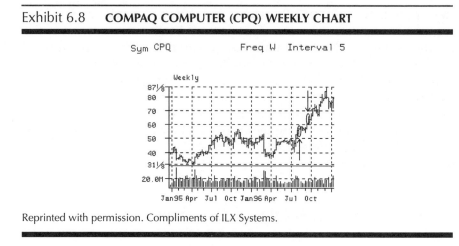

Sym CPQ   Freq W Interval 5

Reprinted with permission. Compliments of ILX Systems.

rectional move in the underlying and a correct call on the timing of the move. When you make both such calls, you can be the beneficiary of a true home-run trade. Failure to meet either one of these conditions, however, often results in a strikeout.

As an example of a home-run trade, you could have purchased the Compaq Computer (CPQ) September 60 call on August 13, 1996, based on a new high in CPQ versus a prior high in late 1995 at 56¾ and confirmed by a new multiyear high in relative strength versus the S&P 500 Index after an eight-week consolidation (see exhibit 6.8). The shares were at 57 at the time of the trade, and you would have paid a premium of 2 for the option. The continuation of the breakout indeed occurred, and the shares experienced a quick 8-point rally to 65 by September 20. You were able to sell the option at a premium of 8 for a 300 percent profit, as your timing and direction assumptions proved correct.

Again, let me remind you that *both* conditions—exact timing and direction—stated at the beginning of this section must be met or a substantial loss is likely to result. If you don't quickly pull the plug on losing positions, all of your capital will likely dissipate on the trade. Time decay will chew up these near-term options more dramatically because they have so little time left until expiration. While timing and direction are two key factors for major options profits, there is a situation where awareness of option volatilities can save you from making a sucker trade. Avoid purchasing options whose implied volatilities have just spiked higher in front of an event, such as an earnings announcement. These volatilities will usually implode after the event occurs. In these cases, you could be correct on both the exact timing and direction, but still lose as a result of the option premium plunging as the implied volatility moves back in line with its historical level.

For example, on July 29, 1996, you could have purchased the Digital Equipment (DEC) August 35 put in anticipation of a negative earnings surprise the next day. The stock was trading at 36½ when the put was purchased. While historical volatility on DEC options was 40 percent before the earnings report, the implied volatility of the DEC August 35 put was pumped up to 69 percent. You purchased the option for 1⅝ and the next day, just as you expected, DEC shares plunged by 2 points (see exhibit 6.9). But you didn't account for the risk of the implied volatilities imploding after the earnings release, as the implied volatility on the DEC August 35 put option dropped to 54 percent, in line with historical volatilities. As a result, the option was *still* trading at 1⅝, and you had no profit on your put. While your timing and direction were perfect, you failed to make money because you didn't anticipate the volatility collapse.

The second type of baseball strategy involves "cheap" at-the-money or in-the-money options. In some cases a speculator will be able to identify a stock that is trading in a tight, definitive uptrend or downtrend. Assuming that this trend is tight, meaning that the stock is not moving in a highly volatile range, premiums on the options can be fairly inexpensive.

Exhibit 6.9   **DIGITAL EQUIPMENT (DEC) DAILY CHART**

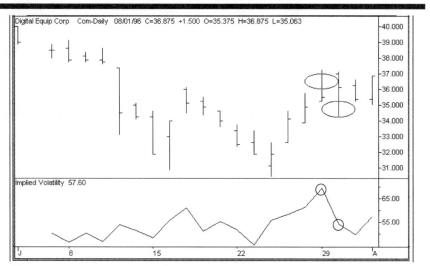

Created with SuperCharts by Omega Research © 1996.

Exhibit 6.10   **U.S. INDUSTRIES (USI) WEEKLY CHART**

Reprinted with permission. Compliments of ILX Systems.

Consider U.S. Industries, which was trading in an upward sloping, tight 9-point range during the last eight months of 1996. During this same period, Charles Schwab was trading in a directionless 8½ point range. Both stocks were trading around 26 in early April (see exhibits 6.10 and 6.11). Even though Schwab stock had no well-established direction, its January 25 calls were more expensive, trading at an asked price of 3¼, while the asked price for the January 25 calls on U.S. Industries was only 2⅜. This illustrates perfectly the fact that the option pricing model overprices directionless volatility and underprices nonvolatile trends. And profit opportunities for options buyers abound in the latter situation.

A less leveraged but still aggressive strategy to take advantage of cheap options on trending stocks is to purchase an at-the-money option that has two to four months until expiration. A target profit of 300

Exhibit 6.11   **CHARLES SCHWAB (SCH) WEEKLY CHART**

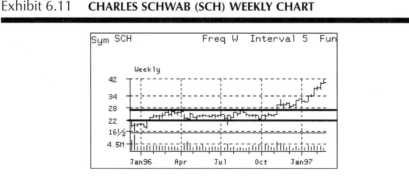

Reprinted with permission. Compliments of ILX Systems.

percent or more is still appropriate. With this purchase, you expect the trend to continue and the volatility on both the stock and the option to eventually increase substantially as the Street begins to pick up on the trend and jump on board. While the stock's expanding volatility could signal that the trend is about to end, a smart speculator could benefit immensely from a blow-off mode to the upside with call positions, as the call premium rises due to the double benefit of a rising stock price and expanding implied volatility.

For example, on August 13, 1996, I recommended the Bank of New York (BK) October 27½ call. As you can see on exhibit 6.12, the shares had been in a tight, longer-term uptrend since early 1995. To fine-tune my entry point to maximize profits, I waited for a breakout above and subsequent retest of the 27 area, which had acted as resistance over the six previous months. Breakouts above resistance areas usually lead to quick, powerful moves higher. To get the most bang for my buck, I could have recommended the purchase of an August or September option. However, BK options were relatively cheap, and to reduce my risk I purchased the October option for 1⁵⁄₁₆. I was able to ride the uptrend over the next month before I determined that an exit was prudent on September 10, 1996. Even with an option that held less leverage than shorter-term expiration alternatives, the payoff resulted in a healthy doubling of the original investment in this position in four weeks.

Exhibit 6.12   **BANK OF NEW YORK (BK) WEEKLY CHART**

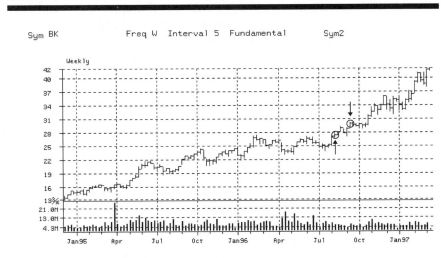

Reprinted with permission. Compliments of ILX Systems.

THE "FREE TRADE" RULE

Traders can have the "best of both worlds" by greatly reducing their risk in an open winning trade while still "letting profits run." This is especially appealing to speculators in very aggressive positions, as profits in the volatile options world can disappear within a matter of hours, potentially turning a profit into a loss. Traders can reduce this potential volatility and guarantee themselves at least a break-even trade when a position at least doubles from the purchase price by selling half of their contracts at a 100 percent profit and holding the remaining half for potentially bigger gains.

For example, suppose you purchase 10 option contracts at $2\frac{1}{2}$ on April 30, and you are targeting for a potential 400 percent gain on this trade. Your capital outlay is $2,500 ($10 \times \$2.50 \times 100$) before commissions. Assume that the underlying equity moves in your direction, and on June 7 you sell five contracts at 5, collecting your original capital outlay $2,500 ($5 \times \$5 \times 100$). You still have five contracts open, for which your target profit of 400 percent remains in place. This is a "free trade" because the original capital outlay is pocketed, guaranteeing you at least a breakeven on the trade even in the worst-case scenario, in which the remaining half of the option position goes on to expire worthless.

The best-case scenario is if the five open contracts go on to achieve the original target profit of 400 percent. In this case, the trader books a 250 percent average profit on the trade [(100% × 0.5) + (400% × 0.5)]. However, there was a *guarantee* of a breakeven on the position (relative to the original investment) after half of the position was sold at a double. This strategy allows you to be more flexible in managing the remaining half of the position. With the risk associated with the total loss of the initial capital outlay now removed, most traders develop significantly greater "staying power" to hold on for the big "home-run" gain.

PROFILES OF BASEBALL TRADES

This section reviews several trades that have netted significant profits as well as some that proved disappointing. Some themes are common to most of these trades, such as strong relative strength patterns versus both the broader market and the relevant sector in the case of call positions, and weak relative strength patterns versus the broader market and the industry group in the case of put trades.

In addition, a contrarian approach was taken in each of these trades, meaning that these profits were generated as a result of jump-

ing onto trends against which speculators with a history of poor timing were betting. I am often asked, "How can it be contrarian to buy
a call on an uptrending stock?" As detailed in chapter 1, contrarianism is about buying low expectations relative to the price movement
in a stock. And when a strong stock is being "faded" by options
speculators, it is often an indication that a trend has staying power, as
a top is rarely reached without speculators adopting a very bullish
posture.

Some of the following trades were the result of identifying a particular equity in a tight trend that enabled me to buy options at fairly
low premiums so that I could look for unusually large profits. In the
first example, Williams Companies, I was able to buy enough time
with a further out-of-the-money option to allow the trend to play itself out, meaning pullbacks within the trend would likely be followed
by higher highs, as long as support levels continued to hold within
this low volatility trend.

Williams Companies (WMB) February 40 Call

On October 18, 1995, I recommended a February 40 call position on
WMB, with a profit target of 300 percent. As exhibit 6.13 shows, WMB
was in a tight uptrend, with support at its 50-day moving average.
With the stock at 26⅝ (adjusted for a 3-for-2 stock split), I recommended this call for purchase at 1⅜. Soon the stock moved higher off
of support at its 50-day moving average and made a new all-time
high above 27. Driving the stock higher was an earnings report that
came in above expectations. In addition, as exhibit 6.14 shows, the equity was displaying tremendous relative strength when compared
with the S&P 500 Index. Despite the bullish price action and the

Exhibit 6.13   **WILLIAMS COMPANIES (WMB) WEEKLY CHART**

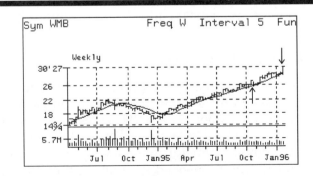

Reprinted with permission. Compliments of ILX Systems.

Exhibit 6.14   **WILLIAMS COMPANIES (WMB) WEEKLY CHART: RELATIVE STRENGTH VERSUS THE S&P 500 INDEX**

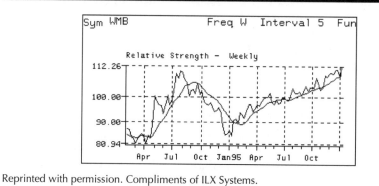

Reprinted with permission. Compliments of ILX Systems.

shares' outperformance, WMB commanded little respect from the Street. In fact, according to figures from Zacks Investment Research, only five of the fourteen analysts who followed the stock considered it a "strong buy," and one analyst actually had a "sell" rating. In addition, I noticed an absence of call accumulation on the shares by options speculators, despite the apparent potential "ease" in making money on WMB when analyzing its trend. Street analysts and options speculators reacting with complacency to the strong upward trend implied from a contrarian perspective that this trend was still playable.

As it turned out, I was correct in my assessment that the trend would continue higher. The shares continued making new highs, with the 50-day moving average providing short-term support within the longer-term uptrend. Management of this trade was important, as I kept holding the position even on pullbacks, keeping in mind that my support levels had not been broken. On February 8, 1996, my 300 percent target profit was achieved on this call after the shares bounced strongly off support into the 32½ area.

United Healthcare (UNH) August 50 Put

This put trade was recommended on June 27, 1996, and the drivers were a mirror image of my successful Williams Companies call position. As can be seen in exhibit 6.15, UNH shares were in a tight trend lower. However, as exhibit 6.16 shows, they were experiencing a short-term upward bounce after gapping lower the prior week. When this gap was filled, I recommended the put position. Usually after a gap down and a bounce, there is an overhead supply of stock, as

Exhibit 6.15   UNITED HEALTHCARE (UNH) WEEKLY CHART

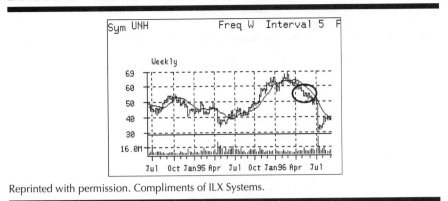

Reprinted with permission. Compliments of ILX Systems.

those who bought the stock just before it gapped lower are eager sellers as they try to break even. In addition, these shares were displaying an extremely weak relative strength pattern versus the S&P 500 Index (exhibit 6.17). With the longer-term trend favoring a put position, and the potential short-term overhead supply just above UNH's closing level on June 26, the time was right to establish a put position, and I recommended this put at 2⅝. Additional downward pressure on the stock came from negative earnings momentum, as UNH's previous earnings report had fallen below expectations. But despite the poor price action and negative earnings momentum, UNH was still a Street "darling." For example, Zacks Investment Research reported that 21

Exhibit 6.16   UNITED HEALTHCARE (UNH) DAILY CHART

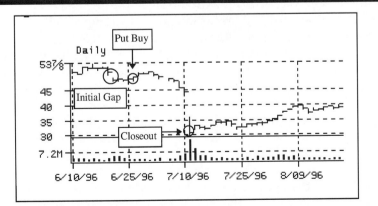

Reprinted with permission. Compliments of ILX Systems.

Exhibit 6.17   **UNITED HEALTHCARE (UNH) WEEKLY CHART: RELATIVE STRENGTH VERSUS THE S&P 500 INDEX: OCTOBER 1993–JULY 1996**

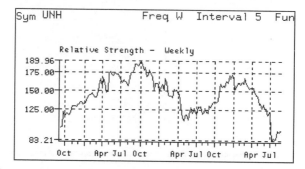

Reprinted with permission. Compliments of ILX Systems.

out of the 24 analysts who followed the equity rated it a "buy." The deteriorating price action was conflicting with the optimism of the Wall Street analysts, and in such cases it is often wise to listen to the market.

Just two weeks later, on July 11, the market proved me correct. UNH indicated that upcoming quarterly earnings would fall seriously below analysts' estimates. The stock gapped significantly lower that morning, before closing 13¼ points lower on the day, and the put position was sold at 17⅛ for a 560 percent profit.

CompUSA (CPU) June 20 Call

CPU presents another example of "going with the trend and against the crowd." On May 3, 1996, with the stock trading at 17⁹⁄₁₆ (numbers adjusted for 2-for-1 split), I recommended the June 20 call at ¹⁷⁄₃₂. The target profit for this particular trade was 400 percent. As exhibit 6.18 shows, CPU shares had been trending beautifully, with support at the shares' 10-day moving average. In addition, CPU shares were consistently outperforming the broader market since January. The fundamentals were also in place to support a continued trend higher, as the company the week before had reported earnings that were 21 percent above consensus estimates. Not only did I find the price action and the fundamentals encouraging, but I found it interesting that "hot money" players had not bought into the trend. This was evident from my analysis of the options crowd, as speculators were fading the rally by accumulating puts at the out-of-the-money 16¼ strike (adjusted for a 2-for-1 split). Such widespread skepticism from this typically

Exhibit 6.18   COMPUSA (CPU) DAILY CHART WITH 10-DAY MOVING
AVERAGE: APRIL 1996–FEBRUARY 1997

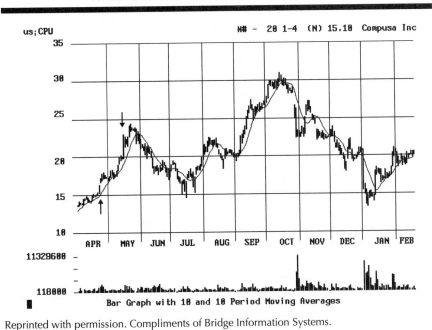

Reprinted with permission. Compliments of Bridge Information Systems.

wrong group, amid a positive fundamental and technical backdrop, set the "contrarian" table for additional robust gains over the short-term.

Two weeks later, Wall Street welcomed news that CPU was acquiring a direct reseller of brand-name computers and peripherals, PC Compleat. CPU shares closed more than 5 points higher, at 22^{7}⁄$_{16}$, and the option trade achieved its target profit of 400 percent.

Newbridge Networks (NN) May 30 Call

I began closely watching NN in late February 1996, after I noticed the shares had held up extremely well amid a rout in technology stocks that began on February 23, as seen in the chart of the Morgan Stanley High-Tech 35 Index (MSH). In fact, as the technology sector continued its decline, NN shares inched higher (exhibit 6.19). I was impressed with this bullish relative strength versus MSH, and expected NN shares to lead the next rally in technology stocks. As the technology group began to outperform the broader market, NN became a call candidate. Also driving this trade was the fact that NN was making

Exhibit 6.19   NEWBRIDGE NETWORKS (NN) VERSUS MORGAN STANLEY HIGH-TECH 35 INDEX (MSH)

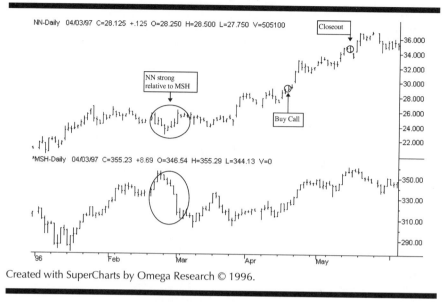

NN-Daily 04/03/97 C=28.125 +.125 O=28.250 H=28.500 L=27.750 V=505100

*MSH-Daily 04/03/97 C=355.23 +8.69 O=346.54 H=355.29 L=344.13 V=0

Created with SuperCharts by Omega Research © 1996.

all-time highs, yet options speculators were ignoring the bullish price action. This lack of speculator enthusiasm implied to contrarians that the stock had room to run.

So on April 18, 1996, I recommended the purchase of this call (numbers adjusted for 2-for-1 split) as the shares were beginning to move higher out of a brief consolidation area. The 28½ level had been acting as resistance since the beginning of April, and as the shares began to move above 28½, I recommended the May 30 call at 1¹⁄₁₆, with a profit target of 300 percent. I expected a quick move to 32½, at which point I anticipated optimism would set in and the rally would fizzle. NN shares, in the previous six months, were notorious for following through with substantial gains after moving higher out of such consolidations.

The 300 percent profit target on this trade was achieved by employing the risk-averse "free trade" strategy outlined earlier. With only two weeks until expiration, the stock moved into profitable territory. I then took profits on half of my position, as I was concerned that the stock could be subject to a bout of profit-taking just prior to expiration. By recommending the sale of half of the option position at a price of 3⁹⁄₁₆, a profit of 235 percent was booked, plus I guaranteed myself at least a 117 percent profit on the trade no matter what subsequently happened to the price of the stock in the two weeks until expiration. Since I was booking more than a 100 percent profit automatically after selling half of this position, I was more aggressive with my target profit for the other half of the position, and bumped this up to 400 percent. Generally, you should not bump the target profit higher, but I had noticed options speculators still were not jumping on the NN momentum and this contrarian indicator gave me added confidence. Finally, on May 15, I recommended closing the second half of the position at a price of 15 for a 370 percent return, resulting in a total profit of 302 percent.

Chrysler (C) April 27½ Call

The Chrysler (C) recommendation that I issued on February 22, 1996, was missing the one common denominator that was present in my past huge successes: a relative strength trend that was in my favor. Therefore, I categorize this trade as riskier than the others, as I attempted to call a more exact bottom in a plunge, which had clipped 14 percent from share values from the early February peak.

How did I call the exact short-term bottom? I used a combination of technical indicators and the contrarian implications of sudden negative sentiment on the automakers as the shares neared their bottom. Of course, I wanted some positive fundamentals in the mix, and at the time, the Big Three were turning in monthly sales numbers that were beating Wall Street expectations.

I recommended the call position when Chrysler shares declined *exactly* to their 200-day moving average. Just three months earlier that average had acted as support before the shares went on to make new highs. The 200-day moving average was at a point that had served as resistance several times in the past, and I anticipated that this former resistance area would lend additional support. Finally, analysts in the press turned negative on the auto sector, citing higher-than-normal inventories. But I viewed the story differently, as sales were sizzling, and the automakers were prepared for continued robust demand. With the stock at 26 (on a post-split basis), I recommended this out-of-the-money call for 1⅜, in anticipation of a quick, strong rebound off this support level. Timing was critical, with only eight weeks to April expiration and the option 3 points out-of-the-money. My timing, however, was "on the money," as a sharp rally ensued within a week of initiating the position. Such precise timing was well rewarded, as the options were closed out on March 13 for a profit of 400 percent.

Of course, not all trades can be winners. Even on losing trades, however, I seek to learn lessons that can improve profits in the future.

EMC Corp. (EMC) July 22½ Call

On June 5, 1996, EMC was breaking out above the key 22 area (see exhibit 6.20), which had served as an important resistance and support level in the past. In fact, prior to this call recommendation, I had a very successful put trade on this stock after calling the top at resistance at 22. This time, however, the shares broke out above 22 on no news and on heavy volume. I was confident I could achieve profits by recommending a call position—so confident, in fact, that I recommended an option that was only 45 days away from expiration and barely in-the-money.

After sending out the recommendation, EMC immediately moved in the expected direction, and the trade was profitable by more than 30 percent in just hours. However, two things happened that would make a contrarian cringe. First, after the market closed, a story appeared on the news wire with technical analysts applauding EMC's "breakout" and predicting that the short term for EMC looked very bright (a contrarian would want this breakout to go unnoticed). Second, an analysis of open interest changes on EMC options the next day revealed that options speculators also believed this was a breakout, as was evident by the heavy out-of-the-money call accumulation at the 25 and 27½ strikes. Suddenly, I realized that I was a part of a potential crowd mania, which is extremely dangerous. The fact that this breakout was so noticed and popular on Wall Street became the kiss of death.

Exhibit 6.20   **EMC CORP. (EMC) WEEKLY CHART**

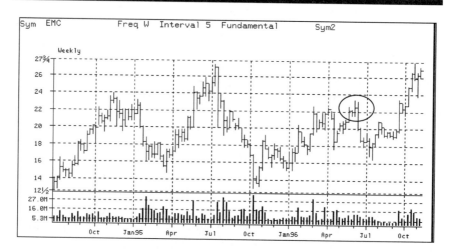

Reprinted with permission. Compliments of ILX Systems.

The next step *should* have been to exit this position. But I didn't stick with this discipline, and the pain of not doing so made this a memorable trade and a powerful learning experience. After all the analyst "happy talk" on the news wire and the options players' frenzy to buy calls on EMC shares, the stock headed directly south after the June 5 close. On June 11, EMC experienced a bearish "outside day" and closed back below potential options-related support at the 22½ strike. At this point I finally threw in the towel, swallowing a 46 percent loss on the trade. I could have been out of this trade a week earlier at a slight profit or at least a breakeven had I followed my contrarian philosophy. Remember that conditions can change soon after you enter a trade, so you must remain open-minded and flexible.

Stone Container (STO) March 15 Call

I recommended the STO March 15 call on January 17, 1997, after the stock broke out above the 15 level on heavy volume (see exhibit 6.21). I believed that this stock was poised for a continuation of this strength, as breakouts on heavy volume are typically very meaningful. Also, the shares closed the day before right at their 10-day moving average, hinting that a bounce was likely. The stock moved against

Exhibit 6.21   **STONE CONTAINER (STO) 9-DAY RELATIVE STRENGTH INDEX: SEPTEMBER 1996 TO MARCH 1997**

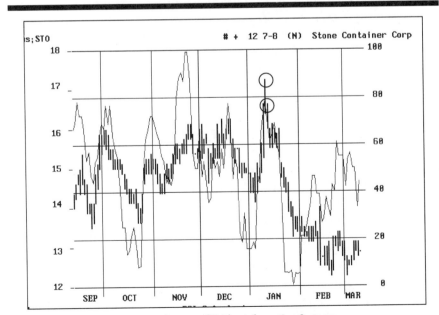

Reprinted with permission. Compliments of Bridge Information Systems.

me almost from the start, however, breaking back below 15 three days later. In hindsight, I would have been better served by an oscillating indicator such as the RSI, which would have better captured the short-term stock moves and usual range-trading behavior of this cyclical stock. The short-term 9-day RSI was coming off overbought levels that have preceded declines in recent months. Many times in a new uptrend, the oscillators will be overbought but the stock will shrug them off as the trend is now up. Yet the cyclical, economically sensitive stocks have shown the least tendency to trend over the course of this bull market, so caution should have been exercised due to the oscillator readings. I recommended exiting this trade on January 27 with STO at 14 and the March 15 call at a 65 percent loss.

CONCLUSION

Opportunities are always available for leveraged options trading, and it is possible to achieve enormous profits. No doubt, it is an exciting game, given the rewards you can reap if you choose to venture into this end of the options trading spectrum. Of course, I cannot stress too strongly that these profits can be achieved only if you are willing to accept the additional risk that accompanies such trading strategies. In other words, you must accept the reality that there will be more losing trades than winning trades with aggressive approaches. You should also be aware that there is an abundance of less risky options strategies that might suit your style equally well. In addition, you must concede that there will be trades on which you will lose your entire investment. However, if you elect to follow these aggressive strategies and are proficient at it, the occasional home runs tend to more than pay for the inevitable strikeouts.

Remember that technical indicators are not infallible. For example, support levels can break down, so on my Chrysler recommendation there was little room for error. If the shares broke below support at their 200-day moving average, the trade would have been in jeopardy, and a quick exit would have been mandated. For instance, if the stock had moved below support and the failed support implied a big decline in Chrysler shares, to cut losses the option might have to be sold at ¾ for a quick 45 percent loss before commissions. Upon entering the trade, a reward/risk ratio of four to one was established: the maximum loss was, of course, 100 percent, while a profit target of 400 percent was established. Fortunately, the latter was achieved.

Along the same lines, an equity can undergo a shift in relative strength or give a false breakout signal. Or company or sector fundamentals may shift for the worse, resulting in a losing trade.

In this chapter, I shared some profiles of my biggest winners as well as some disappointing trades, which will hopefully help you discover some major potential profit opportunities in the market while understanding that losses are inevitable in aggressive options trading. Of course, there is no method that is always successful, but I do believe that the common denominators in my big winners and the lessons that were learned from my losers can assist you in defining future winning trades. Chapter 7 discusses a specific strategy for short-term options trading that I call the "Quick Trade" method.

7

Quick Trade

INTRODUCTION

My investment philosophy dictates that the individual options trader needs to have an edge when buying options, and that edge usually occurs with position trades as you seek to ride trends over a period of days or weeks. As a rule, I don't recommend day trading options, because you then compete directly with the floor trader, who is likely to have better information on events that may move the stock over very short time periods. Floor traders' concerns relate mostly to what happens this minute, this hour, today; tomorrow appears only as a glimmer in their eyes, and next week may well be an eternity away. Also, floor traders have an edge intraday because of lower commissions and their ability to buy at the bid price and sell at the asked price. Don't expect to trade against the floor intraday and make consistent money.

However, I have developed a short-term approach by which you can hold a position for a maximum 7-trading-day period and expect a major edge in your options trading. I call it the Quick Trade (QT) methodology, and it uses regression channels to find acceleration points within trends.

THE POWER OF ACCELERATED TRENDS

Before defining regression channels, let us discuss the benefits of buying options just ahead of an acceleration within a trend. If the market expects a stock to move in a range of ±30 percent over a particular time period, if the options are priced for such a move, and if the stock ends up behaving in that manner, you ultimately have no edge trading options. Play this game frequently enough and you will lose due to commissions and slippage. But if the stock were to move at a 60 percent clip when the market expected just 30 percent, you would have a major advantage, particularly if you could predict the correct direction.

Remember that a 1 percent gain in a week annualizes at a 52 percent per year pace (1 percent × 52 weeks) with no compounding. Using the QT approach, I look for stock gains of as much as 10 percent in one week, which translates into as much as a 520 percent annualized gain. When I find such acceleration points by using regression channels, I typically have an edge of ten times or more relative to the movement the market actually expects over that short holding period.

REGRESSION CHANNELS: ZEROING IN ON THE TREND

Regression channels are lines that define a certain rate of trend. The traditional approach is to define a fixed period of time and draw a best-fit line from the beginning to the end of that period. Roughly half of the points will fall above this best-fit line and half will fall below. Most traders are taught to expect resistance at the top of a regression channel, and I would agree with this concept in principle. But those who expect such resistance and sell at the top of this channel are likely to change their bearish views if that resistance is penetrated and the stock holds above that former resistance area for at least two consecutive sessions.

For example, if a stock is sold short at 100 with the expectation of resistance at 100 and it surges to 105, the short seller is sitting on a 5-point loss. If the stock then pulls back to 100, the bear now has a chance to cover the short at a breakeven. As a result, previous resistance may now become support, as former sellers look to buy back positions at 100.

Note that regression lines can be drawn using the daily opens, highs, lows, closes, or the average of any combination of these reference points, but the closing price is the most meaningful data point on any particular bar chart over time. The majority of the crowd will tend to make their investment decisions earlier in the trading session in response to prior activity, whereas the smart money will look to move prices near the day's close in an effort to drive future activity.

Exhibit 7.1 shows the CompUSA (CPU) daily chart from early January 1996 to January 1997. It portrays a standard interpretation of a fixed time of 120 days (simulating six months of trading) to create a regression line[1] between any two points 120 days apart. Statistically, the regression line is a function of the following formula:

---

1. These regression lines are drawn with TradeStation and SuperCharts software by Omega Research, 9200 Sunset Dr., Miami, FL 33173–3266. TradeStation, which includes intraday charting and advanced system writing capabilities, is the more advanced product. Super-Charts is an excellent tool for those who need only to monitor daily data.

$$\sum_{i=1}^{n} (\chi_i - M)^2 + (\chi_{i+1} - M)^2 + \ldots + (\chi_{n-1} - M)^2 + (\chi_n - M)^2$$

where n is the number of days, M is the mean over n days, and χ represents each daily data point. This is known as the "least squares" formula, which finds the best-fit line, for which the sum of the squares of the deviation of each data point from that line is a minimum.

Line A in exhibit 7.1 shows a 120-day upsloping regression line, as prices were headed higher in the first half of 1996. Line B shows a flat 120-day regression line, as prices began to move higher initially after the bottom in mid-1996, where this 120-day regression line begins. In both of these cases, the regression line is not drawn to begin and then end at a relevant high and low point, since the channel is inflexible and measures only a fixed number of days. Let us see how much more meaningful the channel becomes when we add this flexibility to the regression line.

Exhibit 7.1   **COMPUSA (CPU) DAILY CHART WITH 120-DAY REGRESSION LINES**

01/29/97 C=18.250   O=17.500 H=18.250 L=17.375 V=5043200

Created with SuperCharts by Omega Research © 1996.

USING REGRESSION CHANNELS TO FIND QT OPPORTUNITIES

Exhibit 7.2 shows why you should not get caught up in fixed units of time to draw regression channels, but rather to look for major market lows and highs. The flexible regression lines on this chart better define the slope of the various uptrends and downtrends in CompUSA shares through 1996. The method used to draw these lines is as follows: After starting the regression line at a relevant closing low or closing high, draw the regression line out to important *secondary* highs or lows within an ongoing trend. (I do this because when I am drawing these channels in real time, I won't know where the absolute high or low will be until it is too late.) As long as you have at least twenty days of price data, you can draw a regression line with confidence and follow the future price movement of the stock to see if that line is meaningful. Note that the regression line itself should act as support under the price of the stock or resistance above the price of the stock. This can help you see if the regression line is in fact containing certain price moves in the stock. Now let us see how to add parallel lines around the regression line to form channels that contain the bulk of the price action.

In exhibit 7.3, first take the regression line, which began with the mid-January 1996 closing low, and extend this upsloped regression

Exhibit 7.2   **COMPUSA (CPU) DAILY CHART WITH FLEXIBLE REGRESSION LINES**

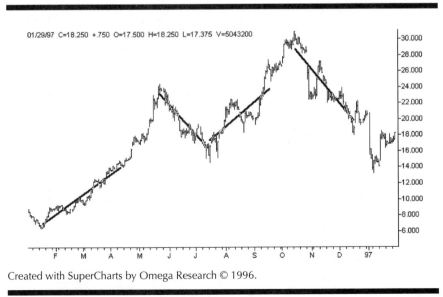

Created with SuperCharts by Omega Research © 1996.

line to the interim high in April 1996. Then extend this regression line out into perpetuity at the same slope. Omega Research's TradeStation and SuperCharts software offers this excellent feature and the ability to draw perpetual lines parallel to the regression line. Then draw two parallel lines, and then fit them initially based off the first significant high and low after the regression line's starting low point. In this case, CPU shares first reached short-term highs in late January 1996, and then made short-term lows in mid-February 1996. As the regression line in this case is drawn to the April 10, 1996, secondary high within the uptrend, you can see that there were a number of highs earlier in April and another high in mid-March that ran into resistance. You now have a number of reference points to line up the upper channel boundary along these highs. You should not adjust the lower boundary line drawn off its first low even though there was a one-day close below the line on March 4, 1996, as CPU subsequently rallied back into the channel the following day and then had a successful retest of this lower channel boundary on March 8, 1996. As you will see from the Quick Trade rules later in this chapter, a one-day move outside the channel does not mark an acceleration point, because such occurrences have a good chance of being noise. You must wait for confirmation via more time outside the channel before you can conclude an

---

Exhibit 7.3   **COMPUSA (CPU) DAILY CHART WITH FLEXIBLE REGRESSION CHANNEL**

01/29/97 C=18.250 +.750 O=17.500 H=18.250 L=17.375 V=5043200

Created with SuperCharts by Omega Research © 1996.

acceleration is likely. Note that the trendline extension actually serves as important support or resistance into the future.

RETESTS AND RETURNS

You can see the acceleration upward (which occurs after a Quick Trade bullish signal, discussed next) in May, followed by the break-down below the channel in late June and the inability to return into the channel in early July. There was a further plunge, and then an-other retest of the channel in August (missing a bearish QT signal by ⅛ point). Afterwards, you then see CPU quickly return to its former upchannel (the quick close back into the channel prevents a bearish QT signal), and then the shares peak again at the top of this now 9-month-old channel in mid-October (note the one-day close above the channel that returns to the channel the next day, again in a display of noise on the one-day event).

Let us look in more detail at the bullish acceleration out of the up-channel in late April and early May. Exhibit 7.4 is a detailed look at CPU during this period. You can see that CPU shares break out of the regression channel on April 23, and after some gains they pull back to just outside but not quite touching the upper regression channel on

---

Exhibit 7.4   **COMPUSA (CPU) REGRESSION CHANNEL BUY SIGNAL**

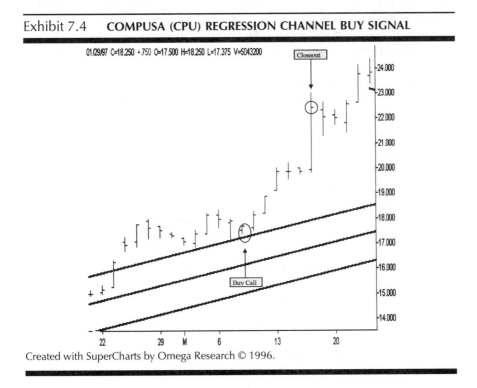

01/29/97 C=18.250 +.750 O=17.500 H=18.250 L=17.375 V=5043200

Closeout

Buy Call

Created with SuperCharts by Omega Research © 1996.

May 2. On May 7, CPU shares pull back as low as 17⅛ (note that these prices are adjusted for a 2-for-1 stock split) to touch the upper regression channel boundary, thereby giving a bullish QT signal. I typically enter at the point the line is touched, or occasionally the next morning if I have some concern that the upper boundary may not hold as support. By entering on the next day's opening price, CPU shares begin the QT trade at 17½. The day the signal is given is called day 0; then begin counting the holding period from the next trading session as day 1, and continue to hold over the subsequent seven trading days after the QT signal is given. On May 16, seven trading days later, CPU shares close at 22⁷⁄₁₆ (share price adjusted for future split), for a gain of 28 percent over just these seven trading days. For options traders buying the June 17½ calls at 1⁷⁄₁₆, the calls closed on May 16 at 5¼, for a windfall gain of 265 percent.

EXTREME FEAR

By focusing on significant highs and lows within the trend, you can gauge the extreme fear at the lows, relative to the counter emotion of greed at or near the highs. You can then position a trendline in the context of these two extremes.

It is very important to understand how to draw regression lines properly. The biggest mistake that can be made is to draw the regression line from the absolute low day. Draw the channel from the *closing* low day rather than the absolute low. Usually the absolute low day will also be the closing low day for a period, but sometimes this is not the case. You will get a better estimate of the angle of the uptrend if you draw the regression line from the low close (or the high close, if regressing a downtrend).

For example, let us look at exhibit 7.5, the daily chart of Nike (NKE). The absolute low came on February 16, but the closing low came on February 26. This slight difference in the point from where the channel is drawn determines whether a future QT put trade signal is registered. The dotted lines show the upchannel drawn inappropriately from the absolute low day to the peak in October 1996. The darker lines show the regression channel drawn properly from the closing low on February 26. This correct darker line rises at a slightly less steep angle than the incorrect dotted line, which causes the following situation to present itself.

As you can see on exhibit 7.6, on November 8, the proper darker line is touched by NKE shares on the bounce in the stock. Meanwhile, the incorrect dotted line is not touched, missing a profitable put trade. From their starting points, the difference in these two trendlines

Exhibit 7.5   NIKE (NKE) DAILY CHART WITH REGRESSION CHANNEL

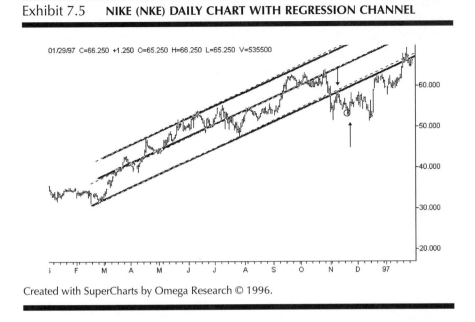

01/29/97 C=66.250 +1.250 O=65.250 H=66.250 L=65.250 V=535500

Created with SuperCharts by Omega Research © 1996.

seems imperceptible. But as time progresses, the gap between the correct and incorrect lines widens. This serves to emphasize the importance of attention to detail in drawing these regression lines accurately, using the lowest close and highest close criteria.

Exhibit 7.6   NIKE (NKE) REGRESSION CHANNEL SELL SIGNAL

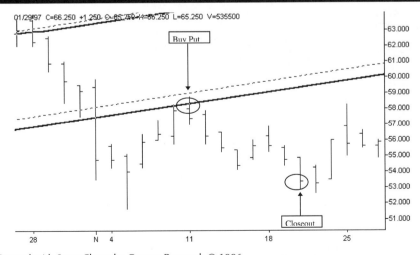

01/29/97 C=66.250 +1.250 O=65.250 H=66.250 L=65.250 V=535500

Buy Put

Closeout

Created with SuperCharts by Omega Research © 1996.

To summarize, the parallel lines around the top and bottom of the best-fit regression line serve as "containment lines," and they will approximate two standard deviations of price action, meaning that about 95 percent of all market activity is likely to be contained within the regression channel. Look for channels that are clearly predictive in defining the high and low points for a stock within its trend. The noisier and less reliable the trend, the less effective regression channels will be, and the less confidence you will have when the QT signal comes along. You really want to focus on tightly trending stocks, with regression channels that are clearly meaningful so you can trade the acceleration out of the channel with confidence.

BEWARE OF HEADFAKES

As shown in exhibit 7.7, although the regression channel for Centocor (CNTO) shares from the first closing low to the last closing high does a reasonable job of containing the bulk of the price action, there can be significant "headfakes" outside of these trendlines. A headfake occurs when you think you have an accurate breakout signal, but it quickly reverses to prove the initial signal incorrect. Acting on these headfakes would cause unsuccessful trades on both sides of the market. Losses would occur at the highs on the May breakout and retest, where an upside acceleration failed to develop and CNTO's share

---

Exhibit 7.7   **CENTOCOR (CNTO) DAILY CHART: AN EXAMPLE OF NOISY PRICE ACTION**

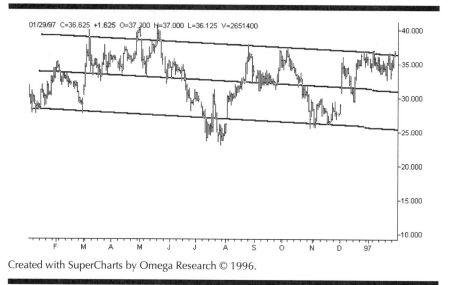

01/29/97 C=36.625 +1.625 O=37.000 H=37.000 L=36.125 V=2651400

Created with SuperCharts by Omega Research © 1996.

price quickly moved back into the channel. Losses would also occur on an expected bearish acceleration near the July lows, where a retest of the bottom band on July 17 would be unsuccessful with a necessary July 19 closeout with the stock gapping back into the band and closing 3 points higher in one day. Note also that the slope of the regression channel is nearly flat, with only a slight downward bias. The flatter and wider the regression channel, the more likely that a stock is not trending and more prone to noisy price action that does not make for reliable QT signals.

Exhibit 7.8 shows a regression channel that is very consistent for Gillette (G) shares. The channel begins at the lows in August 1995 and is drawn to the secondary high in October 1996. The three bold lines represent the *original* regression channel, which gives a correct bearish signal in early April and an initially correct signal in early May 1996, and also two useful bullish signals in early October and early November 1996. The dashed lines added *outside* the original channel are the "outer rails" of the trend. An outer rail is a second parallel line drawn off the first significant high or low outside the original channel. On the next breakout, the outer rail tells the best case to expect for a targeted move in the stock over the 7-day holding period. The outer rail on the first downside move out of the original channel is not touched again in this example, whereas the outer rail above the original channel proves to be significant resistance, and later significant support. When G shares move above the bullish outer rail in January 1997 and then come back to retest this line as new support, there is another bullish QT situation. Just like the high end of the original regression

Exhibit 7.8   **GILLETTE (G) DAILY CHART: AN EXAMPLE OF A TIGHT TREND**

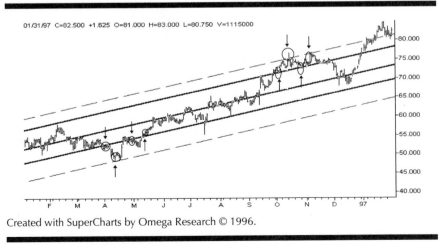

01/31/97 C=82.500 +1.625 O=81.000 H=83.000 L=80.750 V=1115000

Created with SuperCharts by Omega Research © 1996.

channel, resistance ultimately becomes support, so these outer rail signals are good on tightly trending stocks.

INTRADAY REVERSALS

The regression channels we have just discussed are drawn based on the daily closing prices. You could get fancy and test the usefulness of open, high, or low data, but it is my belief that "the battles are fought intraday, but the war is won at the close." I have seen too many situations where a stock looks to be breaking out of a channel intraday only to return within the channel by the close. Such tests are often significant when a stock looks one way intraday and reverses to close in the other direction, as bulls or bears give the breakout their best shot but fail, as shown by the reversal. This often leads to further follow-through in the direction of those who were victorious at the close.

A breakout on a closing basis outside the containment channel signals the stock has the potential to experience a new short-term accelerated trend, and if this breakout comes on news, such as a major earnings surprise, you can have added confidence in the breakout. For example, let us look at exhibit 7.9, the daily chart of Electronics for Imaging (EFII), and let us focus on the April–May 1996 period.

Exhibit 7.9   **ELECTRONICS FOR IMAGING (EFII) DAILY CHART**

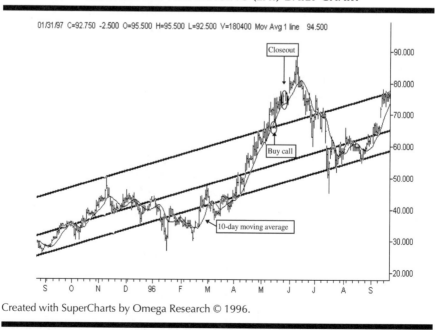

01/31/97 C=92.750 -2.500 O=95.500 H=95.500 L=92.500 V=180400 Mov Avg 1 line 94.500

Created with SuperCharts by Omega Research © 1996.

In April 1996, EFII reported quarterly earnings that blew out Wall Street estimates, and the shares started to march higher, first breaking out above the 50 level that had been resistance. Once the stock broke above the uptrending regression channel and then came back to retest it on May 16 at 65¾ intraday, the stock then took off. This retest of the regression line came in conjunction with another retest of the 10-day moving average, which had been acting as perfect support on this uptrending stock. By that day's close, EFII had reversed off its new QT support line and closed 8 points higher at 73¾, and after seven trading days, it finished at 76¾. This example shows that when the shares are in the process of being "revalued" as more investors jump on board the earnings estimates revision bandwagon (or any other fundamental driver such as restructuring, new management, or new product launches, all of which were discussed in chapter 6), the QT method can help pinpoint quick moves for aggressive option traders within the revaluation trend.

THE "RULES" FOR A REAL BREAKOUT

Note that there must be rules so you can have confidence that a breakout is real as opposed to simply a headfake. First, one day's close does not provide enough price action to confirm that the acceleration is under way; two consecutive closes above (or below) the containment channel are better, as the second close confirms the previous day's closing breakout. If after the first day's breakout, the next session sees a close back within the containment channel, this failure suggests no action under the QT methodology. Once we have had two consecutive closes outside the containment channel, note the level at which a pullback will touch the containment channel on a retest. This retest is the optimal risk/reward point to initiate a QT recommendation. This level should hold as support after an upside breakout, or serve as resistance after a break below the lower containment line. In some cases, you may want to see a day where the retest occurs successfully, and then initiate the trade on the following morning. In either case, as long as the stock is fairly close to the outer regression boundary, the risk/reward is very attractive for these short-term trades of up to seven trading days. Why seven days and not seventy days? My research shows that the first seven days marks the greatest annualized performance in the stock. The options buyer also benefits because the underlying stock moves at a more accelerated rate of trend, creating a better value on the option purchased relative to the

Exhibit 7.10   **ATC COMMUNICATIONS (ATCT) DAILY CHART WITH
REGRESSION CHANNEL AND OUTER RAIL**

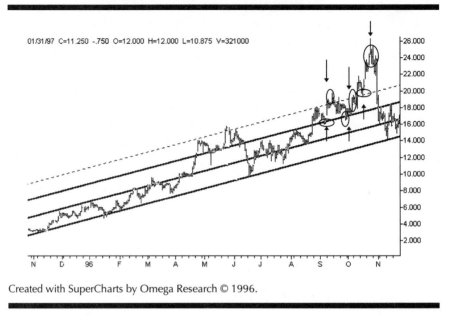

01/31/97 C=11.250 -.750 O=12.000 H=12.000 L=10.875 V=321000

Created with SuperCharts by Omega Research © 1996.

stock's increased short-term potential. Let us look now at two more examples, one bullish and one bearish.

In the bullish example of ATC Communications (ATCT), the up-trend (see exhibit 7.10) was again driven by strong positive earnings momentum, which made for a very consistent and tight channel. The channel not only contained the most price action but also gave good signals on the upside breakout outside the channel in May. This led to very high confidence QT trading signals in early and late September, in which ATCT shares gained nearly 20 percent within seven trading days in each case. Note the QT signal based on the bullish outer rail in early October, when the shares gained approximately 30 percent before ultimately hitting the top. Only when the company had a negative reaction to earnings did the uptrend cease.

Newbridge Networks (NN) (exhibit 7.11) had been in an uptrend from October 1995 to June 1996. The downside break in June and the subsequent retest in early July proved to be a classic bearish signal to buy puts on NN. Note that there are *two* outer rails below the original uptrending regression channel. This suggests there is another way to play an unfolding bearish move. The first is the traditional way: short the retest of the lower regression channel that was support and is now

Exhibit 7.11   **NEWBRIDGE NETWORKS (NN) TWO BEARISH OPPORTUNITIES**

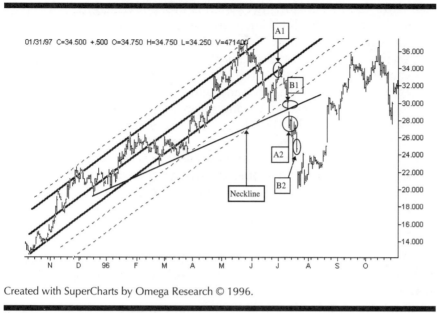

Created with SuperCharts by Omega Research © 1996.

resistance. This leads to a very profitable short position at around 34 on July 1, which plunges to as low as 27½ on July 12, the seventh trading day thereafter, denoted as point A on the chart. The other way to play this move is to wait until the outer rail is broken and short on a close below that point, as downside momentum in some cases doesn't allow a retest of the lower regression boundary. If this occurs, you have a short on the close below the bottom outer rail at a price of 30⅛ on July 10, which seven trading days later, on July 19, closes at 24¹¹⁄₁₆, shown at points B on the chart. In either case, the profits are substantial for put traders based on such sharp stock price movement over the seven subsequent trading days.

REGRESSION CHANNEL ANALYSIS AND TRADITIONAL TECHNICAL FORMATIONS

Technicians should also note the impact of regression channel analysis on traditional technical formations. In the example in exhibit 7.11, we can see what looks like a "head and shoulders" top from April to

June, with the absolute high in NN at $37\frac{1}{8}$ and secondary highs around 34 on each side of the top. Technicians know that the bearish case is in force when the "neckline" is broken, which indicates that major support has been violated. In this case, our neckline is the flattish line drawn around the 29 level. For traders using traditional pattern analysis in this case, their short signal comes on the open when NN shares gap down below the line, at a price of $28\frac{3}{4}$. This is still a successful short-term bearish trade under traditional technical analysis, but look at how the entry point improves with regression channel analysis. In essence, the close below the outer rail can be considered a neckline of its own, as this signifies, soon after the head and shoulders top was formed, that support under the stock had disappeared in the short term. This first close below the outer rail occurs at $30\frac{1}{8}$, a full $1\frac{3}{8}$ points better than shorting on the gap down the following session. So it pays to be aware of exactly where the regression channel is broken, even when you are using other traditional forms of analysis.

Headfakes remain an issue, especially with stocks that are noisy or moving into trading range—instead of trending—conditions. And there is another concern: If the stock is overbought after a short-term breakout, how can you expect to buy and anticipate an even more dramatic accelerated short-term run? My experience says that the most probable winners under the QT methodology are the solid trenders with the least noise in their trend, and an overbought oscillator is often ineffective on such uptrending stocks. One measure to screen for in determining which underlying stocks to follow for the QT methodology is to divide the 52-week price change by the standard error (SEE) term. The standard error measures the tightness of the data points around the best-fit regression line. The better the fit, the lower the SEE. Thus, dividing the 52-week price change by the SEE adjusts the stock's performance for the amount of volatility or unpredictability in achieving this performance. Therefore, stocks with high volatility will see a reduced ratio of price range to SEE relative to lower volatility stocks with similar 52-week price performances. Bridge Information Systems[2] offers a screening tool known as Rank & Filter, which produces a list of the best-performing stocks for any set of criteria. Exhibit 7.12 lists the most attractive stocks as of February 24, 1997, based on 52-week price change divided by the standard error term.

---

2. Bridge Information Systems, 717 Office Parkway, St. Louis, MO 63141.

Exhibit 7.12   **BRIDGE RANK & FILTER: A TECHNICAL SCREEN TO FIND TIGHT TRENDS**

PRTSYM	NA	(W52P/SEE)
US;CNC	CONSECO INC	26.209
US;DELL	DELL COMPUTER CORP	22.196
US;AES	AES CORP	21.302
US;WDC	WESTERN DIGITAL CORP	20.983
US;SPW	SPX CORP	20.499
US;PSUN	PACIFIC SUNWEAR OF C	20.307
US;GPT	GREENPOINT FINANCIAL	19.973
US;CCE	COCA COLA ENTERPRISE	19.408
US;NBTY	NBTY INC	19.401
US;STT	STATE STREET BOSTON	18.977
US;NKE	NIKE INC	17.818
US;VON	VONS COMPANIES INC	17.678
US;KEA	KEANE INC	16.865
US;SOTR	SOUTHTRUST CORP	16.527
US;FINL	FINISH LINE INC	16.388
US;WLA	WARNER LAMBERT CO	16.334
US;STB	STAR BANC CORP	16.082
US;INTC	INTEL CORP	15.876
US;CEI	CRESCENT REAL ESTATE	15.697
US;ASFC	ASTORIA FINANCIAL CO	15.459

Found: 2110

[BIR]RF   <--- Main Menu   24-FEB-97   Page: 1 of 106
[BIR]RF/PRT=OPT/RNK=(W52P/SEE)/PG2█   (c)BRIDGE

Reprinted with permission. Compliments of Bridge Information Systems.

LOW NOISE, TIGHT TRENDERS

The stocks listed in exhibit 7.12 are "tight trenders"—they post excellent upside performance relative to their standard error, or the volatility incurred in achieving this performance. Tight trenders have the least noise within their trends relative to their price movement, meaning you are getting the biggest bang for your options investment with minimal noise.

To summarize the QT entry and exit parameters, seek to enter bullish and bearish trades once the stock has had at least two closes outside of the regression channel, and then the stock has a retest of that regression line. This point offers the optimal risk/reward entry point, because if it closes back into the channel for two consecutive sessions, you should close it out. Give bullish trades seven trading days; on bearish trades you can go out up to seven trading days if the position is working well, but give these trades a shorter leash if they are not working, since the put trades must typically work very quickly.

Note that the QT methodology can be applied to weekly and monthly charts as well, with appealing results for intermediate and longer-term traders.

Weekly Regression Charts—Power Trend

Exhibit 7.13 shows that Becton Dickinson (BDX) had been in a steady weekly uptrend since April 1994, and when the stock broke out to the upside in late 1995 and retested the upper regression channel boundary at 35½ (post-split) in late December 1995, BDX shares were then off to the races. The stock surged from 35½ to 44½ over the next seven weeks making for profits of more than 300 percent in the March 37½ call. This strategy is an adaptation of my original QT research, and I call this weekly analysis Power Trend, as you can experience some really powerful moves in a span of less than two months with weekly regression channel analysis.

Exhibit 7.13   **BECTON DICKINSON (BDX) WEEKLY CHART**

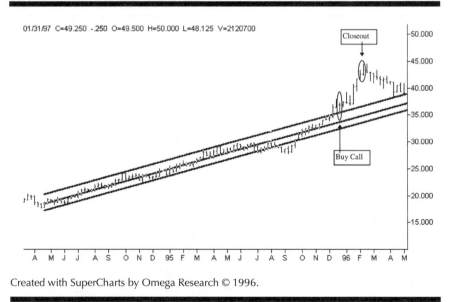

Created with SuperCharts by Omega Research © 1996.

Exhibit 7.14   **DUPONT (DD) MONTHLY CHART**

01/31/97 C=109.625 +15.250 O=94.375 H=112.750 L=92.750 V=42565900

Created with SuperCharts by Omega Research © 1996.

Monthly Regression Charts—Longer-Term Options

This same regression channel analysis can again be applied to monthly charts to spot likely acceleration points. In the case of DuPont (DD), a multiyear uptrend was penetrated to the upside in January 1996, and the retest officially occurred in March 1996 at a price of 75¼ (see exhibit 7.14). Even though DD took a few months to move, the stock over the seven months after the retest finished at the end of October 1996 at 92¾, with a high that month of 97⅝. I use this methodology in *The Option Advisor's* LEAPS Portfolio, discussed in chapter 8.

REGRESSION CHANNELS AND FILTERS—PROS AND CONS

Should you use regression channels alone or in conjunction with other filters? When I first started looking at regression channels, I saw many instances where it looked as if the low end of the channel caught the exact low, and the top end of the channel called the exact high. So naturally I began to paper-trade based on "buying low" and "selling high" on stocks' regression lines. What I found was that occasionally I would call the low or high quite accurately, but there were many instances where I ended up waiting too long for a reversal to occur. This was especially true in betting on a decline at the top end of an uptrending regression channel, or buying the low end of a downtrending regression channel. This makes sense, as such trades would be fighting the broader trend, and the subsequent price action is likely to be a sideways consolidation within an uptrend, or a basing period within a downtrend. The well-known saying, "don't fight the trend," rings as loudly using regression channels as with other approaches.

I also found that, even when buying at the low end of an uptrending channel or selling at the top end of a downtrending channel, the moves still did not happen as quickly as my mind's eye initially perceived. Further examination revealed the popular brain trick of "subjective distortion," where my brain directed my eyes to the good trades while I missed some of the slower-developing trades, or the trades that didn't work. My primary conclusion from this second phase was that I was still fighting a trend. While I was on the side of the longer-term trend, I was buying short-term weakness or fading near-term strength. I decided to incorporate a short-term trend filter to make sure I was favorably aligned with the trend in both the short-term and the broader time scale. My tests revealed that using 200-minute and 600-minute moving averages filtered the short-term trend quite effectively. Exhibit 7.15, the intraday chart of Philip Morris (MO), shows the 200-minute crossovers under and then over the 600-minute trendline as being very meaningful for a 5-point drop on one day, followed by a 7-point rally in one day after the bullish crossover.

The intraday chart of Intel (INTC) in late February 1997 (exhibit 7.16) also includes the "fast" 200-minute moving average and the "slow" 600-minute moving average. When INTC broke below its 600-minute trendline on February 26, the shares went into a steady downtrend. Note also that near the end of this short-term decline, the 200-minute line holds as resistance on the final leg down. Only when the shares close back above these moving averages is the downtrend ended. The benefits of such filters were a higher winning percentage on QT trades, as the shortest-term trends were now in my favor, not against me. The more time frames in which I could get the technicals in synch, the better. Potential buyers (or sellers if all the time frames are negative) may purchase the stock with all types of expectations and different holding periods, but the bottom line is that they are all

Exhibit 7.15   **PHILIP MORRIS (MO) INTRADAY CHART**

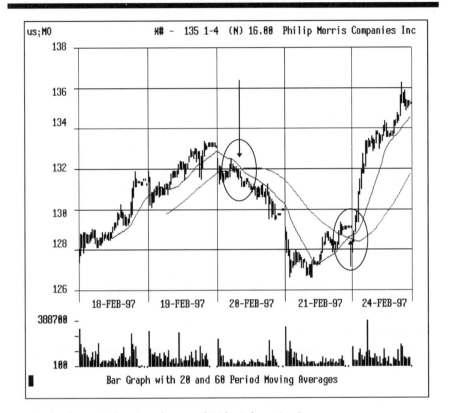

Reprinted with permission. Compliments of Bridge Information Systems.

buying. The primary issue with waiting for confirmation from the intraday charts is that the ideal risk/reward is right at the regression line, as the expectation is that this line provides key support at the top-end retracements for bullish call trades, and important resistance on the retest of the low end for bearish put trades. By using the trend filters, some proof is required that this level has held and the stock has thus already moved away from the regression channel line somewhat at that point. So my entry prices will suffer a bit. To an extent, this is a price I'm willing to pay if I can be more confident in the accuracy of my QT signal.

Exhibit 7.16   **INTEL (INTC) INTRADAY CHART**

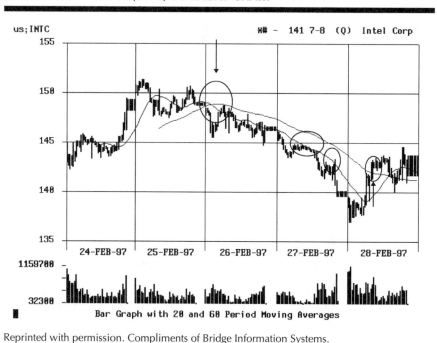

Reprinted with permission. Compliments of Bridge Information Systems.

DECIDING WHEN TO USE TREND FILTERS

There are several factors that determine whether trend filters make sense. First, volatility can be great if the expected regression support or resistance fails to hold, as the stock then often moves rapidly back into the old channel on this failure. The use of trend filters reduces this potential volatility significantly, although some reward is given up for this assurance. Another deciding factor in using such a filter is the existing market condition. Ideally I prefer to enter at the optimal risk/reward point, so the trade can be stopped at a smaller loss if the regression line doesn't hold, while squeezing out more profits if this line is as important as is believed. However, if on a bullish QT opportunity the market as measured by the (OEX) is weak in the short-term (defining weak on the OEX as below its 200-minute and 600-minute averages), I have noticed a definite drag on QT situations and prefer to use the intraday filter to avoid getting caught in market-related weakness. This saved me from issuing many bullish trades during the July 1996 correction, for example, as broad market declines were causing most prior technical uptrends in individual stocks to take a rest before they resumed in August as the broad market firmed up again. One notable exception to these guidelines occurs when you see a retest of the QT line that coincides with an important moving average, usually the 10-day, 20-day, or 50-day moving average for bullish trades, or the 100-day or 200-day moving averages for bearish trades. As we saw in the Electronics for Imaging (EFII) example earlier (exhibit 7.9), this additional trend support made for optimal purchasing of options at the exact retest of the regression line support or resistance.

NOISY NONTRENDERS

What do you do if a stock appears noisy or nontrending? Cull it from your list of QT opportunities to track. There are simply too many other good opportunities to bog your mind and resources down with noisy underlying stocks. If you later notice that the stock appears to be back into a trending mode again, you can always return to it. I spend a great deal of time not only monitoring my various databases for QT opportunities, but also actively culling noisy stocks and adding active optionable stocks that have moved into new trending modes. If you cannot follow the market daily, pick up *Investors' Business Daily* on Fridays, and look at their Weekend Review on the back page of the Section A, which shows charts and tables of attractive stocks with impressive relative strength versus the market. Some of these charts will grab you due to their trending channels, and you can investigate whether these stocks are optionable to leverage the short-term accelerations within these trends. *Investors' Business Daily* also lists in bold the big movers over the past week on higher-than-usual volume on the same Weekend Review page. A screening tool such as Bridge also offers an excellent source of studies to find trending names for further investigation, as discussed earlier with Bridge's Rank & Filter capability.

QUICK TRADES AND OPTIONS

What types of options should you trade under the QT methodology? The front-month options (which I generally avoid) are typically the best options to play with an accelerated trend, as that is where you get the biggest bang for your buck in catching others off guard, as they are pricing the options based on the old trend's rate of speed.

Second-month options are also appropriate for this strategy. Out-of-the-money front-month options are the most aggressive way to play this strategy, but I tend to like options that are near-the-money for the QT approach, as this serves to more closely simulate the stock's movement while providing respectable leverage. Experience shows that a double or slightly more can be achieved with these options over a seven-day holding period, while risk is reduced and some respectable option premium is salvageable if the trade is not working and an exit is required. Occasionally, signals will be given in the final week before the front-month options expire, in which case recommendations typically will go out to the next month's options using an out-of-the-money option; the second-month position will not get hurt too badly if the stock has essentially remained unchanged after seven trading days when an exit is dictated by this approach, whereas the front-month position would likely sustain a total loss.

WHEN TO EXIT A LOSING QT TRADE

Certainly not all trades can be winners, no matter how well researched the approach. However, the QT method gives a clear signal to exit when the underlying stock closes back into the channel. One close back into the channel sends off alarm bells to be ready for an exit. Two consecutive closes back into the channel dictate a closeout, as this invalidates the theory that the stock should accelerate out of its former channel. Losing trades will also occur if the stock fails to accelerate but meanders only slightly higher. This will cause time decay in these short-term options, but by exiting after seven days regardless, you minimize the impact of the loss in such situations.

CLOSING THOUGHTS ON QUICK TRADES

Some final thoughts about regression channels:

1. The less volatile the channel, the better the trend. A tight channel by definition means there is less day-to-day volatility within a trend, which makes that trend steadier and more predictable. These are the trends to watch for breakouts, because they can be traded with higher confidence that the breakout is something more than just noise.

2. There are differences between bullish and bearish opportunities. In general, bullish moves tend to occur more slowly but on a more regular basis, and downdrafts tend to be brief but sharp in nature. In the same way, acceleration points in uptrends usually take more than one or two days to play out—seven days is the average optimal holding period. Downside potential in bearish QT situations can often be more dramatic, with a one-day or two-day downdraft of several points not unusual. As a result, when bearish QT option trades are made, expect a quick windfall profit, which can occur within three to five days as a typical holding period, although you can still hold put trades for up to seven trading days if they are working out properly. The general rule is that if the plunge is going to happen, you expect it to happen quickly. And when panic does set in and the stock downdrafts rapidly, the rule is to take windfall profits when you have them—don't get stuck thinking there could be more downside on the put trades. Usually such behavior prevents the trader from capitalizing on the market's panic by taking profits quickly on the puts.

3. Longer-term trends can develop from these QT acceleration periods. Your goal should be to make quick profits of 100 percent or more on trades lasting up to seven trading days. I have had trades where I took such profits, as my method dictated, yet the stock continued to surge in the direction of the initial acceleration. I noticed that fundamental news such as earnings can be the driver for a new accelerated trend slope that can last for an extended time if powerful enough, as in the case of Electronics for Imaging (EFII) discussed earlier in this chapter. Profits of 11 points were taken on the EFII example, yet the stock tightly channeled even higher still. The 20-day moving average served as support in the new, more dramatic uptrend, as did the new steeply uptrending regression channel I could draw off the new high and low reference points. The lesson here is there are some intermediate-term opportunities for traders who see the importance of the news to the trend's ultimate direction. But I stick primarily with the QT shorter-term approach because there are ample opportunities in most cases, and I find more comfort in catching fresh situations as they begin to accelerate before the market catches on to the new accelerated trend.

4. Similarly, a breakout of a short-term downtrending or sideways channel within a longer-term uptrend can make for an attractive buying opportunity for longer-term traders. Situations such as Schwab (SCH; see exhibit 7.17) are attractive because a downtrending or sideways regression channel that is broken to the upside shows that the stock has already had a significant correction in either price or time, so the ensuing uptrend can last for a significant period before drifting lower. The key decision in this methodology is whether to wait for a retest or to go with the breakout. Again, the decision is

Exhibit 7.17   **SCHWAB (SCH) WEEKLY CHART WITH CHANNEL BREAKOUTS**

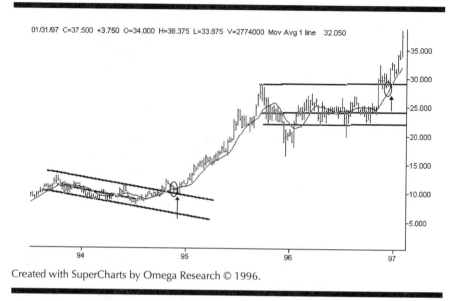

01/31/97 C=37.500 +3.750 O=34.000 H=38.375 L=33.875 V=2774000 Mov Avg 1 line   32.050

Created with SuperCharts by Omega Research © 1996.

likely to rest with what factors support the trade. If earnings are a driver, the stock may not retest, as the new events may have radically changed the trend. In the case of a stock breaking out on no news, you will be better off in most cases waiting to buy the first pullback either the old regression downtrend or at least to a significant moving average such as SCH's 50-day moving average.

5. Be prepared to miss some trades that never retest the former regression channel. The nature of my methodology is such that if I do not see a retest of the former channel, I cannot define an optional risk/reward point to purchase such positions. I have experimented with the 10-day and 20-day moving averages as filters, but even though such levels are sometimes significant, they often temporarily break and the former channel is retested. I would rather have optimal risk/reward to define my entry where possible, rather than chase a trade that could backfire.

CONCLUSION

Why does the Quick Trade method work? Because former resistance becomes support (and vice versa). This classically simple concept serves as the basis for the QT method, which adds the regression line to tell you at what price level the stock should pivot as resistance turns into support and former support becomes new resistance. Many money managers and advisors will tell you that it is too dangerous to play the "blowoff" move in a stock or market. The QT method gives you a systematic way to play blowoffs without being in the market very long if the move fails to happen or if a reversal starts to occur. The QT approach is also ideally suited for options trading, since the accelerated trend is a classic way to beat the static assumptions of the options pricing model as well as to achieve the speed of movement that is so essential to the success of options buyers. Now that we have discussed short-term option buying strategies in detail, chapter 8 will focus on how to use longer-term options to reduce risk and profit from the big moves that sometimes require more time to develop.

8

LEAPS

INTRODUCTION

When you invest in options, you can easily feel that you are hurtling along in the financial fast lane. But you can move over and still enjoy the ride in the driving lane by investing in longer-term options, known as LEAPS.

Long-term Equity AnticiPation Securities (LEAPS) were introduced in 1990, and the first LEAPS underlyings were selected stocks in the Dow Industrials, followed later by other major equities. There are now more than 200 stocks with LEAPS options. You can also buy LEAPS for specific industry sectors as diverse as the Biotechnology Index and the Mexico Index, or on such broad-market barometers as the Major Market Index and S&P's Midcap 400 Index, as well as on the ever-popular S&P 100 Index.

LEAPS are assets with a finite life; like short-term options they will expire at a predefined date. But the rate of time decay for LEAPS is much slower than that for the typical shorter-term option. This is beneficial if you want to hold a position for a number of months, or even for a year. LEAPS typically are initiated with one to two and one-half years until expiration. LEAPS expiration months are in January, which offer tax benefits if you intend to close these positions near expiration in a subsequent tax year. Once a LEAPS series has between six and eight months remaining until expiration, the LEAPS are converted into the normal shorter-term options cycle of the underlying stock, and the symbol changes from the LEAPS option root to the standard shorter-term option root. You need to be aware of that change in option root to follow such options on a quote terminal.

Why devote a whole chapter to LEAPS? You can use LEAPS for a variety of purposes—for trading an intermediate-term stock or market outlook, as long-term insurance against a declining stock or portfolio, or as a stock replacement. You can also use LEAPS in a variety of time spreads and covered writes to add income and value to your portfolio, while lowering the cost on your initial investment. When you buy LEAPS, you are giving up some of the upside leverage you would get with shorter-term options, but you are also dramatically reducing your risk of a large loss. You can thus take advantage of longer-term trends while minimizing worries about daily market swings and accelerated time decay.

Like regular options, each LEAPS contract represents 100 shares of the underlying security, and you have the flexibility to buy either calls or puts. You can take advantage of LEAPS whether you are bullish or bearish on a stock or index. If you, like many investors, are reluctant to sell stocks short, LEAPS can help diversify your portfolio between bullish and bearish positions with strategically selected LEAPS puts in addition to LEAPS calls.

The average option speculator might argue that LEAPS give up too much leverage relative to short-term options. And the average stock investor might be concerned that LEAPS take on too much leverage relative to stocks. This middle ground is precisely what excites options traders who have had the experience of being hammered by a temporary market blip that caused a loss in a short-term expiration month, only to see their view play out as expected a month or two thereafter. And stock investors can lower their total dollar risk in the market and retain similar upside dollar potential with certain LEAPS strategies.

Much has already been written about the strategic possibilities of LEAPS. But I have found that shorter-term options speculators can have a difficult time applying their approach to these longer-term options. Their speculative mind-set tends to lead them to want too much, too fast. The LEAPS discussion here presents a broader perspective on what I call the "big-picture trend." This involves a combination of longer-term technical indicators and, more uniquely, a perspective on the expectations for various sectors and stocks. This perspective is vital to ride out the shorter-term blips (which we care about with short-term options, but must look beyond if we are going to stay aboard the big-picture trend) without experiencing the inevitable shakeouts that cause many who are accustomed to trading shorter-term options to exit prematurely along the way.

This leads to the fundamental premise of LEAPS trading: LEAPS are not to be traded in the same way you trade shorter-term options, and yet you still cannot view them the same way you do a stock investment. It is the successful synthesis—this middle ground—that we will focus on here, and I will show you techniques you can use to effectively trade this relatively new and more conservative options vehicle.

BULLISH LEAPS STRATEGIES

In the following discussion of strategies, we differentiate the bullish situations from the bearish ones due to a fact that many traders overlook: The indicators that work best for bullish trades are not necessarily the ones that work best for bearish plays. Why? Because the character of advances and declines is different in bull and bear markets. In a bull market, rallies are slow but regular in nature, as buyers steadily enter to ride the trend and drive prices higher. When there are corrections in bull markets, they are usually brief but sharp, as quick profit-taking emerges and fear of a top is abundant. So a bull market environment would require call trades structured to take advantage of a steady—although sometimes slow—uptrend, whereas you would need to make bearish trades in a bull market just as the quick drop begins and exit your puts more quickly as the low is more rapidly reached. While the appeal of a faster move to the downside seems alluring, many put traders will be hurt either by poor timing of put purchases against the ongoing uptrend, or by getting complacent about an initial gain on a quick drop that evaporates as the next rally occurs.

Note that in a bear market these conditions reverse. Declines are slow and steady, and bear-market rallies are sharp and brief. Call speculators hope for a bottom that typically doesn't occur until after a more dramatic final leg downward. Traders will want to generally stay with puts in a broad downtrend, since the quick and sharp rallies are too infrequent to risk your capital on calls in such situations.

Bullish LEAPS Strategy #1: Straight Call Purchase

The straight call purchase is the simplest yet most effective LEAPS strategy for options traders and stock investors alike and is the strategy used exclusively in *The Option Advisor's* LEAPS Portfolio. The LEAPS Portfolio contains four LEAPS recommendations each month, screening for attractively priced LEAPS that can approximately double in value on a 15 percent to 20 percent move in the underlying stock.

Table 8.1 shows a sample LEAPS recommendation. Here we see that I recommend buying the January 1999 60-strike call on Coca-Cola. LEAPS option roots differ from those of standard options because they must signify not only the underlying stock, but the year in which the option expires. All LEAPS options symbols begin with Z, W, or V. Each letter is used for a specific expiration year. For LEAPS expiring in January 1999, V is used; afterward, that letter will

Table 8.1   **SAMPLE *OPTION ADVISOR* LEAPS RECOMMENDATION**

	Stock Re-Cap (1-3)		Option Re-Cap (4-5)	
(1)	(2)	(3)	(4)	(5)
Underlying Stock	Ticker Symbol	Closing Price	B=Buy	Expiration Month/ Striking Price
Coca-Cola	VKO	60	B	January 1999/60

(6)	(7)	(8)	(9)	(10)	(11)	(12)
Closing Price	Exchange	Maximum Entry Price	Target Profit	Closeout Date	Volume/ Liquidity Class	Delta
4	C	4¼	100%	04/02	D6	50%

be on hiatus until 2002. LEAPS beginning with W expire in 2001, and Z LEAPS expire in 2000.

There are several key rules that you, as a straight-call LEAPS buyer, should keep in mind:

1. *Buy LEAPS calls only on uptrending stocks.* One of the great temptations beginning traders face is the desire to "pick a bottom" by buying calls just after a stock has experienced a severe decline. LEAPS traders may be tempted to conclude that because they have purchased more time on the option, they have more time to wait if the stock undergoes a drawn-out bottoming phase before it significantly recovers. This is a "time trap" that can lull stock investors accustomed to waiting out a bottom, and lure them into trouble with LEAPS.

Remember, a LEAPS option is still a decaying asset, even if at a slower rate per day than a shorter-term option. As a result, buy LEAPS on stocks that are poised to move higher after a pullback within the uptrend, or after a breakout that confirms the uptrend is still intact.

The moving average is a very familiar concept among technically oriented investors, and it is also one of the easiest to which you can apply entry and exit rules. For LEAPS trading, research shows that the 20-month (about 400 trading days) moving average is one of the most useful for determining the direction of the long-term trend, and it is also much overlooked. For example, on the monthly chart of discount brokerage firm Charles Schwab (SCH) (exhibit 8.1), the 20-

Exhibit 8.1   **CHARLES SCHWAB (SCH) MONTHLY CHART WITH
20-MONTH MOVING AVERAGE**

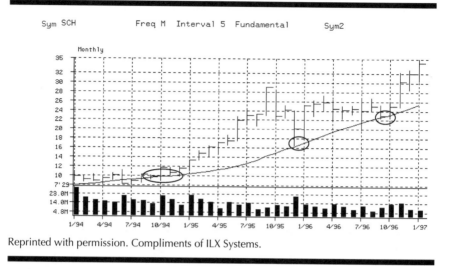

Reprinted with permission. Compliments of ILX Systems.

month moving average has beautifully contained pullbacks within the longer-term perspective. My experience has been to recommend LEAPS calls as the stock comes off this support and begins to break out of the former congestion zone. This most recently occurred for Schwab in December 1996, as the stock broke out above the 30 level after coming off the 20-month moving average, and my recommendation of the Schwab January 1998 30 call on January 7, 1997, took advantage of the breakout in the shares and resulted in a 100 percent gain in the LEAPS call when my target profit was reached on February 14.

Of course, you can use various moving averages to find good buying opportunities. For example, my August 22, 1996, recommendation of the Equifax (EFX) January 1998 25 call was bolstered by major support at the 100-day moving average shown in exhibit 8.2. As long as this line held as support, this point defined optimal reward/risk within the uptrend. Within three months, this recommendation had doubled. Of course, not all technical signs of an uptrend play out successfully. My recommendation on December 21, 1995, of the Lowe's (LOW) January 1997 35 put was made on the basis of a rally back to long-term resistance in the 35 area. As exhibit 8.3 shows, this was also the site of resistance at the 400-day moving average. In March 1996 the shares moved above this resistance, and I rapidly closed this put position after a 41 percent loss. Note also the "whippiness" of the LOW chart, as it regularly crossed above and below the

Exhibit 8.2 **EQUIFAX (EFX) WEEKLY CHART**

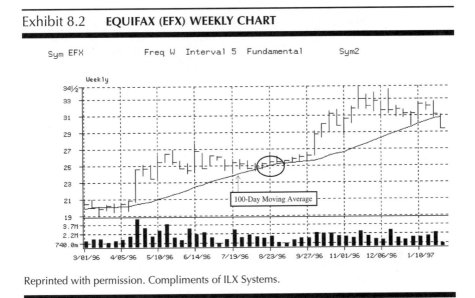

Reprinted with permission. Compliments of ILX Systems.

moving average. In retrospect, I would have been better off avoiding such a nontrending situation as an options play.

2. *If you are shooting for returns of around 100 percent, buy nearer-the-money LEAPS.* The pricing of LEAPS options tends to be such that if a typical stock made a steady 5 to 10 point upleg, you receive

Exhibit 8.3 **LOWE'S (LOW) MONTHLY CHART**

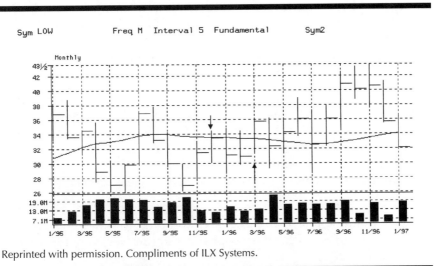

Reprinted with permission. Compliments of ILX Systems.

Table 8.2 **LEAPS PREMIUMS FOR A HIGH AND LOW VOLATILITY STOCK**

February 4, 1997
Microsoft Options (High   versus
Volatility) Stock at 103⅛

February 4, 1997
Merck Options (Low Volatility)
Stock at 91¾

Call	Strike Price	Option Price	Intrinsic Value	Time Prem- ium	Call	Strike Price	Option Price	Intrinsic Value	Time Prem- ium
OTM	105	23⅞	0	23⅞	OTM	95	13⅝	0	13⅝
ATM	100	26⅛	3⅛	23	ATM	90	16⅛	1¾	14⅜
ITM	95	28¾	8⅛	20⅝	ITM	85	18⅞	6¾	12⅛

Put	Strike Price	Option Price	Intrinsic Value	Time Prem- ium	Put	Strike Price	Option Price	Intrinsic Value	Time Prem- ium
OTM	95	10	0	10	OTM	85	6½	0	6½
ATM	100	12⅝	0	12⅝	ATM	90	8½	0	8½
ITM	105	14½	1⅞	12⅜	ITM	95	11	3¼	7¾

approximately a double whether you buy near-the-money or out-of-the-money LEAPS. Only when you expect a more massive rally do you want to consider buying farther out-of-the-money LEAPS. Although the temptation is great to own more contracts for the same dollar investment, the reward/risk profile is better on near-the-money LEAPS if you are expecting a typical percentage gain in the stock on a rally, as opposed to something more extraordinary.

This is particularly true on higher-volatility stocks (see table 8.2). The extra time you are buying really gets priced into the farther out-of-the-money LEAPS relative to their nearer-the-money counterparts.

3. *Accelerated uptrends are very profitable.* The current LEAPS listings tend to be on the more active stocks that have bigger market capitalizations, and thus lesser potential for big gains than their small cap brethren. But occasionally a LEAPS stock can accelerate for significant gains over a relatively short period.

I use two primary methods to find such acceleration candidates:

A. *Modified "Quick Trade" Method* Using monthly bar charts, I examine retests of key regression lines to find the behaviors of LEAPS stocks that appear to be accelerating out of the channel.

Exhibit 8.4   **AVON PRODUCTS (AVP) WEEKLY CHART: ACCELERATION ABOVE THE REGRESSION CHANNEL**

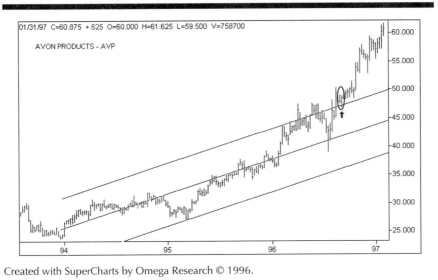

Created with SuperCharts by Omega Research © 1996.

In the Avon Products (AVP) example shown in exhibit 8.4, I made this recommendation knowing on September 9, 1996, that short-term resistance was less than 1 point overhead at 50, yet I did so also knowing that my big-picture regression analysis showed AVP above its multiyear channel and ready to accelerate. For a number of days the 50 level did act as resistance, but my time horizon was much longer than this. The eventual acceleration did occur, and when combined with the short-term resistance at 50 being broken, it led to a quick 8-point rally over the next two months.

In the case of the Procter & Gamble January 1998 110 call I recommended on August 22, 1996, this normally sedate blue chip stock moved out of a channel that had been in place since the 1987 crash (see exhibit 8.5). The shares went on to surge from 90½ to 110¼ to double the call in less than three months.

If LEAPS call trades are not initially accelerating as expected, be patient. I recommend closing such call trades only if they experience a monthly close below the top regression line, as this would show their acceleration potential to be diminished. For example, my August 22, 1996, recommendation of the Federal National Mortgage (FNM) January 1998 32½ call was off to a good start, but it did not reach its target profit and then began to decline. The monthly close back into the re-

Exhibit 8.5   **PROCTER & GAMBLE (PG) MONTHLY CHART: ACCELERATION ABOVE THE REGRESSION CHANNEL**

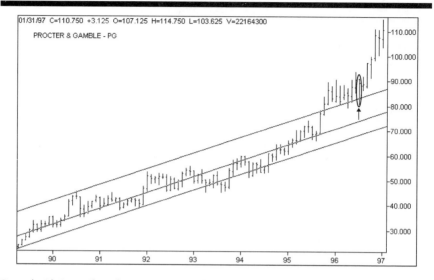

01/31/97 C=110.750 +3.125 O=107.125 H=114.750 L=103.625 V=22164300

PROCTER & GAMBLE - PG

Created with SuperCharts by Omega Research © 1996.

Exhibit 8.6   **FEDERAL NATIONAL MORTGAGE (FNM) MONTHLY CHART: EXIT ON CLOSE BACK INTO CHANNEL**

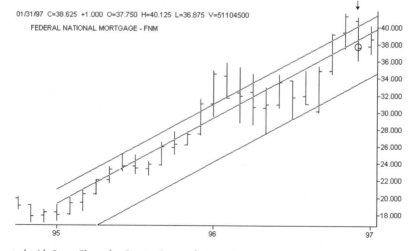

01/31/97 C=38.625 +1.000 O=37.750 H=40.125 L=36.875 V=51104500

FEDERAL NATIONAL MORTGAGE - FNM

Created with SuperCharts by Omega Research © 1996.

gression channel shown on exhibit 8.6 suggested the acceleration potential for FNM shares was diminished in mid-Decem-
ber 1996, and I recommended exiting this position the
following week on a final short-term bounce in FNM shares
for an 80 percent gain.

As mentioned earlier, the acceleration out of the regression channel often foreshadows some development that will
ultimately lead to higher share prices. Often the breakout
comes in conjunction with a better-than-expected quarterly
earnings surprise, as happened with Oracle Systems (ORCL;
exhibit 8.7). Oracle had pulled back to this key regression line
and ORCL's relative strength versus the S&P 500 Index was in
a very favorable uptrend. The stock shot up 10 points after I
initiated the LEAPS call recommendation on September 9,
1996, and reached my 100 percent target profit in less than
three months.

Such buying opportunities can also emerge based on a
temporary drop in a strong stock that is likely to hold up as
support. A prime example of this came in late 1996. Safeway's
1996 gain of 76 percent into early October was briefly reduced
by a 14 percent correction when news hit that Safeway was
taking over the Vons grocery chain in a $1.57 billion merger.

**Exhibit 8.7   ORACLE SYSTEMS (ORCL) MONTHLY CHART: QUICK PROFIT
ON ACCELERATION BEFORE REVERSAL**

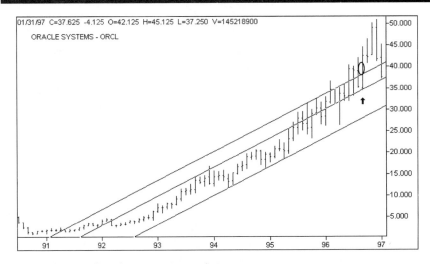

01/31/97 C=37.625 -4.125 O=42.125 H=45.125 L=37.250 V=145218900

ORACLE SYSTEMS - ORCL

Created with SuperCharts by Omega Research © 1996.

Exhibit 8.8   **SAFEWAY (SWY) WEEKLY CHART: BUY ON RETEST OF PRIOR CHANNEL HIGHS**

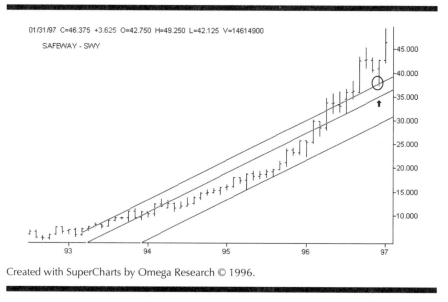

01/31/97 C=46.375 +3.625 O=42.750 H=49.250 L=42.125 V=14614900

SAFEWAY - SWY

Created with SuperCharts by Omega Research © 1996.

The acquiring company often gets temporarily hit on fears of earnings-per-share dilution, but I often see this as a buying opportunity in longer-term uptrending stocks. As exhibit 8.8 shows, Safeway pulled back to its upper regression line, marking a great buying spot for my December 20, 1996, recommendation of the January 1998 45 call. The position went on to nearly double over the next five weeks as the stock gained 20 percent over that brief period.

B. *"Out of Bands" Behavior.* Similar to the regression channel method (where we look for movement outside a range that usually contains 95 percent of the stock's price action), movement outside of volatility bands often shows that something significant is happening with a stock. These "deviant" price moves offer the most potential for big trends. Famed hedge-fun manager George Soros once said that it is in these few percent of the price movements that are unexplained by the standard distribution of the price action (known as the "tails" of the distribution) where he made his biggest money. From the examples that follow, you will see the power of these price moves out of volatility bands that usually define the expected normal range for a stock.

Exhibit 8.9   **AMERICAN HOME PRODUCTS (AHP) MONTHLY CHART**

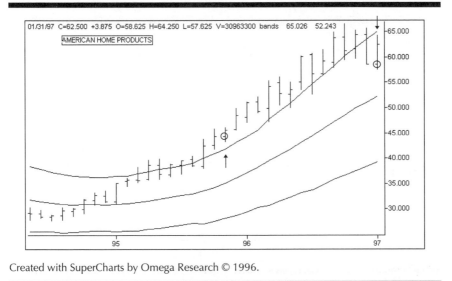

01/31/97 C=62.500 +3.875 O=58.625 H=64.250 L=57.625 V=30963300 bands 65.026 52.243

AMERICAN HOME PRODUCTS

Created with SuperCharts by Omega Research © 1996.

My preference is to take a volatility band that is a function of the high and low over the last 20 months, and thus place a high band and a low band around the 20-month moving average. I then look for breakouts above the high band to find bullish out-of-bands moves. Once a stock has had two monthly closes above the high band, I look to buy the next retest of this high band, as what once was resistance now becomes support (as shown in exhibits 8.9 and 8.10). Only when the stock has a monthly close back under this high band does an exit then become required (see exhibit 8.11). At this point, a retest of the upper band may even be considered a shorting opportunity, as the uptrend is likely to be ended and the upper band is now apt to act as overhead resistance.

I use two other methods to produce longer-term buy signals:

A. *Relative Strength Reversals* Stocks that give new relative strength buy signals versus a relevant index or benchmark are excellent candidates for further upside potential. Watch for a stock that begins to act stronger than the market after a period of underperformance. At a threshold that has been tested to be meaningful over a certain holding period, the strengthening stock gives a relative strength buy signal. I am particularly fond of fast and slow relative

Exhibit 8.10   **COLUMBIA GAS (CG) MONTHLY CHART**

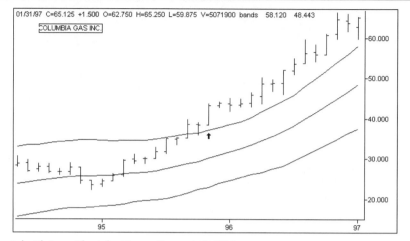

Created with SuperCharts by Omega Research © 1996.

strength averages, which can be adjusted depending on the desired holding period. For LEAPS trading, I look at a 10-week relative performance line (fast) and a 40-week relative performance line (slow) of a stock versus the S&P 500 Index. The crossing of the fast line over (or

Exhibit 8.11   **JOHNSON & JOHNSON (JNJ) MONTHLY CHART**

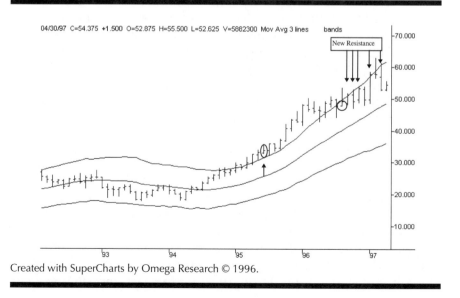

Created with SuperCharts by Omega Research © 1996.

Exhibit 8.12   **ADVANCED MICRO DEVICES (AMD) WEEKLY CHART:
RELATIVE STRENGTH CROSSOVER**

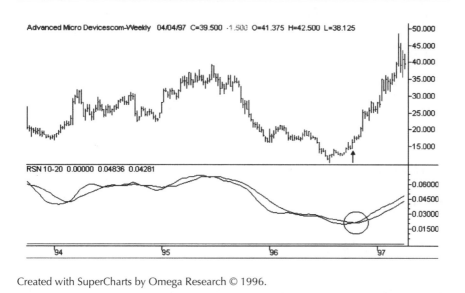

Advanced Micro Devicescom-Weekly   04/04/97 C=39.500 -1.500 O=41.375 H=42.500 L=38.125

RSN 10-20 0.00000 0.04836 0.04281

Created with SuperCharts by Omega Research © 1996.

under) the slow line gives you buy (or sell) signals that, for a number of stocks, can be surprisingly accurate.

For example, my recommendation of the Advanced Micro Devices (AMD) January 1998 15 call on October 24, 1996, was driven by a 10-week/40-week relative strength crossover (see exhibit 8.12). I became even more confident when I looked at the last five crossover buy signals, four of which had produced gains of anywhere from 8 points to as much as 20 points on this relatively cheaply priced stock. So the relative strength buy signal on AMD on October 24, 1996, was a golden opportunity, and the recommended option doubled in less than one month.

The AMD situation raises the questions, Why set profit targets on the option? Why not just let it ride until a new sell signal occurs for that stock? My experience with such an aggressive approach is that although you will hit some bigger winners that way, you will also experience plenty of painful reversals where option profits turn into break-even or losing situations. Either approach can work in theory. But in reality, sticking with your initial profit target enforces one of the keys to successful options trading: developing the discipline to follow your plan. Many traders cannot emotionally handle the volatility inherent in the "let it ride" approach (even though many like to think they can). As a result, they let it ride until a few large losses occur, at which point the questioning begins: "What's wrong with my plan?" "Do I need a new method?" "Should I stop trading this system to see if it is faulty?" And, as Murphy's Law would have it, the trader sits out future trading signals after that loss of confidence only to watch the next big winner from the sidelines. One of my primary goals is to devise options trading plans you can stick to through the inevitable thick and thin, so you can have the confidence to take all the trades to end up on the profitable end of the spectrum.

B. *Systematized sell signals on uptrending stocks* Many traders wait for a new buy signal to occur before purchasing a strongly uptrending stock, but these big winners often offer excellent *buying* opportunities on *sell* signals using the same parameters. For example, Safeway's short trades using the 10-week line crossing under the 40-week relative strength line showed only one out of nine trades profitable. In every case, the stock was higher or the same when the relative strength buy signal reversed the relative strength sell signal. So the sell signal actually produces a better buying opportunity for traders (exhibit 8.13). Note that this strategy is appropriate only on strongly uptrending stocks. Why? Because the shorts take their shot at drag-

Exhibit 8.13   **SAFEWAY (SWY) WEEKLY CHART: RELATIVE STRENGTH VERSUS S&P 500 INDEX**

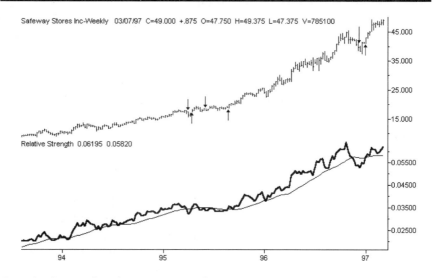

Safeway Stores Inc-Weekly 03/07/97 C=49.000 +.875 O=47.750 H=49.375 L=47.375 V=785100

Relative Strength 0.06195 0.05820

Created with SuperCharts by Omega Research © 1996.

ging leading stocks down, but they fail on these strong stocks because smart money is willing to buy this temporary weakness. The result is that the sell signal occurs very near the short-term bottoms in these strongly uptrending stocks. Don't try to use this strategy with stocks in a longer-term trading range, as the lack of any longer-term uptrend will make the sell signals more effective than they are in uptrending situations. And, of course, you must avoid fading sell signals on downtrending stocks (in fact, in downtrends you may want to consider fading buy signals).

Bullish LEAPS Strategy #2: Deep In-the-Money Leaps Call Purchase as a Stock Substitute

If you are concerned about a correction in a stock or in the stock market, you might try this strategy, which closely simulates the movement of the stock with much less dollar risk than actually owning the stock. For example, let us assume you like the outlook for Philip Morris (MO) shares, but you are somewhat concerned about the possibility of legislative risk in its tobacco operations, or you are worried that a stock market decline of 10 percent to 20 percent could occur. Assuming Philip Morris at $118 per share, instead of buying the stock for $11,800 per 100 shares, you might buy a deep in-the-money LEAPS 90-strike call expiring in two years for just $3,200 to control those same 100 shares. The remaining $8,600 can be placed in safekeeping in a money market fund, not at risk if MO stock should decline.

Examining the LEAPS option purchase further, we see that with the stock at 118, the 90-strike call is intrinsically worth 28 (118 − 90), or $2,800. So by paying a total premium of $3,200, you are paying only $400 in time premium for the right to hold this position until January 1999. The other cost you will implicitly incur relative to owning the stock is that, as an options investor, you won't be able to collect dividends. So as a LEAPS owner you would be giving up this aspect of MO's total return, currently at 4.4 percent.

If MO shares should rise to 150 by LEAPS expiration, the stock owner makes a profit of $3,200, for a 27 percent gain. In comparison, the LEAPS 90-strike call will be intrinsically worth 60, meaning that your profit would be $2,800, or 88 percent. So on a major upside move, you, as a LEAPS owner, closely track the absolute dollar performance the stock owner receives, excluding dividends. And you have only 27 percent of the dollars at risk in the LEAPS call relative to owning the stock ($3,200/$11,800 = 27%).

On the downside, let us say MO drops to 100 by LEAPS expiration. The stock owner loses $1,800, or 15 percent, offset somewhat by dividends. Your LEAPS option is intrinsically worth 10, or $1,000, resulting in a loss of $2,200, or 69 percent.

In a "crash scenario," if MO dropped to 59 at LEAPS expiration, the stock owner experiences a 50 percent loss, amounting to $5,900. Meanwhile, the LEAPS option holder can lose no more than the $3,200 initially invested. And should MO shares decline even further, the loss on your LEAPS position remains capped at the original $3,200 investment. Finally, if MO finishes where it started at 118 at LEAPS expiration, the stock owner has finished flat (prior to dividends) and your LEAPS has an intrinsic value of 28, or $2,800, resulting in a $400 loss, or 13 percent.

You can see that the common denominator of these scenarios—the factor that creates the difference in the deep in-the-money options profile relative to the stock owner's profile—is the time premium paid ($400 in this example). But in exchange for paying this time premium and foregoing dividends, you are able with the LEAPS to significantly reduce your dollar exposure.

If you have a shorter view that you expect to play out in one year or less, the time premium can be reduced (for example, a one-year MO LEAPS 90-strike call would have only $200 of time premium). Or you can still buy the longest-term LEAPS options available but go even deeper in-the-money if you are willing to place more dollars at risk. An MO two-year 80-strike LEAPS call would sell for $4,000 in this example, just $200 above its intrinsic value.

Bullish LEAPS Strategy #3: Debit Spread—LEAPS Call Purchase Versus Shorter-Term Options Writing

Financial ingenuity occurs when an investor can figure out ways to reduce the net cost of a position by selling calls without losing the position in the process. Before LEAPS were introduced, investors could write short-term calls only against stock they owned, or against other short-term options. Now, you can write short-term calls against a LEAPS call you own to significantly reduce the ultimate cost of the position if handled properly.

You would want to buy a LEAPS call option that is approximately at-the-money and plan to sell out-of-the-money shorter-term options against your LEAPS call when the stock is overbought. Your bet is that the short-term options will expire worthless, and you can pocket the short-term premium while maintaining your longer-term position. For example, with Philip Morris at 118, buy a two-year 120-strike LEAPS call at 10, or $1,000. Every time MO rallies 10 percent from a recent low, sell a two-month call that is 5 points out-of-the-money. So when MO rallies to 130, you might sell the two-month 135-strike call for a premium of $100. Assuming MO shares do not finish above 135 at the expiration two months from now, you pocket the $100 premium, and the net cost of the 120-strike LEAPS call is now effectively reduced by $100 to $900. If this pattern repeats itself every six months, you could potentially implement this strategy four times over the life of your LEAPS call and reduce your cost by approximately 40 percent. The key is to have a method to indicate when your uptrending stock is due for a rest. Typically, I recommend looking at intermediate-term overbought indicators and watching for momentum shifts that suggest a consolidation in the stock for two to three months. The caution with this method is that if the stock rallies well above the short-term strike price you sell, the negative delta of the short call will begin to exceed the positive delta of the LEAPS call you own, so you must exercise discipline and shut down the short call should it move significantly into the money.

Bullish LEAPS Strategy #4: LEAPS on the "Dow 5"

You may be familiar with the "Dogs of the Dow" theory. At the end of each year, purchase the ten Dow Jones Industrial Average stocks with the highest dividend yield. You seek to invest an equal dollar amount in each of these ten highest-yielding stocks, and hold these stocks for one year, after which the process starts over again. Since 1973, this strategy has produced a 17.7 percent average annual return, compared to the Dow Jones Industrial Average's 11.9 percent average annual return over that same time (as reported in *U.S. News & World Report*, July 8, 1996).

A unique twist to leverage the normal 10 Dow Dogs stocks is to focus solely on the Dow 5. The Dow 5 consists of the five *lowest-priced* stocks among the 10 Dow Dogs. Investing equally among the Dow 5 each year has produced a 20.9 percent average annual return since 1973, versus the 17.7 percent annually posted by the 10 Dow Dogs (as reported in *U.S. News & World Report*, July 8, 1996).

A way to further leverage the outperformance of the Dow 5 each year is by purchasing LEAPS on those 5 Dow stocks. For optimum leverage in the upcoming year, select the LEAPS that expire thirteen months out, and sell these options after twelve months, at the end of that year.

As you can see from table 8.3, the five lowest-priced Dow stocks with available LEAPS options produced an average return of 20.9 percent in 1996. (Note DuPont and General Electric LEAPS were unavailable at the end of 1995, so Texaco was the next available lowest-priced

Table 8.3   1996 "DOGS OF THE DOW" AND DOW 5

		Price 12/31/95	Yield (%)	Price 12/31/96	1996 Return (%)
MO	Philip Morris Cos.	90¼	4.43	113	25.2
TX	**Texaco Inc.**	**78½**	**4.08**	**98⅛**	**25.0**
JPM	Morgan (J.P.)	80¼	4.04	97⅝	21.7
CHV	**Chevron Corp.**	**52⅜**	**3.82**	**65**	**24.1**
XON	Exxon Corp.	80½	3.73	98	21.7
DD	DuPont	69⅞	2.98	94⅛	34.7
MMM	**Minn. Min. Mfg.**	**66⅜**	**2.83**	**83**	**28.7**
IP	**Internat'l Paper**	**37⅞**	**2.64**	**40½**	**6.9**
GE	General Electric	72	2.56	98⅞	37.3
EK	**Eastman Kodak**	**67**	**2.39**	**80¼**	**19.8**
10 Dow Dogs Average					24.5
Dow 5 with LEAPS Available Average					20.9

stock with LEAPS. Also note that while the Dow 5 usually outper-formS the 10 Dow Dogs, this was not the case in 1996.)

Table 8.4 shows the leveraged impact that the five LEAPS pur-chases have relative to their stock counterparts. Compared to the av-erage stock performance of 20.9 percent, the average performance of the five LEAPS held for 1996 was 130 percent, providing leverage of over six to one.

Let us now look at the Dow 5 projections for 1997, for the stocks and then for the LEAPS. Table 8.5 shows the top 10 yielding stocks as of December 31, 1996. From these ten, we choose the five cheapest

Table 8.4   DOW 5 LEAPS (JANUARY 1997 EXPIRATION): 1996 PERFORMANCE

		12/31/95 close	12/31/96 close	1996 Return (%)
Texaco (TX)	Jan. 80 call	5⅛	18¾	+266
Chevron (CHV)	Jan. 50 call	5¾	15⅝	+172
Minn. Min. Mfg. (MMM)	Jan. 60 call	9⅛	23	+152
Internat'l Paper (IP)	Jan. 40 call	3⅜	1	−70
Eastman Kodak (EK)	Jan. 70 call	5⅝	12⅞	+129
Dow 5 LEAPS Average				+130

Table 8.5   1997 "DOGS OF THE DOW" AND DOW 5

		Price 12/31/96	Yield (%)
MO	Philip Morris Cos.	113	4.19
JPM	Morgan (J.P.)	97⅝	3.53
TX	Texaco Inc.	98⅛	3.44
CHV	**Chevron Corp.**	**65**	**3.25**
XON	Exxon Corp.	98	3.18
T	**AT&T**	**43⅜**	**2.99**
GM	**General Motors**	**55¾**	**2.88**
IP	**Internat'l Paper**	**40½**	**2.45**
DD	DuPont	94⅛	2.38
MMM	**Minn. Min. Mfg.**	**83**	**2.31**

stocks with LEAPS to determine our Dow 5 on which we will trade. The five cheapest equities among the top 10 yielders are International Paper, AT&T, General Motors, Chevron, and Minnesota Mining & Manufacturing.

If you are studying the past year's performance, you might be tempted to throw out the weak performer last year among the Dow 5, International Paper. Don't succumb to this temptation. While IP has been an obvious laggard, it is often these "repeat offenders" that can offer the best value in this full-year strategy, and potentially have the most room to run as they begin to move to the upside.

Table 8.6 shows the Dow 5 LEAPS selections for 1997, and their prices as of 12/31/96. (Note that these are January 1998 expiration LEAPS, which are to be exited on the last trading day's close of 1997.)

Table 8.6   1997 DOW 5 LEAPS

		12/31/96	1998 LEAPS	12/31/96 Price
CHV	Chevron Corp.	65	Jan. 65 call	6
T	AT&T	43⅜	Jan. 60 call	3⅛
GM	General Motors	55¾	Jan. 55 call	6¼
IP	Internat'l Paper	40½	Jan. 40 call	5¼
MMM	Minn. Min. Mfg.	83	Jan. 85 call	6

BEARISH LEAPS STRATEGIES

The strategies the LEAPS player must use for put trading must, by necessity, be different from the strategies used by the call trader. The central point is that the character of declines is different from the character of advances. In a bull market, gains are slow, steady and prolonged, with sharp but temporary corrections along the way. In a bear market, the declines are slower and more enduring, and while bear-market rallies are dramatic, they may not last more than a few days before the downtrend resumes. If you can develop methods to catch the quick countertrend, you are better off applying those methods to shorter-term options, because the entry and exit of such spikes must be speedy. So for LEAPS put trades I exclusively focus on methods for determining where the uptrend has broken and a new downtrend is beginning to unfold.

Bearish Leaps Strategy #1: Straight Put Purchase

The straight purchase is the simplest and easiest way to participate with LEAPS puts in a new downtrend. I use three primary methods to screen for potential new downtrends:

1. *Relative Strength Rollovers*   A deteriorating relative strength line is one of the best signs that something is not right with a stock. Poor relative strength stocks will have more of a tendency to be in a downtrend relative to the average stock, which fits my first criterion of defining downtrending stock situations. If relative strength is rolling over *and* options speculators are viewing the decline as a bargain to accumulate calls, this confirms from a contrarian perspective that the stock is likely to decline further to shake out this complacent sentiment.

One of the most memorable examples of a steady downtrend that option speculators greeted complacently was in the United Health-Care (UNH) August 50 put I recommended on June 27, 1996 (see chapter 7 for a complete discussion of this trade—in that example I used a shorter-term option on this downtrending stock, as there were no LEAPS puts available at reasonable option prices). The stock had been in a steady downtrend (see exhibit 8.14), yet options players were accumulating call positions, with no interest in the put side. This complacency simply bred more downside potential. So when the stock gapped down 10 points on a poor earnings outlook, it did not come as a surprise that the "bottom-fishers" had collectively failed to call the bottom.

2. *Channel Breakdowns*   The regression channel methodology is a good one to define the nature of the trend. Moves below the bottom

Exhibit 8.14   **UNITED HEALTHCARE (UNH) DAILY CHART**

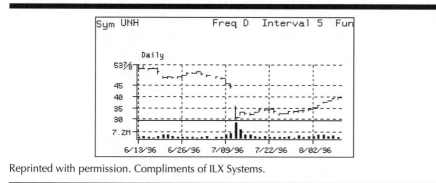

Reprinted with permission. Compliments of ILX Systems.

channel line can forewarn of a new downtrend. One bearish example in my LEAPS portfolio was a LEAPS put recommendation on GTE. This rate-sensitive utility had started to underperform the S&P 500 Index, yet the financial press was extremely optimistic on the outlook for interest rates heading into 1996. An uptrending channel that had been in place since the secondary low in May 1995 was broken and successfully retested as resistance on the monthly chart in February 1996 (see exhibit 8.15). GTE shares failed to return above this lower trendline, and this methodology suggested the odds were higher than normal that the stock could move still lower. Although the stock market as a whole performed impressively in 1996, GTE shares lagged. My GTE put position was closed for a 22 percent gain, which was a decent profit on a put position in a bull market.

3. *Event-Driven Trading* This element of put trading involves monitoring the fundamental events that have been driving a com-

Exhibit 8.15   **GTE CORP. (GTE) WEEKLY CHART: CHANNEL BREAKDOWN**

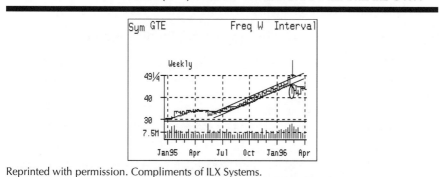

Reprinted with permission. Compliments of ILX Systems.

pany's stock price. The primary tool here is earnings momentum. If a stock has been beating consensus Wall Street forecasts, and the stock is responding well to these quarterly earnings reports, the stock is said to have positive earnings momentum. The first sign of a crack in the armor is when a company reports earnings above analyst estimates, but the stock actually falls in response to the earnings report. This tells me the stock is fully priced in the short-term, and may have further downside potential. The thinking here is that "if a stock can't rally on great news, what can it rally on?" Such events hold added potential for a negative surprise when option speculators are aggressively accumulating short-term call options in the days heading into the earnings report.

One classic example of a high-expectation stock that had nowhere to go but down in light of heavy call option activity was Micron Technology (MU) in the fall of 1995. Micron reported earnings on September 20, 1995, and in the week prior to the report had reached a high of 94¾, plunged as low as 83½ two days before the report, and then started to rally. Options speculators saw the pullback as a "gift" to buy calls heading into what everyone knew would be a great earnings report. The problem was, of course, the fact that "everyone knew." From a prior day's close at 90, MU's initial response on the earnings was to gap open 1½ points higher to 91½. The opening price was the high for the day, and MU shares steadily fell to close down 2⅝ at 87⅝, beginning a steady decline from there. MU was a name that had been experiencing heavy put activity by skeptical options players throughout its big 1995 rally. But just prior to its earnings release, activity was very heavy on the call side, and this pattern continued. Couple this speculative overenthusiasm with disappointing postearnings price action in MU, and you have a recipe for a potentially serious pullback. MU went on to massively downtrend, as shown on exhibit 8.16, reaching a low of 16⅝ by late July 1996, less than one year later.

Bearish Leaps Strategy #2: Hedging a Stock Position with Leaps Puts

If you are worried about a stock position over the next year or two, whether due to company-specific or market-related reasons, and you still want to maintain your long-term position and/or wish to avoid capital gains taxes, you can protect your bullish stock position by buying LEAPS puts as a hedge.[1] For example, if you bought IBM back

---

1. The CBOE Website (www.cboe.com) was very helpful in sparking ideas about various hedging strategies, and this site is also informative on hedging strategies with LEAPS and with OEX options.

Exhibit 8.16   MICRON TECHNOLOGY (MU) DAILY CHART

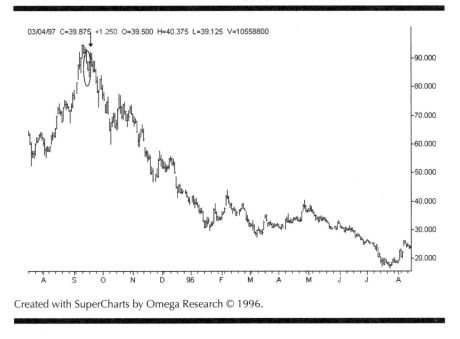

03/04/97 C=39.875 +1.250 O=39.500 H=40.375 L=39.125 V=10558800

Created with SuperCharts by Omega Research © 1996.

in 1993 when Louis Gerstner was named the new CEO. Let us say you purchased 1,000 shares at an average price of $50, and with IBM at $160, you are concerned about protecting your profits. However, you don't want to incur a huge capital gain, and you may want to own the stock longer term despite any short-term bumps in the road. It is early 1997, and you buy ten contracts of the January 1998 150-strike put on IBM (to protect all 1,000 of your shares) at 8. Let us say you think that there is a reasonable chance IBM could drop to 130 over the next six months, and assume that this occurs and that your put option is now trading at 22. Of the 30 points you gave up on the decline in IBM shares, you made up for 14 of those points with the gain in your LEAPS put, so 47 percent of your loss was hedged in this transaction.

There are advantages to hedging long stock positions by buying LEAPS puts relative to buying short-term puts, as you reduce the cost of your hedge per unit of time and you reduce your commission costs by avoiding frequent "rollovers" to new expiration months as your short-term puts expire. But the same general caveat that I always provide regarding the purchase of put protection still applies to LEAPS puts: they represent a significant expense and most investors buy them when they don't need them, and don't own them when they do need them. In fact, one of my most bullish indicators in the 1990s has been the continuing desire by nervous investors to waste their money on put protection in a bull market.

CONCLUSION

LEAPS offer both options and stock investors an excellent vehicle to profit by allowing a big-picture trend on a stock to play out, with much less capital required than buying the stock. Yet LEAPS are less risky than their short-term option counterparts. With the time frame of many investors falling into the one-year to two-year horizon, LEAPS offer an investment alternative that should continue to grow in popularity. In the next chapter, we discuss lower risk strategies using short-term options.

9

Conservative Approaches to Options Trading

INTRODUCTION

Options traders should take note of Benjamin Disraeli's words of more than a hundred years ago: "The secret of success is constancy to purpose."[1] All traders must have a thoroughly tested trading plan and the discipline to make every trade according to that plan, thus creating the ability to take profits out of the market consistently over time. Many traders spend a great deal of time trying to find the most profitable methods and systems possible, which may ultimately result in some huge winning trades. But during the heat of battle, how will they react when their methodology is churning out losers before producing future winners? Will they be able to follow their plan consistently, or will they give in to the emotional and financial strains? Many traders who think they are big risk-takers in reality may need a more risk-averse method that allows them to frequently take "singles" out of the market instead of "swinging for the fences." Aiming for home runs often puts a trader on an emotional roller coaster of highs when successes occur and lows when strikeouts take place.

Once you have done your research into the risk and reward of various approaches, one of the best ways to gauge where you fit on this spectrum is to get your risk down to your "sleeping level." If you can sleep at night with the volatility of the more aggressive approach, and if you don't feel emotionally drained by the roller coaster's highs and lows that you must endure to ultimately reach your objectives, aggressive trading is a path you should consider. Otherwise, you should seek to add more conservative options strategies to your trad-

---

1. Benjamin Disraeli, from a speech on June 24, 1872.

ing arsenal. In fact, many successful traders balance their aggressive options trading with conservative options strategies, to build stability into their trading results. We discuss several of the more attractive conservative approaches in this chapter.

If you are going to trade options for greater consistency, the first thing you need is a much higher batting average than the typical home-run hitter's approach to options buying. You won't always clear the bases in every at-bat, so you need to generate steady returns in a more predictable fashion. At the same time, you want to manage volatility to keep strikeouts to a minimum, and thus form a reward/risk ratio that will give you an edge in the markets.

There are numerous options-selling strategies. With covered writing strategies you write calls against stock you own. We won't discuss covered call writing strategies here, as abundant literature is available on the subject elsewhere. Instead, let us focus on profitable approaches with which you may be less familiar. Uncovered equity put selling, for example, can be an excellent approach to generating income or acquiring quality stock at lower prices; we'll discuss put selling later in this chapter. In addition, you may not be aware of another powerful strategy that can generate 15 percent to 20 percent returns in one month or less, with winning trades achievable more than 90 percent of the time if you are a good market timer. This strategy is known as credit spread investing.

In 1992, I set out to develop an approach that would allow investors to stick to a trading program that would achieve both steady rewards and controlled risks, so that they would then have the confidence to take every trade over the life of this trading method. As a result, I created the *OA Wealthbuilder* methodology, which combines my market timing techniques with an options trading strategy designed to produce the consistency of profits that is essential to the success of a "singles hitting" approach to option trading.

Table 9.1 shows the *OA Wealthbuilder* track record. You are probably wondering how I could possibly have achieved an accuracy rate of more than 90 percent in options trading. The beauty of the *OA Wealthbuilder* strategy is that instead of paying premium money up front (as you do when *buying* options), you collect premium dollars into your account up front as a net *seller* of options premiums. Your goal in this case is to have the options expire worthless, and pocket the entire premium. Let us now explore the basics behind the index credit spread strategy, which is basic to this methodology.

Table 9.1   **OA WEALTHBUILDER TRACK RECORD FROM INCEPTION TO DECEMBER 1996**

Date	OEX Option Sold/ Bought		Average Credit	Close	Gross Profit (%)
02/23/93	Mar.	390p/385p	0.750	0	+17.6
03/16/93	Apr.	400p/395p	0.594	0	+13.5
04/23/93	May	395p/390p	0.688	0	+15.9
06/11/93	Jul.	400p/395p	0.563	0	+12.7
09/03/93	Sep.	420p/415p	0.813	0	+19.4
10/28/93	Nov.	420p/415p	0.906	0	+22.1
01/03/94	Jan.	425p/420p	0.938	0	+23.1
02/07/94	Feb.	430p/425p	0.844	0	+20.3
03/07/94	Mar.	425p/420p	0.875	0	+21.2
03/07/94	Mar.	440c/445c	0.563	0	+12.7
04/21/94	May	420c/425c	0.750	1.875	− 26.5
07/07/94	Jul.	420c/425c	0.750	0.688	+ 1.5
09/01/94	Sep.	430p/425p	0.750	0	+17.6
10/27/94	Nov.	420p/415p	0.750	0	+17.6
02/27/95	Mar.	450p/445p	0.938	0	+23.1
04/03/95	Apr.	465p/460p	0.938	0	+23.1
08/01/95	Aug.	520p/515p	0.781	0	+18.5
10/05/95	Oct.	545p/540p	0.750	0	+17.6
03/05/96	Mar.	615p/610p	0.750	0	+17.6
04/11/96	Apr.	590p/585p	0.750	0	+17.6
05/07/96	May	605p/600p	0.813	0	+19.4
06/09/96	Jun.	640p/635p	0.813	0	+19.4
07/03/96	Jul.	635p/630p	0.750	5.000	−100.0
08/23/96	Aug.	630p/625p	0.750	0	+17.6
11/04/96	Nov.	670p/665p	0.875	0	+21.2
12/10/96	Dec.	715p/710p	0.750	0	+17.6

Totals: 24 wins of 26 trades = 92.3% profitable
Cumulative return is +301.4%
Average return is +11.6% per trade

AN INTRODUCTION TO INDEX OPTION CREDIT SPREADS

A credit spread involves two options: an out-of-the-money option that you *write* (sell) and a further out-of-the-money option that you *buy* as a hedge. Both the option sale and the option purchase are opened simultaneously, at a net credit to your account for the spread. The question immediately arises: "Why don't you just sell the one option and *not* buy the other option, to maximize the dollars you collect into your account?" I prefer to buy another option as a hedge to protect my position from a large adverse market move, just in case an unexpected event hits the market. By always having a hedge in place, not even a crash scenario can severely damage my portfolio. I also employ proper money management techniques so that the 10 percent of the trades that *are* losers can't do much damage to the bottom line of my credit spread portfolio. Of course, even with such a high winning percentage, if you are investing 100 percent of your funds in every trade, it only takes one 100 percent loss to wipe you out. I have experienced a 100 percent loss once in the history of my *OA Wealthbuilder* service, and I have always maintained that credit spread investors must be prepared for such an event by allocating no more than 50 percent of their trading capital to this strategy. You never want to have all your options portfolio dollars allocated to any one trade, as that is the recipe for potential disaster, even if you are right 99 times out of 100.

The S&P 100 Index (OEX) is the only vehicle I currently use to implement credit spreads. It is the most active optionable security available to traders today, which provides excellent liquidity in entering and exiting trades. Also, the strategy can be better managed with an index than with an individual stock, as there are 100 large-capitalization stocks in the OEX, and event risk related to one stock will not have an excessive impact on the index (i.e., on earnings or another event-related gap in a specific stock).

Credit spreads can be created on either side of the market, depending on your market view. With the OEX at 776.30 and if you are bullish, in late January 1997 you could *sell* the February 760 put and *buy* the February 755 put, for a credit of 1 point, or $100.00 per contract. If the OEX does *not* fall below the 760 strike by February expiration (the third Friday in February), both options expire worthless and you collect the full $100 credit less any commissions you paid when initiating the spread. If you sold ten contracts of this spread (I recommend a minimum of ten contracts on this strategy to reduce the impact of commissions on your total return), you would collect $1,000 minus commissions.

You would need *margin* in your account to cover the worst case loss (see chapter 10), which in this example is a net margin of $4,000 (in the case of ten contracts on this 5-point spread, $5,000 minus the $1,000 you collected). The worst-case loss occurs if on expiration day the index closes below the strike price of the option you bought as a hedge. In this case, you would be committed to buying an OEX contract at 760 while having the right to sell an OEX contract at 755, so your loss would be $500 on each spread. However, you collected $100 on each spread up front, so your net loss on each would be $400 or $4,000 for all ten spreads. Of course, commissions would be added to this loss. This calculation also demonstrates why you must post a margin equal to $4,000, since this is your maximum loss. Your maximum return on margin is calculated by dividing the credit collected ($1,000) by the net margin required ($4,000), which in this case equals 25 percent. I prefer to collect a credit of at least three-quarters of a point on each credit spread, whereby the gross return on margin is 17.6 percent.

CREDIT SPREAD ADVANTAGES

There are two primary attractions to the credit spread approach. First, you can profit from a broad range of outcomes. Returning to our previous example, you were bullish with the OEX at 776.30 when you initiated the 760/755 put credit spread. If the OEX closes even as low as 760.00 at expiration, you would *still* collect the full credit and earn your maximum profit, even though you would have been wrong on the market by 16 OEX points, or more than 2 percent. With the credit spread strategy, you win if the market finishes higher, flat, or even 2 percent lower in this case, and you have a predefined maximum loss. That is a broad range of winning outcomes as opposed to the narrower range of winning outcomes associated with my FAR rule for success at options buying from chapter 3.

If you are an out-of-the-money options buyer, the market must move in your predicted direction for you to make money. If the market is flat or lower, the call buyer loses; the call buyer can also lose if the market is slightly higher but doesn't rise far enough to overcome the initial cost of his calls. But in credit spread investing, you flip the range of probable outcomes in your favor, knowing that while you give up the chance for the occasional home run, you enjoy a high probability of taking consistent profits out of the market.

The second significant advantage in credit spread trading occurs when you ride a position out to expiration and both options expire worthless: you incur no commissions to close the trade. The trade "closes itself" because the options no longer exist after expiration.

Note that in the put spread example, the one scenario under which you do get hurt is if the index plunges well below 760. The break-even point in this trade is the written strike (760) minus the initial credit collected (1), or 759.00. Your worst-case loss, as stated earlier, is the margin ($400 per spread) if the OEX closes at or below the strike price of the put option purchased for protection, in this case, 755 or lower.

Some credit spread traders like to close out their positions with a few days to go until expiration even it if costs them an eighth of a point to close their spread position. That is because they have seen the market on or near expiration day make a sharp directional move and turn a winning spread into a loser. They feel that discretion is the better part of valor. My general preference is to let the options expire worthless if there is sufficient breathing room heading into the expiration, but in a few cases I have shut these trades down early to control risk. If the index is trading near the written strike price with only a few days until expiration, any signs of technical weakness can prompt a closeout. At the same time, I don't want to panic out of such positions, because if the index stays flat to higher, the out-of-the-money put premiums will collapse in the final days before expiration and the full credit will be collected as the options expire. This is where real-time monitoring really pays off.

You can generate a variety of credit spread possibilities, depending on the conviction of your bullish or bearish outlook. The February 765/760 put spread nets out to a "fatter" 1½ point credit, but the trade-off is that the break-even point would rise to 763.50. If the market never looks back from here, the higher strike price is obviously a better sell. However, I find it easier to sleep if I provide a cushion equal to at least 1.5 percent between the option strike I sell and the market level, as no one can time the market perfectly.

If you are bearish on the market, you can analogously construct call credit spreads. You could, for example, sell the February 800 call at 4 and buy the February 805 call at 3, also for a credit of 1. As long as the index closes at or below 800, you collect the full $100 minus any opening commissions. Your breakeven here would be 801.00 (800 plus the 1 point credit).

FACTORS AFFECTING INDEX CREDIT SPREAD PRICING

In my view, the four most important factors that affect credit spread pricing are volatility, time until expiration, upcoming events, and faulty pricing assumptions.

Volatility in the OEX options is best measured by the CBOE Market Volatility Index (VIX). You will typically see extremes in VIX volatility expectations at major turning points in the market. For example, when the market is plunging, the VIX generally rockets up. In chapter 5, we discussed the bullish implications of "spikes" upward in the VIX and how these spikes marked fear-induced put buying right near the lows in the market. Such instances occurred at the major market low in November 1994 as well as at the July 1996 bottom (see exhibit 9.1). These spikes in volatility often provide opportunities for selling bullish credit spreads.

During strong downward price movements, the market reacts by projecting that this downside volatility is likely to continue. But market volatility rarely expands once it has neared a historic extreme; it usually then begins to contract. Typically, once it is clear that this volatility spike is reversing and the market is not going to plunge further, selling one put and buying a further out-of-the-money put in the form of a bullish credit spread is attractive. This strategy becomes doubly attractive because these higher volatility assumptions mean you can collect more net option premium on your credit spread, and you are often selling the bullish credit spreads at or near market bottoms.

Exhibit 9.1   **CBOE MARKET VOLATILITY INDEX RELATIVE TO S&P 100 INDEX**

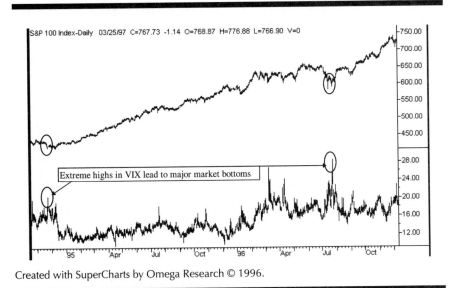

Created with SuperCharts by Omega Research © 1996.

You can also see from exhibit 9.1 that the VIX has tended to hit low points right near market peaks, as complacency sets in and market players show a lack of worry about a market decline. The tricky part is that such tops can often take days or weeks to form once the low volatility point in the VIX has been reached. As a result, you also must apply other expectational indicators to confirm when to implement bearish call credit spreads after low VIX readings.

Time until expiration is another key factor that takes a surprising turn in credit spread pricing. When you *buy* options, you pay an increasing premium as you buy more time, since the odds of the underlying security moving deeply into the money at some point increase with time. Interestingly, with credit spreads the difference in premium received is minimal the farther out you go in time, while your risk increases dramatically the more time you sell. For example, if you initiated the February 760/755 put spread on January 30, 1997, it would bring you a credit of 1 point, but initiating the March 760/755 put spread on the same date only nets a credit of 1¼ points. Clearly, you are not getting much added compensation for taking on one more month of risk of an adverse market move. As a result, I recommend only front-month options (those options closest to expiration) for credit spreads to take maximum advantage of time decay just before the expiration date.

Time value erodes rapidly in the final month of an option's life, as you recall from the chart of time decay in chapter 3. And since you expect your options to expire worthless in a credit spread, you want to be near the expiration date where the time premium erodes most rapidly, as opposed to farther away from expiration where the decay is slower over a comparable period. In credit spread trading you want to accomplish two primary objectives:

1. *Minimize your risk* by having positions exposed to the market for the shortest time possible, which is accomplished by using only front-month options. By restricting positions to those that expire in one to four weeks, you can take a nice profit out of the market and then soon be safely back on the sidelines waiting for the next low-risk entry point.

2. *Maximize your reward* by "turning over" your investment as many times as is prudent over the course of a year, which is also accomplished by using only front-month options. If you collect a $1,000 credit on ten contracts, you put up margin of $4,000. Thus your return on your investment is 25 percent before commissions. As we saw in the prior example, initiating credit spreads farther out in time produces little incremental return, yet you incur more risk in the time they must be held

open. Plus, by turning over your margin more frequently using front-month options, you significantly increase your annual return.

Important *upcoming events* such as Federal Reserve meetings, unemployment reports, quarterly earnings releases, and other key news may be profitable for options buyers at times, but for premium selling with credit spreads, I generally prefer to "wait until the dust has settled." This allows me to analyze the market's reaction to the event.

As a rule, the market's first intraday reaction to news may be a short-term headfake in one direction, followed by a reversal in the direction of the market's broader trend. Many times when the Federal Reserve makes a decision on interest rates, stocks have an initial move in one direction followed by a much bigger move in the opposite direction. So wait for the initial shakeout after the news and then go with the market's bigger trend.

For example, in 1996 the key event each month was the employment report, because the perception was that this measure of the strength of the economy would determine whether the Fed would tighten. On November 1, 1996, the October employment report was released, and it suggested no Fed tightening. The market initially reacted poorly, and then firmed up somewhat into the close, but finished under the key 680 strike. The next Monday's trading session saw stocks begin to surge, with the OEX retaking the 680 mark. I then recommended the November 665/660 put credit spread with the OEX at 681.93. This trade was never in the red, as the OEX finished more than 30 points higher in just two weeks.

The final important factor affecting credit spread pricing is what I call *faulty pricing assumptions* of the options market. We have already discussed volatility and how the options pricing model reflects extreme volatility assumptions after major declines or advances, just as those conditions are prone to reverse after such extremes have been reached. This creates one set of opportunities in that it sometimes results in wide disparities between the implied and historical volatilities. As a credit spread investor, the high VIX levels that occur near market lows offer a significant opportunity for net sellers of options premium.

Another market assumption you can exploit for profit is the efficient market theory, where prices are assumed to be normally distributed and have for all intents and purposes an equal chance of going up or going down. The bottom line is that the options pricing model assumes that you cannot predict the direction of an underlying instrument. The price of the underlying at expiration is assumed to be equal to the current price plus a modest carrying cost that is a function of the current level of interest rates. By applying technical and sentiment indicators in conjunction with fundamentals to determine the direction of the index, you can achieve a significant edge over those operating on the assumption that the index price is static or random. And the greater the magnitude of the predicted trend, the more massive is your edge as a directionally oriented trader over the efficient market crowd.

INDEX CREDIT SPREAD TECHNIQUES

To help identify the short-term and longer-term condition of the market in order to time our entry into index credit spreads, we can use a variety of indicators—technical, sentiment, option-related, and event-driven. When these indicators come together to confirm each other, we can obtain very high confidence trading signals for conservative strategies such as selling index credit spreads.

Among technical gauges, I like to examine not only trending measures but also overbought/oversold indicators. One example of such an indicator is the Relative Strength Index (RSI; see chapter 2 for more details). I frequently use a nine-day period for the RSI when analyzing the OEX (see exhibit 9.2). This gives me a short-term overbought/oversold indicator on the OEX. Readings under 30 show an oversold market that could soon rally, and readings above 70 show an overbought market that may turn lower.

Other technical oscillators include MACD, standard deviation bands, and regression channel analysis for the OEX. In addition, sentiment indicators such as the put/call ratio, sentiment surveys, and other measures can be useful to gauge expectations, all of which are discussed in detail in chapter 2 and chapter 5. The key is to have a set of indicators that give you a sense of when the market has reached a significant turning point.

You also need to be aware of "round numbers" on the OEX. Just as the press has talked about the Dow Industrials tackling each new 1,000 point milestone (Dow 5000, Dow 6000 and Dow 7000), traders likewise watch the "century marks" (600, 700, 800) on the OEX with great interest. Exhibit 9.3 shows the OEX weekly price movement since 1994. Technical support and resistance appear around these century marks, precisely because people are willing to bet more heavily on whether such round numbers will be penetrated. As a result, heavy call and put open interest tends to accumulate at these century-mark striking prices. Likewise, the "half-century marks" (550, 650, 750) can tend to be important as a midpoint from one century mark to

Exhibit 9.2   **S&P 100 INDEX DAILY CHART WITH 9-DAY RELATIVE STRENGTH INDEX: AUGUST 1996 TO FEBRUARY 1997**

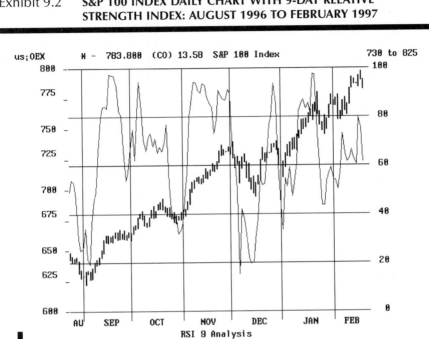

Reprinted with permission. Compliments of Bridge Information Systems.

Exhibit 9.3   **S&P 100 INDEX WEEKLY CHART WITH CENTURY MARKS**

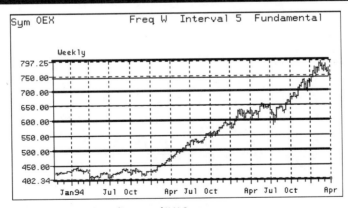

Reprinted with permission. Compliments of ILX Systems.

the next. Never bet on a breakout above or below one of these key levels until it occurs on a closing basis.

Exhibit 9.4 shows a comparison of the OEX divided by the S&P 500 Index (SPX), with a 10-day moving average of this ratio. Typically, when this line is rising the OEX is performing well, perhaps because big players are doing more program buying than selling. When the line starts to fall dramatically, the risk of program-induced sell-offs gets more dramatic.

This OEX/SPX indicator traded in a slightly upsloped regression channel through most of 1996. As exhibit 9.4 shows, every time the ratio reached the low end of its range, the market was ready to rally. Meanwhile, at the top of its range, this indicator successfully called pullbacks within the uptrend. On the first trading day of 1997, the OEX/SPX ratio broke out to new highs. Once out of the trading range, the OEX/SPX ratio trended steadily higher, which foreshadowed the stunning advance of nearly 70 OEX points in only sixteen trading days. Within trading ranges on the OEX/SPX ratio, you want to be wary of the OEX at the high end of the range and be looking for a low in the OEX at the bottom of the range. When the ratio breaks out of this range, you want to bet that the direction of the OEX/SPX trend will lead the direction of the OEX and the market in general over the near term.

Exhibit 9.4   **S&P 100 INDEX: RELATIVE STRENGTH VERSUS THE S&P 500 INDEX**

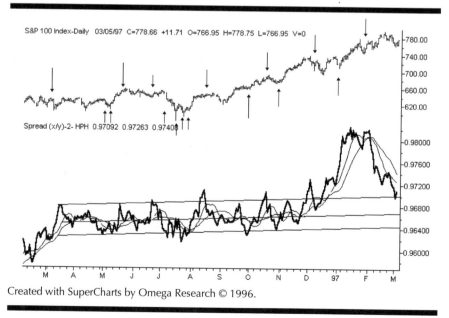

Created with SuperCharts by Omega Research © 1996.

Note that no indicator is foolproof, and the OEX/SPX ratio gave a breakout signal in early December 1996 that proved to be a fakeout. I recommended an *OA Wealthbuilder* December 715/710 put credit spread on December 10, 1996, partly based on this OEX/SPX signal. I was initially wrong by some 30 OEX points, as the market steadily drifted lower from 725 to under 700 intraday. The main factor that kept me in this trade and allowed my initially poor timing on this headfake to still result in a profitable trade was the substantial put support below the market, especially at the 700 "century-mark" strike price. We discuss the significance of major OEX open interest next, and this example reminds us that we need to have a layer of indicators supporting these trades so that even if one indicator proves faulty, the credit spread retains a high probability of success.

The Importance of OEX Open Interest

There is a tendency for striking prices with big open interest to serve as pivot points for the market. In the above example from December 1996, the December 700-strike put open interest dwarfed other put open interest levels. What we saw on December 16, 1996, was a test at 700, with put open interest of 26,000 contracts on this retest that held as options-related support. The 700 level was also the site of the 50-day moving average. The OEX bounced off the 700 level very sharply. Note from exhibit 9.5 how the OEX went below 700 intraday on December 17 and then closed above the 700 put support. This marked a key reversal for the OEX, as a battle was won by the bears intraday to get the market significantly below 700, but the bulls won the war at the close with the market finishing back above 700. Look for such key reversals off a major put open interest level as a key inflection point for the market that leads to a rally. In this case, the OEX rallied 30 points in just three trading days.

By the same token, when key open interest levels break down, volatility often increases, and I tend to avoid credit spreads until it appears that volatility has peaked and is on the way down. For example, in March 1994 the biggest put open interest was at the March 430-strike. This level should have held as support on a closing basis, but, as exhibit 9.6 shows, the market started to break down and plunged 5 points below this key strike on March 25, 1994, beginning a vicious "hedging cycle" that pushed the OEX down from 425 to 402.34 in a matter of four trading days. Note that this 6 percent decline in one week came in a period of the lowest annualized volatility in many decades. During the period from 1992 to 1994, annual volatility in the OEX was a very modest 11 percent from high to low each year. So a

Exhibit 9.5   **S&P 100 INDEX DAILY CHART WITH 50-DAY MOVING AVERAGE**

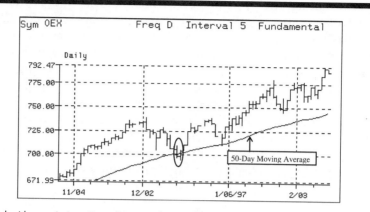

Reprinted with permission. Compliments of ILX Systems.

decline of more than one-half the full year's expected range in just one week clearly was a major event. The 52-week volatility was low, yet this one-week volatility was high, showing the importance of this break in the put open interest that should have held on a closing basis.

Hedging cycles occur because the options floor has tended to be short OEX puts on a net basis since the 1987 crash, as there has been strong demand from institutions and individual speculators for OEX

Exhibit 9.6   **S&P 100 INDEX WEEKLY CHART: 1994 PERFORMANCE**

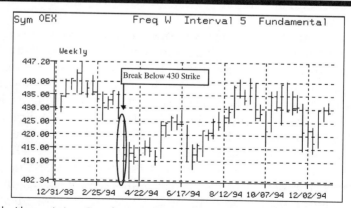

Reprinted with permission. Compliments of ILX Systems.

puts to hedge a portfolio or to speculate on the downside potential of the stock market. Consequently, these floor traders have an incentive to support the market on retests of key strike prices to the extent that they are not fully hedged by being short stock index futures or baskets of stocks. They want to see those options expire worthless. But when a strike price is broken on the close, it shows that the floor has lost the war. As those put options go deeper in-the-money, they gain delta, and the floor traders' losses accelerate on their unhedged put positions. The floor will then further hedge its short put positions by shorting stock index futures, which only further accelerates the decline.

My strategy is to also examine OEX option pricing very closely, and I keep an eye on the ratio of prices for equivalent out-of-the-money calls and puts. For example, assume that the OEX is at 725, so 20 points out-of-the-money on the call side, the January 745 call is asked at $\frac{7}{16}$, while 20 points below the market the January 705 put is offered at $1\frac{1}{8}$. In this instance the out-of-the-money put is about two and one-half times more expensive than the equivalent out-of-the-money call. These pricing differences result from simple supply and demand. If there is strong demand for puts for protection, and there are few sellers, the puts are going to increase in price until supply equals demand. Conversely, if call sellers are more aggressive than call buyers, call options will be cheaper than usual. An analysis of the pricing for out-of-the-money options equidistant from the current OEX price provides a good contrarian indicator.

Typically, if the out-of-the-money index puts and calls are priced similarly, it is bearish, because these puts have almost always been priced higher since 1987 (see chapter 5 for more details on put/call pricing heading into the 1987 crash). This post-crash pricing behavior is due mainly to trader bearishness and because the market has tended to drop faster than it rallies over the short term. I have seen pessimistic extremes where puts are five and even seven times more expensive than calls. At that point, you want to be very bullish on the market due to the bullish contrarian implications of this extreme pessimism.

Credit spread investors need to be aware of such pricing discrepancies, because bullish strategies will involve selling one relatively expensive put and buying another relatively expensive put. The risk is that the put purchased for protection is priced more aggressively in such extreme times than the put sold. Be sure to examine the implied volatility for each of the puts in the spread, otherwise the net premium you collect will provide too little profit potential relative to the risk incurred.

Loss Control with Index Credit Spreads

I try to collect at least a ¾-point credit on credit spread trades. As an exit rule of thumb, should the market go against me to the point where I would lose the amount I collected (in this case where I would have to buy the position back for 1½), I will strongly consider abandoning the position.

This strategy helps to set a definite limit on the capital at risk on the trade. Moreover, since I am confident that my credit spread trades will have a 90 percent success rate, I know that the next couple of trades will likely restore any capital lost on an unsuccessful trade. I tend to measure the loss on my positions based only on the closing prices, because there can be many battles fought during the trading day among big-money investors seeking to drive the market one way or the other. However, the war is won or lost on the close.

NAKED EQUITY OPTION SELLING

Uncovered (naked) option selling on individual stocks is another example of an excellent conservative strategy that can bring substantial profits with controlled risk. Generally speaking, stocks tend to advance over time, so it is wiser to focus on selling puts at opportune times rather than selling calls. Also, puts often tend to be overpriced due to the fear factor, which leads to greater initial credits. Option selling takes advantage of the concept of time decay—an option's premium declines on an accelerated basis as the option approaches expiration. Having time decay working in your favor relieves you of much of the pressure to precisely predict the future direction of a stock's price. Time premium will decay at a fairly predictable rate, and will deteriorate more rapidly the closer the option gets to its expiration. Decay is most dramatic in the last forty-five days before expiration.

With naked put selling, you want to choose a stock you believe will rally or at least will not decline significantly from its current levels, and then you sell an out-of-the-money put. The proceeds from this sale are credited to your account, whereas, with option buying your account is initially debited by the cost of the options. Because the put option is out-of-the-money, it has no intrinsic value. If the stock rallies or at least stays above the strike price at expiration, this option will expire worthless, allowing you to keep all the premium as your profit from the trade.

As an example, suppose with eight weeks until September series options expire, you notice Charles Schwab shares have been holding above 35 and the stock is currently at 36. Even when the overall market declined, Schwab managed to stay above 35, suggesting that this level may be significant technical support. You are convinced the stock won't close below the support at 35 any time soon, so you sell an out-of-the-money September 35 put for 1½. At expiration, Schwab closes at 37, so the 35 put expires worthless, and you keep the 1½ points you collected for selling the September 35 put.

But what if you wanted to be even more certain that your trade would be profitable? You might be fairly confident that the 35 level would hold as support, but you are really confident that the 30 level won't be broken to the downside. As an alternative, you could have sold the September 30 put for ¾. Even if Schwab fell as low as 30, you would pocket the ¾-point premium, whereas the 35 put sale would have posted a loss on such an occurrence. Selling the 30 put gives you another 5 points of "insurance" to the downside, because Schwab would have to remain only above 30 instead of above 35. But note that your "reward" for selling the 30 put was only half that for selling the 35 put, so you have to measure the risk and reward of selling one striking price versus another. This requires an analysis of the underlying stock's potential movement over the time until expiration relative to the premium received.

Let us see how the example of selling the 35 put would look as a percentage return on margin. To sell an equity put, there is a margin requirement equal to 20 percent of the current value of the underlying stock, plus the option premium received, less the out-of-the-money amount. In this case, this margin would be $690 per contract sold: [($37 per share × 0.20) × 100] plus $150 from the initial premium received minus $200 for the out-of-the-money amount. Therefore, should you ultimately pocket the 1½-point credit ($150), the return on the $690 margin would be 21.7 percent.

If the stock were to close below the 35 strike at expiration, or moved significantly below 35 prior to expiration, it could be *assigned* to you. The term "assignment" means that if the option you sold is exercised by the buyer, you will be assigned to fulfill the right you sold him. In the case of put selling, you are giving the buyer the right to *sell* the stock to you at a certain level (the striking price) in exchange for receiving a premium from him. If the buyer exercised his put, you would be required to buy 100 shares of stock at the striking price for each put you sold. However, you would keep the $150 credit you had received for each put sold, allowing you to purchase the stock for a net price of $3,350 for each 100 shares, or $33.50 per share (the 35-strike less the 1½-point put premium), excluding commissions. The risk of assignment in put selling should limit you to writing puts on high-quality shares that you would want to own on any temporary dip in price.

For example, in my Put Selling portfolio for *The Option Advisor*, I recommended selling the Schering-Plough (SGP) February 65 put on December 20, 1996 (see exhibit 9.7). With the stock trading at 67⅛, subscribers were able to collect a premium of 1¹¹⁄₁₆. I initiated this recommendation based on the long-term uptrending nature of SGP and the likelihood of major support in the 64 area, which had marked previous peaks in April and July 1996. The 100-day moving average was also at 63, to provide likely trendline support. The odds suggested the stock would not fall further, and even if it did it would be an excellent buying opportunity given SGP's consistent earnings growth. The stock did, in fact, rally within two weeks and never looked back, reaching a high of 81⅜ in the February expiration week. Based on the minimum margin requirement of $1,293.75 per contract, the SGP February 65 put provided a 13 percent return on investment in two months.

To sell naked puts effectively, you must understand that there will be occasions when even quality stocks will decline, whether based on market-related weakness, stock-specific concerns, or purely technical factors. So you need to be financially positioned to buy the stock at the lower price if the put options you sold are exercised. Most people who sell naked puts do not do so with the thought of ever acquiring the underlying stock. They simply want to sit back and collect pre-

Exhibit 9.7   SCHERING-PLOUGH (SGP) WEEKLY CHART

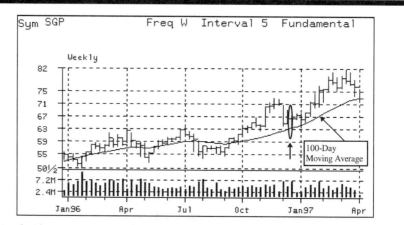

Reprinted with permission. Compliments of ILX Systems.

mium. If you do not want to buy stocks in some situations where they are temporarily sold off, or if you do not have the capital to do so, you should not use this strategy. In such situations, the capital commitment can be significant, and you should expect to be assigned the stock 15 percent to 25 percent of the time.

Many brokerage firms will require you to have a portfolio of at least $50,000 to implement put selling strategies, because the potential capital commitment to buy the stock is much larger than the margin required for selling options. At the same time, most brokers allow the purchase of an assigned stock on 50 percent margin, which I prefer for two reasons:

1. It keeps your capital commitment down.
2. If the quality stock has experienced a temporary dip, that is just the time to leverage yourself by betting the stock will recover, so this could prove to be a major buying opportunity.

My goal is to monitor the fundamental and technical outlook on quality stocks I recommend for put selling so that I can ride out such temporary volatility as just a blip, rather than as something more serious. If conditions do change, I will shut down the position, whether this change in outlook occurs before the option is exercised or after the stock has been acquired.

IN-THE-MONEY OPTIONS

As discussed in chapter 3, understanding options pricing is essential to estimating the profitability of a trade. Options pricing is based on volatility, time until expiration, stock price, distance out-of-the-money, as well as the minor impact of interest rates and dividends. However, these factors act differently on in-the-money options than they do on out-of-the-money options. In-the-money options offer a unique blend of characteristics that allows in some cases a larger profit from a given move in the underlying security than might occur with out-of-the-money options.

We focus here on the straight in-the-money option purchase. If used properly, in-the-money options can offer a relatively conservative approach to investing. As we shall see, the time premium and intrinsic value profile of in-the-money options work in your favor by giving you more control of your position if there are no strong moves in the underlying.

First and foremost, an options buyer has to predict the direction of the underlying stock correctly. Without this simple understanding, the trader is doomed to failure. In-the-money and out-of-the-money options buyers have the same general criteria for initiating a position. The predicted stock move has to occur within the time frame of the option's life, and the option has to increase in value above the initial purchase price to yield a profit.

My own in-the-money philosophy is centered on combining market timing analysis and specific stock scenarios—determined by technical and sentiment indicators and option activity—with the powerful benefits of buying options with substantial intrinsic value. It is also important to realize that in-the-money strategies can still result in losses as large as 100 percent, although the odds of such a loss are far lower than with out-of-the-money options. The key to a successful in-the-money strategy is as much about successfully managing losing trades as picking winners. As unpleasant as losing trades are, they must be managed properly to maximize your account's profitability.

Intrinsic Value and Option Pricing

The single biggest disadvantage you face as an out-of-the-money options buyer is the perpetual decay of time premium throughout the life of the option contract. For example, assume a company reports earnings that are sharply above estimates—after the market has closed for the day. When the options on that stock open the following day, they will often be priced at a substantially lower volatility than the day before. Due to the high volatility built into the pricing of the options before the earnings report was released, the stock will have to make a large move after the earnings report for any options purchased before the report to be profitable. In other words, the event had been "priced into" the option. When you are buying out-of-the-money options, you need to be keenly aware of this, because your ability to make a profit on the position strongly depends on the time and volatility assumptions built into the option price, both when entering and exiting the position.

Once an option is in-the-money, it has intrinsic value. Remember, the intrinsic value of an in-the-money option is equal to the stock price less the striking price for a call, and is equal to the striking price less the stock price for a put. Essentially, it is the price of the option less the time premium.

As options move deeper into the money, their pricing characteristics change. As discussed in chapter 3, the delta is a frequently used measure of the amount that the option price is expected to move for a 1-point move in the underlying stock. Delta approaches zero for call options that are far out-of-the-money and approaches 100 for call options that are deep in-the-money. For example, suppose you purchase a call with a striking price of 55 that will expire in 30 days while the underlying stock is at 60. Assume the option is selling for 6 and the delta is 0.90. An increase in the stock price to 61 should result in the 55-strike option being priced at 6.90. So, as an in-the-money buyer, you will in this case achieve nearly "point-for-point" participation in the movement of the stock and you will have much less concern about the impact of volatility assumptions on the pricing of your option.

One other way to help you think about delta is that it is a good approximation of the probability that an option will finish in-the-money. A delta of 0.90 implies that the option is already in-the-money and in nine out of ten cases it will remain there. A delta of 0.10 implies an out-of-the-money option that has only a one-in-ten chance of finishing in-the-money. The market assumes an at-the-money option will have a 50–50 chance of finishing in-the-money, so it carries a 0.50 delta. Note also that for a given striking price for a call option, the more time before expiration, the higher the delta.

Buying deep in-the-money options significantly helps in the battle against time erosion; however, time and volatility are always key considerations in selecting any option. As with out-of-the-money options, time premium is a significant factor in determining in-the-money option pricing, but the time premium as a percentage of the option's cost is far less for in-the-money options than for out-of-the-money options. For example, assume that a stock's price is at 31, the 25-strike calls are priced at 6¾, the 30-strike calls are priced at 2, and the options expire in thirty days. The deep in-the-money buyer is paying ¾ point in time premium on top of 6 points of intrinsic value. That's an 11 percent time premium component relative to the total premium. The 30-strike option buyer is paying 1 point of time premium on top of 1 point of intrinsic value. That's a 50 percent time premium component. Should the stock remain at 31 until expiration, the deep in-the-money buyer would have suffered an 11 percent loss whereas the slightly in-the-money buyer would have suffered a 50 percent loss. Of course, the out-of-the-money call buyer would have incurred a total loss in this situation.

I view the in-the-money approach as a good compromise for the options trader who is not aggressive enough to trade out-of-the-money but who wants to retain the advantages of limited risk and theoretically unlimited profit potential that accrue to options buyers.

CONCLUSION

It is clear from this discussion that relatively conservative options strategies can be tailored to the individual's taste for risk. This chapter detailed several strategies that offer higher winning percentages with still respectable returns. This concludes our discussion of various option strategies. We next discuss setting up a brokerage account so you can begin to trade these strategies.

10

Selecting an Options Broker and Establishing an Options Trading Account

CHOOSING A BROKER

You have read this far and feel you understand my contrarian trading philosophy and the options basics. You are excited about the potential for big profits in the options market, you understand the risks involved, and you would like to start your own options trading program. So what's the next step?

If you have not done so already, you must establish an equity options account with a brokerage firm. The following are some important factors to consider when choosing an options broker:

1. *Options Expertise.* Does the firm have brokers available who specialize in options (preferably Registered Options Principals (ROPs), who must pass the Series 4 test to show their options knowledge) to handle your orders and answer questions?

2. *Account and Margin Requirements.* What is the minimum account size for options trading at the firm, and what margin requirements does it demand?

3. *Commissions and Fees.* What are the firm's commissions for options trading and its fees for maintaining an account or using other services?

4. *Service.* What kind of personal service and attention will you get with your account, and what kind do you need?

5. *Automated and Electronic Services.* Does the firm offer touch-tone trading or Internet/PC trading?

6. *Features.* Can you download quotes cost-free from the firm's computer for options positions you either hold or are analyzing? Does the firm offer electronic trading and written confirmations on each trade? Does the firm offer such account features as check writing, bank wires, and monthly statements?

7. *Reputation.* Does the firm have an established reputation for executing trades promptly and going the extra mile for its customers?

You should begin the process of selecting a brokerage firm for your options trading by gathering information on several firms and consulting with colleagues, friends, and relatives for referrals. Before you make your decision, weigh your various needs and resources to see what type of broker would best fit your situation. For example, a very experienced options trader looking for low commissions, minimum margin requirements, and the ability to trade via fax, phone, or computer may choose to establish an account with a no-frills, deep-discount broker. On the other hand, an investor relatively new to options trading who prefers personal service may decide to go with a full-service broker who is knowledgeable in options, can take orders over the phone, and has a walk-in office. Your personal situation will determine the most appropriate type of broker for you.

TYPES OF BROKERS

Full-service brokerages seek to offer just that: full service. If you establish an account with a full-service broker, you will be assigned an individual broker who will personally handle your account. The minimum account requirements and commissions of full-service brokers are generally higher than those for discount or deep-discount firms, and they often specialize in higher net worth clients. You may be able to negotiate lower commission rates with a full-service broker based on your account size and your frequency of trading. The payscale of brokers at full-service firms is usually based largely on commissions generated. This has the potential to create a conflict of interest between the broker's need for commission income and your need for winning trades, which heightens the importance of recommendations from satisfied clients. The full-service firm may offer a wide variety of services and abilities that are not available at other firms, such as personal investment advice, an increased opportunity to buy Initial Public Offerings (IPOs), a fully staffed bond desk, and an in-house investment research department. Full-service brokers who accept retail options accounts include Merrill Lynch, PaineWebber, Smith Barney, Dean Witter, and Prudential Securities.

Discount brokers came into existence in 1975 when the New York and American Stock Exchanges agreed to abandon the minimum commission schedule previously imposed on all members. These new, less-binding regulations encouraged the emergence of discount brokerage firms that charged lower commissions in return for less personalized service. Discount brokerage houses vary widely, but almost always have cheaper fees and commissions than full-service houses. Personal attention and specific investment advice are generally not part of the picture, but the discount broker usually offers convenient access to trading and customer services through a toll-free telephone number. Brokers at discount firms are often paid relatively more in salary and relatively less in commissions than their full-service counterparts, giving them less incentive to induce you to trade. On the other hand, the lack of sales incentive may make your dealings with a discount firm more impersonal, and often you will not deal with the same individual on a regular basis. Note that the gap in the degree of service between full-service and discount firms has narrowed considerably over the past decade, as has the gap in commission rates. Discount brokers include Charles Schwab & Co., Fidelity Investments, Quick and Reilly, Waterhouse Securities, and Jack White & Co.

Deep-discount brokers arose from the discount broker camp as the gap between the discount firms and full-service brokers narrowed. Basically, deep discounters offer the lowest commission rates along with stripped-down service. These firms are geared to knowledgeable investors who need little hand-holding. Because many options traders are in this category, the options market share of the deep discounters has been growing steadily. Personalized attention at a deep discounter may be virtually nonexistent, as may be additional features such as twenty-four-hour customer service, bond trading, or foreign stock investing. Some examples of deep-discount brokers include PC Financial, National Discount, Pacific, and Accutrade.

Options-specialized brokers have grown in recent years by filling a niche that was long neglected by full-service firms and by many discounters—serving the special needs of options traders. These firms generally employ ROPs to interact with clients and will often handle difficult or complex option orders or transactions that less specialized firms tend to avoid. Although not all options-specialized brokers offer deep commission discounts, most offer very attractive commission rates. Options-specialized brokers include Benjamin & Jerold, E. D. F. & Man International, R. F. Lafferty, and PTI Securities.

Internet brokers allow clients to enter their own trades via the World Wide Web, a proprietary online service, or a bulletin board. We will discuss Internet trading in more detail later in this chapter.

SETTING UP AN OPTIONS TRADING ACCOUNT

Once you have selected your brokerage firm, all that remains to establish an account for options trading is completing the paperwork and depositing the assets required to open an account. The paperwork includes the following components.

Brokerage Account Application: Includes your vital information, including employment, bank accounts (optional), and net worth. Net worth, including liquid and total net worth, is required by the brokerage house as part of the "know your customer" guidelines of the National Association of Securities Dealers (NASD). The know your customer rules are designed to make sure that brokers do not place you into inappropriate investments at odds with your financial situation, goals, and knowledge. Some brokerage houses may have stricter net worth requirements if you indicate you plan to write naked options, because that strategy has the potential for theoretically unlimited losses.

Characteristics and Risks of Standardized Options: This booklet, published by the Options Clearing Corporation (OCC), is provided to all prospective options account holders. Usually you must affirm to your broker that you have read and understood the material contained in the booklet. The booklet gives a basic explanation of equity and index options, as well as the risks incurred in various types of positions.

Options Agreement/Application: To trade options in your brokerage account, all brokerage firms require you to complete a separate options agreement. It will ask for information regarding your investment experience and knowledge of various types of options trading strategies, as well the number of options trades you have initiated in the past. This is designed to help your broker determine if options trading is suitable for you and understand what types of trading may be most appropriate for you.

Deposit of Assets: Your broker will require a deposit in the form of cash or securities for you to make your first trade. Assets can be brought into an account in many forms, including check, wire transfer, electronic transfer, or a transfer of assets from another broker. Your particular brokerage house may have other paperwork requirements to establish an account for you. Additionally, specific types of accounts—such as trusts and retirement accounts (IRAs, for example)—usually have their own regulatory requirements.

MINIMUM MARGIN REQUIREMENTS

Various types of equity option trades have minimum initial margin and maintenance margin requirements. There may also be separate margin requirements for index option trading. Please consult a broker or a Registered Options Principal for specific margin requirements for any type of trade not listed here. You should also keep in mind that individual brokerage firms may have different margin requirements than others on trades that involve naked option sales. The minimum margin is usually 10 percent, but most brokers require more, with 20 percent being the typical margin requirement. Following is a brief summary of margin requirements for several common options strategies (note that firms may have minimum margin requirements that exceed the amounts required for these individual trades):

Long Put or Long Call: Option premium must be paid for in full. For example, suppose you buy one XYZ December 100 call at 4½ ($450). You must have $450 in available cash plus the opening commission in your account to place this trade. Many brokers will require a larger minimum equity in the account before an option trade can be initiated.

Short Put or Short Call: Generally 20 percent of the underlying stock value plus any premium received and less any amount by which the option is out-of-the-money. The minimum requirement is 10 percent of the underlying stock value. For example, suppose you sell one XYZ November 90 put for a credit of 1½ ($150) when XYZ is at 102. The margin in this case is:

$$[20\% \times \$102 + \$1.50 - (\$102 - \$90)] \times 100 \text{ shares} = \$9.90 \times 100 = \$990$$

The term in brackets represents 20 percent of the underlying stock price of $102, plus the credit of 1½ points received from the sale of the put, minus the 12 points that the 90-strike put is out-of-the-money. However, since $990 is less than 10 percent of the underlying stock value, you would be required to put up the higher amount, which in this case is $1,020 ($102 × 100 × 10%), plus commission.

Put Credit Spread or Call Credit Spread: The difference between the strike prices minus any premium received. For example, suppose you sell one XYZ December 110 put and simultaneously buy one XYZ 105 December put, for a net credit of 1 ($100). Your margin requirement for each spread contract is the difference in the strike prices (110 − 105 = 5, or $500) minus any premium received (the $100 credit) for a total margin of $400 per contract.

Covered Call or Buy/Write (Long Underlying Stock and Short Call): No requirement on short call; 50 percent of long stock position less call premium received. The reason no margin is required on the short call position is that if the call holder exercises his option, you already own the stock needed to satisfy his exercise. It would simply be called out of your account. For example, if you buy 100 shares of XYZ at $115 and sell one December 125 call at 1½, the margin requirement for the stock purchase is 50 percent of the underlying stock value ($115 per share × 100 shares = $11,500 × 50%) less call premium received ($150), or $5,600, plus commission.

Note that margins are calculated each evening after the market closes and if one or more positions have moved strongly against you, the brokerage firm may issue a "margin call," asking you to supply additional funds to maintain your position. If you are unable or unwilling to deposit the required additional funds, either a portion or all of your account will be liquidated to satisfy the call.

COMMISSIONS

A commission is paid on both the entry and the exit of an options position and is added to the total cost or deducted from the proceeds of the trade. In the event an option expires worthless, only entry commissions are paid.

Commissions vary widely by brokerage firm and can be adjusted by factors such as account size, account activity, and trading method. They are generally calculated based upon the premium of the option and the number of contracts traded, although some firms calculate commission based purely on the dollar value of the transaction. For example, a broker may charge a minimum commission of $32, plus $4 for every contract traded. An order for ten contracts would then cost $72. As in the case of stocks, the commission rate (as a percentage of the total cost of the trade) will generally decline as the total dollar amount or the number of contracts increases. Spreads, straddles, buy/writes, and other orders are generally charged two commissions, one for each side of the trade.

With the explosive growth of the deep-discount firms, options-specialized firms, and Internet and PC-based firms in recent years, the level of commissions available to options traders has ratcheted downward, which is a very welcome development in an area of investing where trading frequency is generally quite high (see table 10.1).

Table 10.1 **COMPARISON OF COMMISSIONS BY BROKER CATEGORY AND TRANSACTION TYPE**

	25 Contracts at $1.00		10 Contracts at $2.50		5 Contracts at $5.00		Average	
	($)	(%)	($)	(%)	($)	(%)	($)	(%)
Full-Service Brokers								
Dean Witter	217.00	8.68	140.00	5.60	142.00	5.68	166.33	6.65
Paine Webber	250.00	10.00	162.00	6.48	115.00	4.60	175.67	7.03
Smith Barney	211.00	8.44	135.00	5.40	81.00	3.24	142.33	5.69
Average	226.00	9.04	145.67	5.83	112.67	4.51	**161.44**	**6.46**
Discount Brokers								
Fidelity	78.00	3.12	68.75	2.75	68.75	2.75	71.83	2.87
Quick & Reilly	81.00	3.24	69.00	2.76	69.00	2.76	73.00	2.92
Schwab	81.00	3.24	69.00	2.76	69.00	2.76	73.00	2.92
Average	80.00	3.20	68.92	2.76	68.92	2.76	**72.61**	**2.90**
Options Specialized Brokers								
Benjamin & Jerold	112.50	4.50	59.00	2.36	36.00	1.44	69.17	2.77
ED&F Man	125.00	5.00	50.00	2.00	35.00	1.40	70.00	2.80
PTI Securities	170.00	6.80	80.00	3.20	48.00	1.92	99.33	3.97
Average	135.83	5.43	63.00	2.52	39.67	1.59	**79.50**	**3.18**
Internet Brokers								
e.Schwab	81.25	3.25	55.00	2.20	46.00	1.84	60.75	2.43
e-Trade	63.75	2.55	37.50	1.50	29.00	1.16	43.42	1.74
e-Broker	60.00	2.40	45.00	1.80	35.00	1.40	46.67	1.87
Average	68.33	2.73	45.83	1.83	36.67	1.47	**50.28**	**2.01**
Deep Discount Brokers								
Accutrade	67.00	2.68	52.00	2.08	42.00	1.68	53.67	2.15
Pacific	56.25	2.25	29.00	1.16	29.00	1.16	38.08	1.52
PC Financial	78.75	3.15	52.50	2.10	43.75	1.75	58.33	2.33
Average	67.33	2.69	44.50	1.78	38.25	1.53	**50.03**	**2.00**

Note: These figures are believed to be reliable, but cannot be guaranteed. Rates are subject to change over time. Data collected via telephone survey, February 28, 1997.

As table 10.1 shows, even discounted full-service rates are not likely to attract much options business. The individual option speculator is most likely to choose among the other four categories. If you focus on the Internet or deep-discount brokers or take advantage of Internet trading discounts from the traditional discount brokers, you can substantially lower your commission costs. Note that if you intend to sell credit spreads or use any other options strategy with a maximum profit level, you are going to need low commissions to produce a worthwhile net profit after the trade is closed.

OPTIONS ORDER CATEGORIES AND WHEN TO USE THEM

There are four basic categories of orders, revolving around buy or sell orders, combined with open or close orders.

1. *Buy to open.* The trader initiates a long premium position. Straight call and put purchases fall into this category.

2. *Sell to open.* The trader initiates a short premium position. Naked put selling is an example of this category.

3. *Sell to close.* The trader closes the long premium position initiated in 1 above.

4. *Buy to close.* The trader buys back the short premium position initiated in 2 above.

Currently, trading hours for equity options were 9:30 A.M. to 4:10 P.M. eastern time, but the exchanges have just received approval to change the closing time to 4:02 P.M. The trading hours for index options are 9:30 A.M. to 4:15 P.M. eastern time.

Generally, all bids and offers as reflected on brokers' quote screens are for market orders up to ten contracts. Larger orders and limit orders may run a risk of a "partial execution," in which only part of the order is filled. The ten-contract rule (sometimes called the "10-up rule") may vary by exchange, market maker, and the liquidity of any given option. Currently, almost every option is quoted 10-up, with an increasing number of options quoted 25-up, or even 50-up or more.

Orders are of several types, as elaborated next:

1. *Market and Limit Orders.* When you place an order to purchase an option, the order is entered either at the current market price or at a specified limit price. Market orders take precedence over limit orders.

A market order to buy will be executed at the lowest available selling price, generally the asked price. A market order to sell will be executed at the highest available buying price, generally the bid price. For example, if an option is currently bid at 1 and asked at 1⅛, and you place a market order to buy ten contracts, your order will most likely be filled at 1⅛. Likewise, if you place a market order to sell ten contracts, your order will most likely be filled at 1. A broker will typically confirm the execution of your market order during the same phone call. You should understand that in fast-moving markets, prices can change, sometimes significantly, between the time you place your market order and the time the floor fills it. With a market order, you are certain that you will be filled but you are uncertain of the price of this fill.

A limit order to buy is an order to purchase at a certain price or lower. A limit order to sell is an order to sell at a certain price or higher. For example, if you place an order to buy 10 XYZ January 100 calls at a limit of 2, you are willing to pay up to a maximum of 2 points for each option contract. If the XYZ January 100 calls are bid at $2\frac{1}{8}$, asked at $2\frac{3}{8}$, your order will not be immediately filled. Limit orders that cannot be immediately executed are generally placed on the specialist's order book or the public order book (depending on the exchange) for potential execution should the market move toward the limit price. If you place the same order (to buy at a limit of 2) when the XYZ January 100 calls are bid at $1\frac{5}{8}$, asked at $1\frac{7}{8}$, your order will likely be immediately filled at $1\frac{7}{8}$. Remember that a limit order to buy means you are willing to pay that price or lower—the market maker or specialist is obligated to fill your order at a lower price if it is available. With a limit order, you are certain of the price of your trade but you are uncertain as to whether your order will be filled.

I recommend that you always place a limit price on entering options positions, as you don't want to "chase" a trade by overpaying. When closing out positions, it is sometimes worthwhile to place market orders to exit quickly. All market orders are placed for the trading day only (day orders). Market orders will always be filled unless the trading is halted in the underlying stock. Limit orders to buy or sell can be good-till-canceled orders (which remain active until canceled) or day orders.

2. *Good-till-Canceled and Day Orders.*   Theoretically, good-till-canceled (GTC) orders can remain on the trading floor's books forever or until the option expires. However, there may be limits to the time period such orders can be maintained, sometimes as little as one month. Check with your broker for specific rules on the life of limit orders. The disadvantage of GTC orders is that a trader may forget the order has been placed; an additional disadvantage of GTC option orders is that they may be executed at very unfavorable prices, particularly on a "gap" move in the underlying stock. Many brokers will send a written reminder stating the name of the security and the quantity and price specified for each open limit order.

Day orders are either filled during the trading day for which they are placed or expire at the end of the day. I generally recommend placing limit orders as day orders, good for the day only.

3. *Stop-Limit and Stop-Loss Orders.* Stop-limit and stop-loss orders are used to exit a position if a certain price level is breached. They are generally used to protect a long position by setting a sell level below the current market price. The options exchanges generally do not accept stop orders on options. However, some individual brokers may accept stop orders on options in-house, so check with your broker for further information. These so-called "desk-stops" are placed at the customer's risk. The broker agrees to watch prices for the customer on a best-efforts basis but usually cannot be held responsible for bad or missed fills. For these reasons and because the options market is so fast moving, I do not recommend placing stop orders in your options trading. You should instead allow time to eventually stop you out by determining in advance how long you will be willing to hold a long option position.

4. *All-or-None Orders.* To avoid a partial execution on market orders for more than ten contracts or on a limit order, an all-or-none restriction can be placed on your order. These are accepted only on day option orders; they are not accepted on GTC option orders. Again, check with your broker for house-specific rules and regulations. You should think carefully about the use of an all-or-none limit on an order. Suppose you are trying to exit a 20-contract position and you enter an all-or-none sell order at 5 where the bid is for ten contracts. The market drops to 4, but your order doesn't get filled. Would you be happier holding all your options at 4 or would you be more pleased having sold half of your position at 5?

5. *Contingency Orders.* Your broker may allow contingency orders to be placed on your trades. A contingency order involves a conditional situation that must be met for an order to be filled. For example, if you are long one XYZ January 115 call, you may instruct your broker to close the option position at the market price if XYZ closes at $120 or higher. Your order to sell the option is contingent, or conditional, upon XYZ reaching a price of $120 a share. Not all brokers accept contingency orders, and those who do may limit the type of such orders they will accept. In some cases, individual brokers may accept contingency orders, even unusual ones, on a "not held" basis, meaning that they are not held responsible if a fill does not occur.

DISCRETIONARY AUTHORITY (LIMITED OR FULL)

Discretionary authority gives the broker the right to trade your account, in some cases with no restrictions on what may be traded or the strategies employed. Limited discretionary authority generally applies to only certain types of trades. Full discretionary authority gives the broker the right to make any trade at any time in your account, without consulting you. I generally do not recommend that you grant full discretionary authority unless you are totally confident in the trading ability as well as the ethics and reputation of your broker.

OPTIONS TRADING AND TAXES

Please consult a tax advisor, accountant, or attorney for specific tax implications of options trading on your particular situation. The following are simply a few basic guidelines on how Internal Revenue Service (IRS) taxes impact options traders.

It is important to keep a record of all of your options trades, including confirmations of the quantities, the purchase and sale prices, the cost of purchases, and the proceeds from sales. Also, keep your monthly or quarterly brokerage statements. Your broker may send you a summary of all options purchases, but the tax regulations do not currently require this. In addition, you will receive from your broker a Form 1099-INT showing any interest paid to you during the year and a Form 1099-DIV showing any dividends received on stocks held in your account. To ensure accuracy, review the data on all of the tax forms you receive.

Every completed options trade (an initial purchase or sale, followed by a closing sale, purchase, expiration, or assignment) results in a realized capital gain or loss of some measure, which must be reported to the IRS. Capital gains and losses on securities are generally reported on Schedule D of your tax forms. If a long option is held for less than one year before the position is closed, that transaction is considered a short-term capital gain or loss. If held for more than one year, the transaction is considered a long-term capital gain or loss. Short positions and other, more complex options positions are, in some cases, considered long-term, whereas others are treated as short-term capital gains for tax purposes. Again, you should consult with a tax advisor, attorney, or accountant for answers to specific questions you may have on tax issues raised by your options trading. You can also contact the IRS for additional guidance.

WWW.INTERNET.TRADING

The Internet has been mentioned briefly in this chapter; now let us take a closer look at how you can make option trades over your computer. Internet and PC-based brokerages that allow clients to enter their own trades via the World Wide Web, a proprietary online service, or a bulletin board are now up and running and open for your business. Some are relative newcomers; others are more established investment names. Before you select an electronic broker, make sure you understand each step of the process. A single mistake on an order could cost you many times what you might save by trading electronically over a number of trades.

In these days of increasing computer-"ease," you don't need to be a cyberpro to make trades over the Internet. If you know the address, you can easily connect to a broker's Website and follow the point-and-click paths from there. If you don't know the address, a simple search can put you in touch. The following is an illustration using a keyword search (under "Go To") on America Online. Typing in http://www.altavista.digital.com pulls up the AltaVista search engine. A search for "pc financial" results in about two million possible matches, ranked in order of their likelihood of fulfilling your search request. In this case, the second possible match reads "PC Financial Network—Home." The capsule description is "Online trading, free real-time quotes, mutual funds, S&P news, Zack's earnings estimates, and more." This leads you to the PC Financial Network homepage.

A few addresses that may help you in your search for the right online trading broker follow:

Schwab: http://www.eschwab.com

Lombard Brokerage: http://www.lombard.com

PC Financial Network: http://www.pcfn.com

E*Trade: http://www.etrade.com

Accutrade: http://www.accutrade.com

As you might expect, you can find all kinds of brokerages that trade options via the Internet, from venerable firms such as Schwab to newcomers such as E*Trade. Following, with information drawn from their Websites, are snapshots of a few of these brokerage firms. You should note that any information reported here is not guaranteed to be reliable and is subject to change, especially given the rapid changes still occurring on the Internet.

Schwab. Part of Charles Schwab & Co., e.Schwab allows you to trade options either through the World Wide Web or through the firm's StreetSmart software. The company offers real-time quotes, news and research, and real-time trading. Your account transactions are consolidated into one computer-accessible file every night. You also get a regular statement, and printed trade confirmations are mailed.

Lombard Brokerage. Lombard offers you online options trading, along with a range of services designed to give you the information to manage your account. These include Realtime Quote Server, which allows you to enter symbols and get real-time and delayed quotes; Realtime Graph Server, on which you can plot every price change in intervals from intraday to yearly; and Portfolio Management, which lets you see your Lombard account data in real time. Lombard's account representatives are salaried. The company does not charge inactivity fees. Links within Lombard's Website lead you to information on opening an account, depositing funds, margin requirements, security issues, and more.

PC Financial Network. PC Financial Network offers free real-time quotes, news and access to your portfolio, as well as online options trading. You can apply for an account online and possibly be eligible to trade right away. PC Financial Network accepts "CyberCash." CyberCash is a means of paying for purchases with a sort of "online currency." The system is based on a MasterCard Debit Card. CyberCash transactions are protected by today's most secure encryption technology. You can get "CyberCoins" in increments as small as a quarter, and use them to make purchases you wouldn't want to charge on a credit card.

E*Trade. With E*Trade, you can trade equity options and manage your portfolio via your PC, using either the World Wide Web or a direct modem connection. Research, market analysis, news, and options analysis are available online. You can place all the common types of orders—market, limit, stop and stop-limit, all-or-none, and good-till-canceled—and use such options strategies as covered writing, spreads, or combinations. You must have full funds, securities, or margin in your account to buy options. Notification of executions is immediate on E*Trade's Web-based message center; a hard copy confirmation is also mailed the day of the order's execution. There are no per-order, connection-time (when you use the Internet), handling, or account maintenance charges—just commission fees for each trade and for any requested special services.

Accutrade. Accutrade is a computer-and-modem-based trading system that gives you access to options quotes, a selection of information sources, Accutrade securities trading services, and information about the performance of your portfolio. You can execute buy-writes, spreads, and straddles in addition to straight option purchases. Accutrade requires a $5,000 minimum equity—in cash, securities or a combination of the two—to open an account. You can use this initial deposit toward securities purchases.

Again, any numbers and services quoted here are subject to change. In fact, since the Internet itself is in a constant state of flux, you will want to verify all information presented here before making any decisions. In summary, a few hours at the computer will turn up a wealth of information. Those hours may be well worth investing.

WHY TRADE OVER THE INTERNET?

A little more than a century ago, the question might have been, "Why trade over the telephone?" The simple answers are that using the Internet is easy, practically instant, and—if you use the services of a discount or deep-discount broker—it can be a means of saving on commission expenses.

When you log onto a broker's Website, you can point and click your way through a universe of information you can use to make decisions, as well as "buttons" you can electronically push to make things happen. Most sites contain links within themselves that act like the pages of a book, leading you to facts or to application forms that you fill in and send with the click of a mouse.

Ease is the name of the game on the Internet. Point and click and you can execute the trade. You can get the latest information and track your account in the middle of the night. You can plan your strategy on the screen of your home computer. You can move money by traditional methods or over the Web. You can send funds by mail or by telephone. You can wire the money. You can use CyberCash.

You will find many discount and deep-discount brokers online, competing to offer you the most appealing per-trade price and the most attractive discount. The price you are likely to pay for such low-cost service is just that—service. The lower the bottom-line commission, the lower the level of personal service you can probably expect from the broker. Generally speaking, these firms are online to execute your trades quickly and cheaply, not to advise you on what to trade, or how to construct your strategy. If you aren't troubled by that trade-off, you may find online option trading to be a positive move in your investment planning.

WHY *NOT* TRADE OVER THE NET?

The Internet has had well-publicized problems with its lack of security. The same features that attract you to the Internet also attract unscrupulous hackers and other undesirables. You are looking for information; and they are looking for information, too—about you. You like the instant communication of e-mail; they would like to obtain your e-mail address and send you junk e-mail. You like the ability to conduct transactions online; they would like to find a way to wiggle an electronic finger in your accounts. And if you don't think they can, guess again.

Your online communications travel a circuitous path from your computer to the destination you intend. Along the way, they may route through many computer systems, where they can be intercepted, copied, altered, or spied upon. What's a trader to do?

Technologically speaking, you do have safeguards available. Netscape Communications has developed a system that offers authentication, data encryption, and message integrity. Secure Sockets Layer protocol, as it is known, provides a high level of resistance to encryption cracking, and that difficulty is itself considered a deterrent.

Your broker can tell you the security practices he follows for online trading. If he does not bring the subject up or include the information in his Website, be sure to ask. The money you save could be your own.

Even with heightened security—the ability to get your information from here to there without anyone picking it off along the way—you still have to contend with the human factor. Do you trust the company you have selected with your confidential financial and personal data? Can you trust the company's employee—the representative to whom you have given these facts? Those questions are as old as commerce itself, and you will have to wrestle with them whether you trade over the Internet, pick up the telephone, or walk through the front door. Which is the best way? That is up to you.

CONCLUSION

This chapter has covered the key elements needed to buy and sell options effectively. You must first select a brokerage firm that meets your needs as an options trader. This fact applies whether you choose a traditional arrangement or decide to trade over the Internet. You must understand the types of orders you need to place, as well as the capital required for a particular options strategy. Armed with this knowledge, you are now poised to trade, but you must also have the appropriate information to trade options well. Again, the Internet is an excellent source of up-to-date options information. We explore this more fully in the next chapter.

11

Navigating the Internet

INTRODUCTION

Gone are the days when you had to scamper to the library and mull over outdated corporate information to research your investments. The proliferation of information and services available on the Internet and the World Wide Web has launched a new era for the "do-it-yourself" investor. With a computer and modem, you now can gain access to free data and information that just a few years ago was privy only to the large institutions that could pay for high-priced terminals and services. Now, through the Internet, you can access more financial information than you could ever hope to digest. With a little bit of hunting, you can find stock and option quotes, corporate press releases, Securities and Exchange Commission filings, earnings statements and outlooks, IPO announcements, analyst estimates, news stories, and insider trading figures.

Does this sound too good to be true? Well, there is a catch—in order to get to this valuable investment information, you must first wade through a never-ending barrage of commercial solicitations, junk e-mail, dead-end links, flashing banners, pyramid schemes, and downright gaudy homepages.

The massive commercialization of the Web has made it a huge success, but this same commercialization is also its biggest drawback. Post a question to an investment USENET newsgroup, and your e-mail account will quickly become stuffed with "get rich quick" schemes, unsolicited commercial messages, people hyping their own stock, and an occasional insulting "flame" or two. Yet, somewhere among the millions of users who comprise the Internet will be a kindhearted soul who will answer your question and provide you with valuable information, tempering the disturbing fact that there are more than a few people out there who hope that you are really gullible.

FREE INFORMATION—BUT BE WARY

The information on the World Wide Web and Internet originates from many sources. As with almost all free information, it comes with no pledge or certification of validity. Some information on the Internet is passed on from person to person and site to site, often changing in the process like the childhood game of "telephone." In fact, by the time you see the message the information may not even resemble the first posting.

While the Internet has catered to the needs of the do-it-yourself investor, the sheer number of users can present its own temptations. For instance, someone who has invested in a stock has an interest in spreading the good word to other investors on the Internet, while "forgetting" to mention any drawbacks or risks. This process can lead to an exaggeration or even the blatant hyping of a stock or company. In fact, rumor has it that some companies have started paying people to say good things on the Internet about their stock or business.

This is not to imply that there isn't any useful information on the Internet—far from it. Some companies provide as much free information as possible to encourage you to visit their sites. In return, these companies may get leads for prospective customers and increase their goodwill.

Other useful information on the Web is provided by those who have a deep passion for a subject. It is not uncommon to find complete dissertations and research papers posted on the Internet by graduate students or professors. But remember, almost everyone who puts information on the Internet has an agenda or reason for doing so. While this agenda will tend to influence the message, it is normally quite easy to decipher the reasons behind the message, then sort through the facts, opinions, and advice. In fact, such a process is ideally suited to the critical thinking approach of contrarians. With the knowledge of how the Internet operates, and perhaps a little bit of luck sorting through thousands of Websites, you might find the Internet a very valuable investment information resource.

Options-related information on the Web began as a trickle and is just now starting to build into a steady stream. This chapter explores the various types of options information currently available on the Web, taking into consideration that the electronic landscape will change rapidly as it relates to options.

FINDING YOUR WAY AROUND

How do you sort through the vast amount of information on the World Wide Web and find the proverbial "needle in a haystack"? First of all, you have to find the right haystack. The World Wide Web is cluttered with thousands of information centers that might lead you directly to the information you are seeking—or perhaps they won't. Instead, they might lead you through a confusing "web" of links only to leave you back at the same place at which you started. Or, they might guide you through promising sites but come to an abrupt dead end, or bring you to an unusual site that might contain something like an extensive list of humorous bumper stickers. While the latter may be interesting and merit a few minutes of leisure time, it is certainly not the valuable investment information you had originally sought.

SEARCH ENGINES AND HOW TO USE THEM

If you are having problems finding an originating site for financial information—or any other interest—you might want to use one of the numerous World Wide Web "search engines." These sites catalog the millions of pages on the World Wide Web and provide an organized guide or directory of related topics. Some search engines are content-based, which means you can prospect for information by category.

If you run out of luck with the content-based search engines and you don't mind sifting through large amounts of data, you will want to try one of the text-oriented search engines. Text-oriented search engines were created after the Web had grown in popularity and had become too large to adequately group every site by a single topic. In particular, text-oriented search engines are helpful when you are searching through very large sites that contain a diverse assortment of information that falls under several different topics.

Text-oriented search engines send automated computerized requests (often called bots, robots, or spiders) to known Web pages. These robots archive and compress the complete text of each page into one massive database. A visitor to a text-oriented search engine can then search for sites that contain a specific word or phrase. The results of the search can be taken from the title and abstract of each site, like content-based search engines, but these engines will also search each and every word and page on a Website.

One of the most popular search engines, Yahoo! (http://www.yahoo.com) provides a content-based directory of Web resources, as

Exhibit 11.1   **YAHOO! HOMEPAGE**

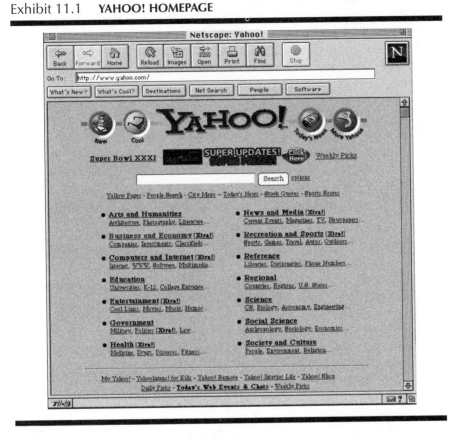

well as a search tool that helps you navigate this extensive directory. Yahoo! was the first online guide to the World Wide Web. Its user-friendly look and feel, as shown in exhibit 11.1, have consistently placed it on the top five of most frequently visited sites on the Web.

Once you connect to the Yahoo! site, you will see an orderly listing of fourteen categories:

Arts and Humanities	News and Media
Business and Economy	Recreation and Sports
Computers and Internet	Reference
Education	Regional
Entertainment	Science
Government	Social Science
Health	Society and Culture

Under each of these categories are directories for numerous related subcategories or topics. You can either use these subcategories to focus on sites of interest or use the "search" command to type a word or phrase to find related subcategories and sites. Sites with information on options can be found on Yahoo! by following the path: Business and Economy . . . Investments . . . Futures and Options.

As for any good Website, Yahoo! Webmasters constantly update their data and add additional areas of interest. Yahoo! offers a "What's Cool" button that pulls up brief descriptions of sites that the Yahoo! staff rates as "cool." In particular, Yahoo! employees have selected specific categories within their World Wide Web directory in which they found amusing, extraordinary, or especially useful content. Another feature of Yahoo! is its "News" button, which provides the top headline news on an hourly basis in addition to news in specific categories such as business, entertainment, sports, and international and U.S. politics. The amount of effort Yahoo! puts into designing, updating, and improving its search site definitely makes it a good place to begin a search—or to return to if a search attempt has resulted in a dead end.

AltaVista. AltaVista (http://www.altavista.com) is one of the most comprehensive text-oriented search engines. The AltaVista Website (exhibit 11.2) allows you to sort through the full text of millions of pages. Since the number of successful matches can be massive, AltaVista also provides the alternative of an "advanced search," which lets you designate some words as more important than others, allowing for more complex searches.

First-time users are often overwhelmed by the massive amounts of data available for review. For example, a search for information related to "equity options" on the AltaVista search engine results in more than 300,000 possible matches. Thankfully, most search engines rank the responses in order of the probability of successful hits for your convenience.

In addition, there are various other search engines that can also be very useful. You may want to take a look at the content-based search sites listed in table 11.1, or the text-oriented search engines included in table 11.2 (see page 258).

INVESTMENT RESEARCH INSTITUTE'S WEBSITE

The Investment Research Institute (IRI) Website (http://www. OPTIONS-IRI.com) is designed to provide online investors with previously hard-to-find information about options trading, investment

Exhibit 11.2   **ALTAVISTA HOMEPAGE**

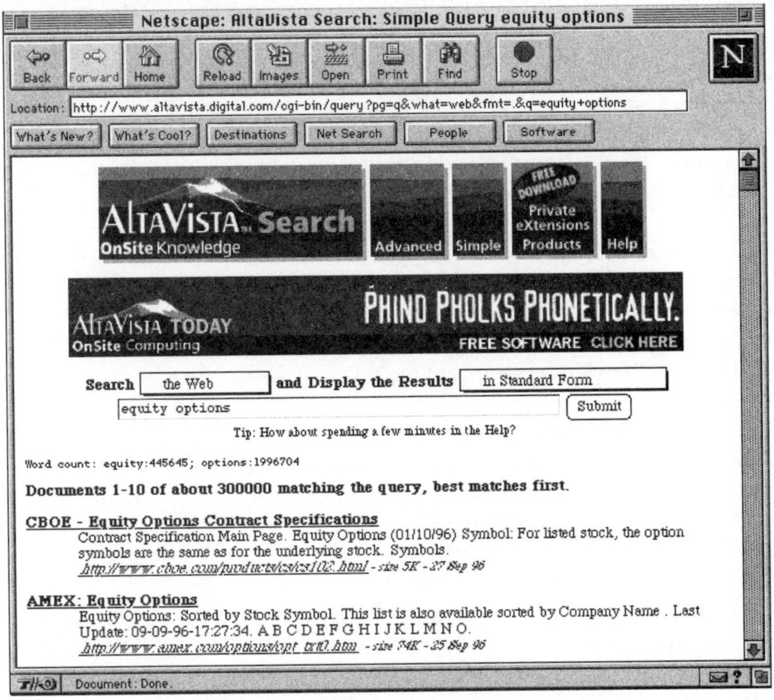

Table 11.1   **CONTENT-BASED SEARCH SITES**

Black Widow
http://www.penetang.com/blackwidow/
Identity
http://www.identity.com
Imagesurfer
http://www.interpix.com
Inference Find
http://www.inference.com/ifind/
Lycos
http://www.lycos.com
Planet Search
http://www.planetsearch.com
Point Search
http://www.pointcom.com/categories/
Yahoo!
http://www.yahoo.com

Table 11.2   TEXT-ORIENTED SEARCH ENGINES

AltaVista
http://www.altavista.com

DejaNews
http://www.dejanews.com
This search engine uses text-oriented searching to archive the Internet USENET news groups. It contains a "Power Search" option that lets users take advantage of Boolean operators such as *and, or, not,* and *near.*

Excite
http://www.excite.com
This search engine is the first to successfully use concept-based searching. When you search on a word such as "paint" it also includes articles on "home improvement." This search engine gives each site a "confidence rating,," ranking the success of the search in terms of the criteria.

Infoseek
http://www.infoseek.com
This search engine provides the convenience of text searching with the added benefit of a relational database. This means that when you type a word such as "cat" you will get articles that include closely related words such as "kitten."

Metacrawler
http://www.metacrawler.com
This site searches lots of search engines simultaneously.

Galaxy Search
http://galaxy.tradewave.com/search.html

HotBot
http://www.hotbot.com

Infoseek
http://www.infoseek.com

OpenText
http://www.opentext.com

Webcrawler
http:/www.webcrawler.com

---

strategies, and market timing. The IRI Website, as shown on exhibit 11.3, contains a daily market summary, including a list of movers and shakers in the high-tech sector, educational articles on options investing, special reports on option strategies, and information about IRI's specialized option services.

IRI's site was one of the first to offer free equity option quotes, and it provides information on intraday bid, ask, last, volume, net change equity option data, and open interest on a daily basis. The IRI Quote Page, as shown on exhibit 11.4, also provides comprehensive

Exhibit 11.3 **INVESTMENT RESEARCH INSTITUTE (IRI) HOMEPAGE**

stock quotes, including such data as open, high, low, previous day's close, 52-week high and low, P/E ratio, bid and ask figures and size, change in dollars, change in percent, volume, volume of the last trade, average volume per trade, and number of common shares. Historical open, high, low, close, and volume figures are also posted. In addition, the IRI Website contains a searchable list of stock ticker symbols and an extensive list of financial links related to investing, and to options investing in particular. The contents of the site are changed and updated frequently. IRI's objective is to create and maintain the best originating point for options investing information.

In addition, a new site devoted exclusively to educating options traders will be operative in August 1997: http://www.bernieschaeffer. com. This interactive site is expected to offer quiz to readers of this book in addition to other information on options strategies.

Exhibit 11.4   **INVESTMENT RESEARCH INSTITUTE (IRI) QUOTE PAGE**

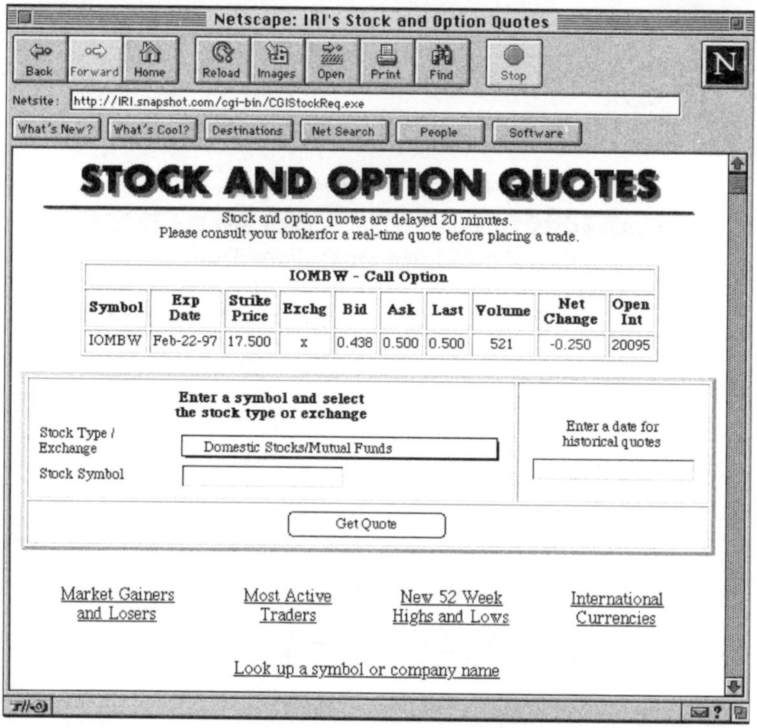

OPTIONS INDUSTRY ORGANIZATIONS ONLINE

The Options Industry Council. The primary goal of the Options Industry Council (OIC) Website (http://www.optionscentral.com), shown in exhibit 11.5, is to educate investors about the versatility of options. The Options Industry Council is the marketing and education arm of a group of exchanges, including the American Stock Exchange (AMEX), Chicago Board Options Exchange (CBOE), Pacific Stock Exchange (PSE), Philadelphia Stock Exchange (PHLX), and the Options Clearing Corporation (OCC).

At the Options Industry Council Website, you can look up free seminar schedules or request a free instructional videotape titled *The Options Tool.* This video comes with the educational guide *Understanding Stock Options* and a copy of *Characteristics and Risks of Stand-*

Exhibit 11.5   **THE OPTIONS INDUSTRY COUNCIL HOMEPAGE**

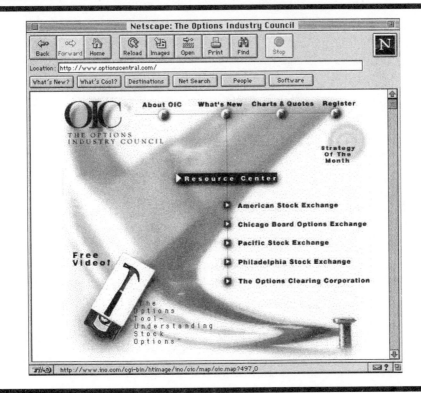

ardized Options. The OIC Website also includes a "Strategy of the Month," an options glossary, and a searchable list of options symbols.

The Options Clearing Corporation. The Options Clearing Corporation (OCC) is the largest clearing organization in the world for financial derivative instruments. OCC issues and clears options on underlying financial assets including common stocks, foreign exchange, stock indexes, U.S. Treasury securities, and interest rate composites. Four participant exchanges share equal ownership of OCC: the American Stock Exchange, the Chicago Board of Options Exchange, the Pacific Stock Exchange, and the Philadelphia Stock Exchange. OCC's clearing membership consists of approximately 150 of the largest U.S. broker dealers and non-U.S. securities firms, which represent both professional traders and public customers.

The Options Clearing Corporation (OCC) Website (http://www. ino.com/occ/), shown in exhibit 11.6, contains the OCC annual report

Exhibit 11.6　**THE OPTIONS CLEARING CORPORATION HOMEPAGE**

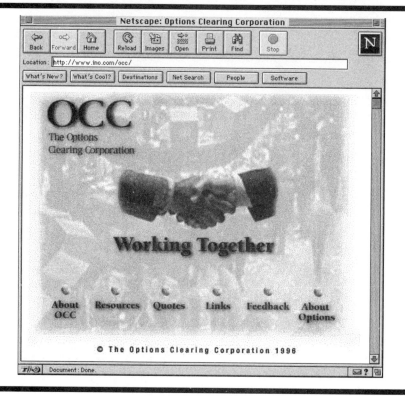

and financial statements, press releases, and information on its clearing members and board of directors. On the OCC Website, you can also find reports and publications on options-related topics, such as LEAPS, taxes and investing, and options market statistics.

The Committee on Options Proposals. Established in 1988, the Committee on Options Proposals (COOP) is an association composed of respected options industry professionals and marketing personnel from forty stock exchange member firms, the four options exchanges, and the Options Clearing Corporation. COOP was formed to improve the environment for trading options as well as to further the investment industry's—and the public's—knowledge of option strategies.

The COOP Website (http://www.coop-options.com), shown in exhibit 11.7, contains the minutes of COOP meetings, letters to the Securities and Exchange Commission, information on the standardization of options, and standardized exchange literature.

Exhibit 11.7   **THE COMMITTEE ON OPTIONS PROPOSALS (COOP)
HOMEPAGE**

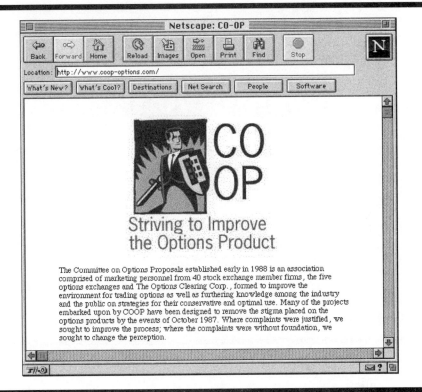

MARKET TECHNICIANS ASSOCIATION

The Market Technicians Association (MTA) is the national organization of technical analysis professionals in the United States. This not-for-profit association has three main goals: (1) encourage the exchange of technician information and collectively explore new frontiers in the area of technical research; (2) educate the public and the investment community about the use, value and limitations of technical research; and (3) uphold a code of ethics and the professional standards among technical analysts. These goals are accomplished through a wide variety of activities and publications and with the voluntary involvement and dedication of many members.

Exhibit 11.8   **MARKET TECHNICIANS ASSOCIATION (MTA) HOMEPAGE**

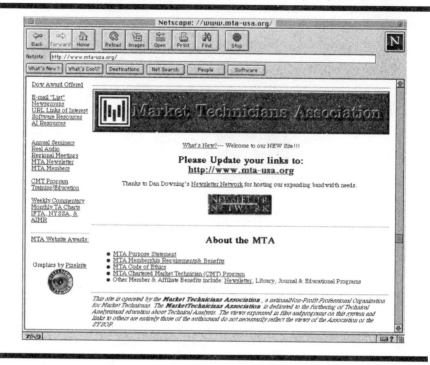

The MTA Website (http://www.mta-usa.org), shown in exhibit 11.8, contains information on MTA's annual four-day seminar, which is held in May. This seminar is devoted to exploring emerging techniques in the field of technical analysis, as well as re-examining changing points of view on more classic styles. The site also contains the minutes of MTA meetings, information on the MTA newsletter, educational efforts, and MTA's library—the world's most comprehensive library devoted to the field of technical analysis.

STOCK EXCHANGES ON THE WEB

There are currently four U.S. stock exchanges that trade options on individual equities: the American Stock Exchange, Chicago Board Options Exchange, Pacific Stock Exchange, and Philadelphia Stock Exchange. Currently, the following exchanges have Websites.

The American Stock Exchange. The American Stock Exchange (AMEX) Website (http://www.amex.com), as previewed in exhibit 11.9, provides a daily market summary of activity on the exchange.

Exhibit 11.9   **AMERICAN STOCK EXCHANGE (AMEX) HOMEPAGE**

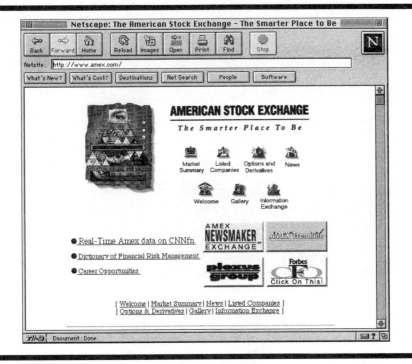

This report includes the day's most active stocks, largest percentage gainers, and largest percentage decliners for companies whose stocks trade on the American Stock Exchange. The report also includes a daily summary of AMEX index and equity option activity, such as option contract volume, dollar volume, advancers and decliners, most active series, and most active classes. The market summary is updated at approximately 6:00 P.M. eastern time each trading day. The AMEX Website also includes the specifications of its international, broad-based, and sector indexes, and a listing of all exchange-listed companies and their ticker symbols. A unique "gallery" section of the Website allows you to see the American Stock Exchange in action through a collection of photos and full-motion video of the trading floor and other sites of interest.

The Chicago Board Options Exchange. The Chicago Board Options Exchange (CBOE) Website (http://www.cboe.com) offers an impressive sphere of investment-related information. The site (exhibit 11.10) contains an extensive options-education section and a broad range of online information resources and tools for quick and direct access to information and assistance. The CBOE online information services in-

Exhibit 11.10   **THE CHICAGO BOARD OPTIONS EXCHANGE (CBOE)
HOMEPAGE**

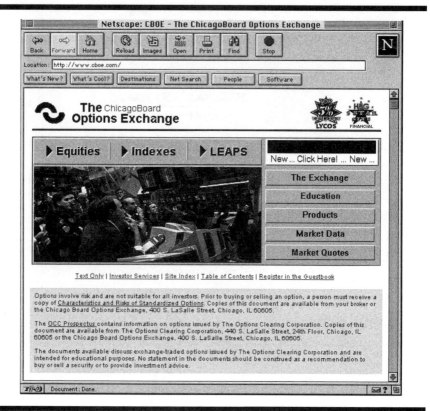

clude an Investor Service FAQ (answers to frequently asked questions) and an options symbol directory. You can contact the exchange's investor service representatives, who can answer options-related questions and requests by e-mail, telephone, fax, or mail. In addition, you can request a free copy of CBOE's educational and informational literature, such as their *Taxes and Investing* booklet, *Understanding Stock Options* booklet, expiration calendar, *Options Tool* video, and *Directory of Exchange Listed Options*.

The CBOE Website is also the home of The Options Institute Website. In April 1985, the CBOE founded The Options Institute to serve the educational needs of the investing community. The focus of The Options Institute is to expand the knowledge and thereby increase the comfort level of options users. The institute provides training on how to manage risk in an increasingly complex marketplace. Classes and seminars for individual investors, retail brokers, institu-

Exhibit 11.11   **PHILADELPHIA STOCK EXCHANGE HOMEPAGE**

tional investors, and federal and state securities regulators are offered on a regular basis and are listed on this Website. The institute also supports the expansion of options knowledge through the development and presentation of seminars for branch managers, brokers, and individual investors in major U.S. cities.

The Philadelphia Stock Exchange. The Philadelphia Stock Exchange (PHLX) Website (http://www.phlx.com), shown in exhibit 11.11, is conveniently divided into six categories: events, exchange information, products, publications, news, and marketplace. The products section contains lists of PHLX equity options and LEAPS, sector index components and contract specifications, and trading examples. You can find information about the PHLX exchange under the exchange section. Upcoming happenings, including the PHLX conference schedule, are listed under the events category. The PHLX also offers information about exchange newsletters under the publications heading.

THE SECURITIES AND EXCHANGE COMMISSION

As time permits, the "do-it-yourself" investor may want to dive into more detailed corporate information. A great place to start is the U.S. Securities and Exchange Commission Website (http://www.sec.com), shown in exhibit 11.12, provides access to the SEC's vast EDGAR database. In addition to the EDGAR data, described below, the commission has also made available numerous investor guides, SEC reports, and other securities-related information—including investor alerts regarding fraudulent investment schemes on and off the Internet.

EDGAR, the Electronic Data Gathering, Analysis, and Retrieval system, performs automated collection, validation, indexing, acceptance, and forwarding of submissions by companies and others who are required by law to file forms with the SEC. EDGAR's primary purpose is to increase the efficiency and fairness of the securities market for the benefit of investors, corporations, and the economy by accelerating the receipt, acceptance, dissemination, and analysis of time-sensitive corporate information filed with the agency, such as prospectus, 10-K, and annual report to shareholder data.

EDGAR listings are posted to this site twenty-four hours after they are filed. Not all documents filed with the SEC by public companies are available on EDGAR. Companies have been phased into EDGAR filing over a three-year period, ending May 6, 1996. It is important to note that not all public domestic companies are required to make their filings available on EDGAR. Some documents are not yet permitted to be filed electronically with the SEC and consequently will not be available on EDGAR.

Other documents may be filed on EDGAR voluntarily, so they may be available electronically. For example, Forms 3, 4, and 5 (security ownership and transaction reports filed by corporate insiders), Form 144 (notice of proposed sale of securities), and Form 13F (reports filed by institutional investment managers showing equity holdings by accounts under their management) may be filed on EDGAR at the discretion of the filer. Similarly, filings by foreign companies are not required to be available on EDGAR, but some of these companies do so voluntarily.

You should be aware that actual annual reports to shareholders (except in the case of investment companies) need not be submitted on EDGAR, although some companies do so voluntarily. However, the annual report on Form 10-K or 10-KSB, which contains much of the same information, *is* required to be filed on EDGAR. The SEC provides search capabilities for both EDGAR and the SEC Website with the results posted in chronological order.

Exhibit 11.12   **SECURITIES AND EXCHANGE COMMISSION (SEC) HOME
                  PAGE**

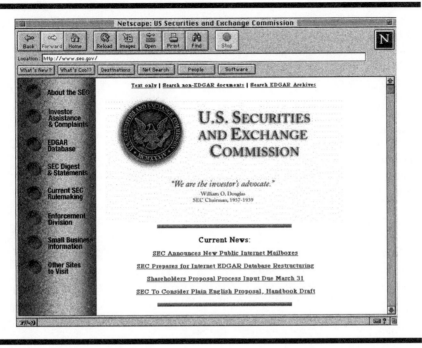

FINANCIAL NEWS SOURCES

With the advent of the modem and online services, publication and distribution costs of news delivery have diminished. Due to this cost reduction, many of the national business wires have taken advantage of the "free" delivery of the World Wide Web in an attempt to gain reader market share. In addition, national and local newspapers are flocking to the Web, posting their articles on a delayed basis. Although many publishers have attempted to set up subscription or "pay as you read" sites, high competition in this industry is forcing them out. Instead, sites that gain their revenue from advertisements are proliferating. The list of financial news sites in table 11.3 is not meant to be exhaustive, but it is a good directory of some of the financial news sites with free content. The sites listed are a great place to start your financial research.

Financial Magazines. With many individual investors using the Internet for investment research, the World Wide Web has become a showcase for financial magazines to exhibit their wares and entice

Table 11.3   **FINANCIAL NEWS HOMEPAGES**

Bloomberg
http://www.bloomberg.com
Businesswire
http://www.businesswire.com
CNBC
http://www.cnbc.com
CNNfn
http://www.cnnfn.com
Financial Times
http://www.ft.com
Investors Business Daily
http://www.investors.com
Nando Times Business Section
http://www2.nando.net/nt/biz/
News Page
http://www.newspage.com
Standard & Poor
http://stockinfo.standardpoor.com
USA Today Money Section
http://www.usatoday.com/money/mfront.htm
Yahoo Business Headlines
http://www.yahoo.com/headlines/business/

visitors into subscribing to their publications. In fact, the periodical section of the Web has become increasingly competitive, and many financial publications give free access to online versions of their publications. Even though these online versions usually don't include all the articles or stories in the printed editions of the magazine, they do contain enough information to make viewing the online magazines worthwhile. In addition to published articles, the online versions will often contain exclusive Web-oriented articles or special reports that are not printed in the newsstand issues. The Web addresses of several well-known financial magazines are listed in table 11.4.

The PointCast Network. The PointCast Network (http://www.pointcast.com) was founded in 1992 to provide current news and information services to users via the Internet. The free news service delivers up-to-the-minute information twenty-four hours a day to your computer screen (see exhibit 11.13, see page 272) to potentially save you the considerable time and effort you would otherwise spend surfing the Internet for news and information. The PointCast Network broadcasts national and international news, stock information, industry updates, weather, sports scores, and more. Sources of information

Table 11.4 **ONLINE MAGAZINE HOMEPAGE LIST**

Advertising Age
  http://www.adage.com
Business Week
  http://www.businessweek.com
Cyber Stocks
  http://www.cyberstocks.com
Economist, The
  http://www.economist.com
Financial World
  http://www.financialworld.com/home.htm
Forbes
  http://www.forbes.com
Futures Magazine Online
  http://www.futuresmag.com
Money Online
  http://pathfinder.com/money/
Money Talks
  http://www.talks.com
Research
  http://www.researchmag.com
Technical Analysis of Stocks and Commodities
  http://www.traders.com

include a variety of publications and services, such as *Time*, *People*, *Money*, Reuters, PR Newswire, BusinessWire, Sportsticker, Accuweather, and CNN.

To use the PointCast Network, you must first download and install the software, available free of charge from the PointCast Network Website. Besides all the news channels, the software package contains an advertisement window that spouts full-motion video advertisements. Essentially, the advertisers pay for the service so users get free access.

With the PointCast Network, you can select general categories of information that you want to receive, including national and international news stories, business and industry updates, current sports scores, and even weather maps and forecasts for cities around the world. Although you must pick and choose from PointCast's topics, the free service lets you personalize the information you download. For example, under the company menu item, you can select up to twenty-five different companies whose stock quotes and news stories you will receive.

Exhibit 11.13   **POINTCAST NETWORK SCREEN**

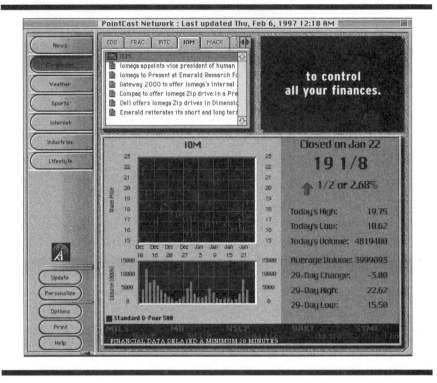

CONCLUSION

With the speed at which financial sites are sprouting up on the Web, it would be impossible to publish a conclusive list of such sites without it being somewhat outdated by publication time. Moreover, if you were to attempt to compile such a list, the result would be a rather thick book, not a single chapter. Use this chapter as a starting point for exploring the Internet and finding the sites that are most beneficial to your own investment strategy. "Knowledge is money" truly applies to the investment world, so dive in and take advantage of the wealth of knowledge available on the Internet.

12

Contrarianism Revisited

MISCONCEPTIONS ABOUT CONTRARIANISM

By now it must be clear to you that I attach great importance to "expectational analysis" as a key factor for success in trading. If you maintain a good understanding of the expectations underlying the market, as well as of individual stocks, you will develop an important trading edge, and such "edges" are what add up to profitable results. Much of my expectational analysis is rooted in traditional "contrarian" theory.

But is everyone a contrarian these days? It sure seems that way from a regular reading of the financial press. Along these lines, the question is whether the "proliferation" of the contrarian philosophy will endanger the accuracy of expectational-based forecasts as contrarianism becomes more and more mainstream or conventional.

It is certainly a credit to the power of the contrarian philosophy that so many seem to be in such a rush to label themselves as contrarians. Clearly, those who remained bullish on the stock market throughout the course of the bull market from 1994 to 1996 were of a contrarian bent, as conventional analysts fought this huge rally every step of the way with their talk of "overvaluation" and "mutual fund manias." As a result, a certain grudging admiration for contrarians has ensued. And who would not prefer to be labeled as someone who stands out from the crowd as opposed to one of the sheep who follow crowd thinking in their investment approach?

Unfortunately for these newcomers (and fortunately for those of us who rigorously apply the contrarian philosophy), the proper application of contrarian theory requires far more than simply labeling oneself a contrarian. And the vast majority of those who call themselves contrarians or on whom the media confers this label would not pass the "Humphrey Neill" test.

As stated in the preface, Humphrey Neill's *The Art of Contrary Thinking* is the classic work on contrarianism. I highly recommend it to you, as it explains the contrarian philosophy in clear, concise terms and provides some fascinating stock market history in the process. Neill defines contrarianism as simply "a way of thinking," and he goes on to explain very clearly in his book how a contrarian should think when analyzing the market.

The discussion of the major misconceptions about contrarianism that follows will also help clarify some of Neill's key principles.

Contrarianism and Conventional Thinking

A "contrarian" is *not* someone who follows conventional thinking, is proven wrong by the market, and then stubbornly clings to his opinion in the face of additional losses. There are many proper choices for labeling such an individual (including some that are inappropriate for a "family" investment book), but "contrarian" is not one of them. Yet the financial press regularly applies the contrarian moniker in such situations, particularly when this individual is "highly respected."

In early 1996, conventional wisdom was that bonds were a superior investment to stocks, as economic growth was sure to slow down. In fact, the chief strategist for a very large brokerage firm was advising investors to go easy on their stock exposure and to "back up the truck" and load up on bonds. A similar view was held by a highly respected manager of a very large portfolio of bonds, who is regularly quoted in the media on the fixed income markets. Several months into 1996, after the bond market began to tank on reports of a stronger-than-expected economy, this bond manager was interviewed in a financial daily. And the newspaper reported that he was sticking to his "contrarian view" on bonds despite the weakness in this market. The moral is that being "long and wrong" based on conventional thinking and then "sticking to your guns" is *not* an act of contrarianism (and is often an act of investment suicide).

Contrarianism and Value Investing

A contrarian is not a "value investor in drag." Value investors specialize in buying beaten-down stocks that they perceive as cheap, in the hopes that these stocks will ultimately prove to be profitable bargains. But as discussed in earlier chapters, cheap stocks can always become cheaper. The key to a successful contrarian approach is to buy low *expectations*, not low *prices*. In fact, high expectations often accompany prices that are considered cheap, and low expectations often accompany prices that many would consider to be expensive.

For example, as we entered 1996, the securities brokerage sector, as measured by the AMEX Securities Broker/Dealer Index (XBD), was trading near its all-time highs. But expectations for this sector were quite low, as the conventional wisdom held that the bull market in stocks was on its last legs and that the brokerage business was still cyclical. I was extremely bullish on this sector for its strong fundamentals and technicals combined with these low expectations. In fact, I recommended a 100 percent invested position in the Fidelity Select Brokerage Fund for the entire second half of 1996, and this fund posted a 19.8 percent gain over this period.

Contrarianism as the Opposite of Trend Following

A contrarian is not an anti–trend follower. A common view is that contrarians are "cantankerous curmudgeons" who automatically adopt the opposite viewpoint from that of the consensus. But this is *not* my conception of a proper contrarian approach, nor is it that of Humphrey Neill. Mindless contrarianism is just as dangerous as mindless trend following (the latter expression may be an oxymoron). The mindless trend follower always gets badly hurt at tops, as he is most likely to be fully invested at those points. And the mindless contrarian puts himself in the untenable position of trying to call tops and bottoms and "getting in the way of the freight train" on stocks whose price trends continue despite the strong affirming beliefs of the crowd.

As Neill has stated, the crowd is "right during the trends but wrong at both ends."[1] And if you always go against the crowd, you will get bloodied during the trends. Contrarianism is a synthesis of the general crowd opinion (the "prevailing thesis" according to Neill) and the contrary opinion ("antithesis") to develop the conclusion at which the contrarian arrives ("the synthesis of the common and opposing viewpoints"). In other words, through a regular thought process the true contrarian allows for the fact that the crowd is sometimes partially or even totally right. As Neill correctly had stated: "If you don't think things through, then you're through thinking."[2]

---

1. Humphrey B. Neill, *The Art of Contrary Thinking* (Caldwell, Idaho: Caxton Printers, 1985), 44.

2. Ibid., 9.

OPTIONS-BASED INDICATORS

Just as there has been a proliferation of those referring to themselves as contrarians, there has also been a significant expansion in the number of analysts who profess to be using options-based data after to develop contrarian conclusions.

Unfortunately, the wise adage "a little knowledge is a dangerous thing" is particularly relevant to the investment world, and an abundance of poorly constructed options data and poorly formulated contrarian conclusions based upon options data now abounds.

Options Volume as an Indicator

Many analysts use options volume or changes in options volume as an indicator for the direction of the underlying stock. It is not difficult to understand why using options volume is so popular, as it is a very simple statistic and it is readily available from quote terminals or from the national business newspapers. The theory often is that big increases in, say, call volume may signal "smart money" activity that precedes a major rally in the underlying stock, often as a result of an actual or anticipated takeover or a favorable corporate earnings report.

The problems with using options volume as a directional indicator are threefold:

1. The money that is creating the volume is more apt to be "clueless" than "smart."

2. You have no idea whether such volume is the result of new positions being accumulated or old positions being liquidated, or is simply the result of day-trading activity. And it is only the volume that results in new positions being accumulated that should be of interest to you.

3. Volume on equity options is often freely mixed with volume on index options. This creates a database that is not homogeneous, as there generally is far more put activity relative to call activity in the index options.

This is not to say that options volume figures are useless as directional indicators. For individual stocks, they provide an important initial "flag," which should then spur a more detailed investigation. And for stock indices such as the OEX and for the universe of all equity options combined, extremes in put or call volume as measured by the put/call ratio have often been very accurate as contrary indicators for calling short and intermediate-term market tops and bottoms because of the general "cluelessness" of options traders as a group (see chapter 5). But note that equity options volume is almost always far better contrarian indicators than index options volume, as a much greater proportion of index options volume results from the activity of professionals whose actions should not be viewed as contrary indicators.

Changes in Implied Volatility as an Indicator

By tracking trends in the implied volatility of the options on individual stocks, one can often pinpoint significant turning points in a stock, which may either be confirmed by trends in volume and open interest or may actually show up before appearing on the volume and open interest "radar screens." One indicator, discussed in chapters 2 and 5, is that of volatility spikes, where the implied volatility takes a big pop to the upside on a decline in the underlying stock. This is often a solid indication that the stock decline has been climactic, as options traders bid up the price of put options dramatically as their fear reaches extreme levels. But you must be careful in reaching a contrarian conclusion in such situations, because if the implied volatility spike is not accompanied by any significant volume, then it is likely that the trading floor is responsible for this volatility pop, and, needless to say, the trading floor is "smart" much more often than it is "clueless."

You can also compare the implied volatility on out-of-the-money calls versus out-of-the-money puts to see if there are any major disparities (see chapter 9). If such disparities exist, this is telling you that the prevailing belief in the options market is that this stock has a much greater chance of moving strongly in one particular direction. Again, the key is whether to interpret this pricing disparity in a contrarian fashion or to "go with the flow," and this is often dictated by the volume flows or, more important, by the trends in open interest.

Option Open Interest as an Indicator

Open interest is by far the most accurate indicator of options trading activity, and changes in open interest are by far the best option-based statistic on which to draw contrarian conclusions. Changes in open interest can tell you whether options volume is translating into overnight positions, and you must know this in order to be able to reach any conclusions about the directional implications of heavy options volume. For example, if you know that 10,000 Microsoft calls traded yesterday and only 1,000 puts traded, you could reach the surface conclusion that option traders are much more interested in accumulating Microsoft calls than Microsoft puts. But it is most certainly possible that the 10,000 Microsoft calls that traded resulted in a net decrease in call open interest, as traders were liquidating existing positions, which gives you a completely different perspective on this activity.

Furthermore, an analysis of overall volume tells you nothing about the activity at the various striking prices. Even if volume is translating into increases in open interest, you would want to know the strikes at which this is heaviest. Why? Because you need to know whether to interpret this activity in a contrarian fashion or whether to go with the options flow. For example, if call volume was heaviest in the front-month, out-of-the-money options, and this translated into big increases in open interest, you would tend to interpret this volume in a contrary manner, as these are the options most favored by "clueless" speculators. On the other hand, if the big open interest increases were in the longer-term options that were on-the-money or in-the-money, you would not want to be a contrarian, as these options are most favored by the professionals and institutions.

THE OUTLOOK FOR EQUITY AND INDEX OPTIONS

The future for equity and index options is very bright for four reasons:

1. Investors are becoming more knowledgeable and sophisticated, and as such they are increasingly more interested in utilizing options in their investment program for the potential to reduce risk and enhance returns.

2. The availability of quality information about equity and index options is expanding dramatically. The Options Industry Council (OIC), an educational organization sponsored by major brokerage firms and the options exchanges, has made information about options available to hundreds of thousands of investors through the medium of videotapes as well as literature. Brokerage firms are beginning to realize that options investors are among their most desirable clients in terms of their sophistication and the size of their overall investment portfolios, and these firms are thus catering more and more to the needs of the options investor. And the Internet is vastly expanding the information base on options (see chapter 11) and effectively reaching even younger and more highly educated investors. Finally, there are organizations, such as Investment Research Institute, that are dedicated to providing investors with the information and recommendations they need to maximize the rewards of options trading.

3. The options industry has become even more investor-friendly, and this trend should accelerate in the future. In the preface, I discussed how the advent of options exchanges twenty or so years ago had transformed a product that previously had been considered arcane and exotic into a mainstream tool for individual investors. In the 1980s, the industry introduced options on indices, and in 1990 the concept of long-term options via "LEAPS" was initiated. The latter resulted in options that were more "stock-like" and thus easier for beginning options investors to approach, whereas options on indices allowed investors to adopt options-trading approaches to industry sectors or to the overall market. In the 1990s, the concept of multiply-listed options was introduced, whereby the same option series traded on several competing exchanges. Although there were some operational hurdles associated with introducing the multiply listed concept, the net result has been significantly better order fills for individual investors. Much of the options industry's progress in the area of investor "friendliness" can be credited to the fine work of the Committee on Options Proposals, an industry committee that has dedicated itself to improving the options product under the outstanding leadership of Michael Schwartz. My "wish list" for future progress in these areas includes the expansion of the number of option series that are multiply listed, and the display on quote terminals of "size of market" for options just as it is displayed for exchange-listed and NASDAQ national market stocks.

4. At the risk of being flip, I must mention the fact that *options trading is fun.* It may not be fun for everyone, and it is certainly not fun for those who trade without a solid foundation of knowledge, but most investors find the world of options to be a never-ending source of fascination, new ideas, and, yes, just plain fun. But ultimately it must never be forgotten that failure is not fun, and in order to ultimately succeed in your options trading you must apply the kind of discipline and focus that has been emphasized throughout this book.

Appendix A

Options: Basic Concepts

At-the-Money. At-the-money is a put or call option whose striking price is equal to the current market price of the underlying security.

Call Options. A call option is a contract in which the buyer has the right, but not the obligation, to purchase an underlying security at a specified price on or before a given date. As a purchaser of a call option, the holder believes the stock value will move higher prior to the expiration date of the option.

Expiration Cycles. Every security's options are assigned to one of three expiration cycles: January, February, or March sequential cycles. A January cycle means a stock's options can be listed in January, April, July, and October. A February cycle means a stock's options can be listed in February, May, August, and November. And a March cycle means a stock's options can be listed in March, June, September, and December. At any point in time, an option will have contracts with four different expiration months outstanding (this does not include longer-term options). For example, after the third Friday in January, options will have two near-term expirations (an expiration date within two months) and two further-term expirations (three to eight months out). The further-term expiration months available depend on which sequential cycle (January, February, or March) the underlying stock follows, which is predetermined by the options exchanges. Sequential cycle expirations give the options investor choices based on time and liquidity, since cycle months tend to be the most active.

Expiration Date. Every option has an expiration date. The expirations for stock options officially occur on the Saturday following the third Friday of the expiration month. For example, if an investor holds a June option, that option will cease trading after the options market closes on the third Friday in June. Not all equity options will have the same expiration months available at their offering, but options on each underlying security trade in one of three expiration cycles.

In-the-Money. In-the-money call options have a striking price that is lower than the market price of the shares, whereas in-the-money put options have a market price of the underlying security that is less than the striking price of the option.

Intrinsic Value. The difference between an in-the-money option strike price and the current market price of a share of the underlying security is the option's *intrinsic value*. For a call option at a 95 strike with a stock price of 100, the option has an intrinsic value of 5 (market price less strike price).

Option. An option is a contract that gives its holder the right, but not the obligation, to buy or sell shares of an underlying security at a predetermined price on or before a given date. There are two types of contracts available: call options and put options. In the case of equity options, a single contract represents an option to buy or sell 100 shares of the underlying stock. For index options, a single option contract represents the right to buy or sell 100 units of the underlying index. If the option holder decides to convert this right and actually buy or sell the 100 shares, or obtain cash settlement in the case of index options, he exercises his option.

Options Quotes. The options quotes on major underlying stocks and indices can be found in the business sections of many newspapers. Although the format of the options quote section will vary across different newspapers, the sections generally contain the components shown in exhibit A.1 and elaborated below.

    A. *The Name of the Company.* In this example, the underlying security is Iomega Corporation. Newspapers will often abbreviate the company name. For example, Compaq Computer, Inc. is abbreviated "Compaq" in the *Wall Street Journal* and is abbreviated "CompaqCmp" in *Investor's Business Daily*. Because of the large number of stocks that have options (currently more than 2,100), newspapers will list only the most actively traded options. If you are interested in quotes of a less frequently traded option, call your broker. Many brokerage firms have automated quote hotlines. You can also check several Web sites that have unlimited free option quotes (as discussed in chapter 10).

    B. *The Closing Price of the Underlying Stock.* The closing price is the price at which the underlying stock traded at the last transaction of the day on the New York Stock Exchange. Newspapers list this quote in several different ways. Some will include this quote with every option listed, and some will

Exhibit A.1

A/B	C	D	E	F	G	H
Option	Strike	Exp.	Vol.	Last	Vol.	Last
Iomega	5	Aug.	25	22⅝	100	¹⁄₁₆
27½	10	Aug.	31	17⅜	65	³⁄₁₆
27½	10	Nov.	50	17⅝	130	¾
27½	12½	Aug.	139	13	16	⁷⁄₁₆
27½	12½	Nov.	40	14¼	54	1³⁄₁₆
27½	15	Aug.	1966	13⅜	260	¹³⁄₁₆
27½	15	Nov.	160	13⅛	161	2
27½	17½	Aug.	22	11½	427	1³⁄₁₆
27½	17½	Nov.	19	12	84	2⅞
27½	20	Jul.	1134	8⅝	3699	⅞
27½	20	Aug.	544	9¾	472	1⅞
27½	20	Nov.	160	11¼	93	3⅞
27½	20	Feb.	42	12⅞	2	4¾

A. Name of the company
B. Closing price of underlying stock
C. Striking price of the option
D. Month the option expires
E. Volume traded on the call
F. Last price at which call traded
G. Volume traded on the put
H. Last price at which put traded

quote it only once—usually in the company heading and after the description "close."

C. *The Striking Price of the Option.* The striking price is the price per share at which the holder of an option can purchase (in the case of a call option) or sell (in the case of a put option) the underlying stock upon exercise. To conserve space, many newspapers will only list a portion of a stock's options. Some newspapers list the most active strike prices and some list the strike prices nearest the current price of the stock.

D. *The Month the Option Expires.* This is the last month that the option can trade. Listed options cease trading as of the close on the third Friday of each month. Most newspapers will list quotes on the nearest two months, and some newspapers list quotes on the nearest three months. It is important to note that the third month may not be consecutive because the schedule of listed options varies among underlying stocks due to different expiration cycles. Furthermore, there may be months that do not contain certain striking prices.

E/G. *The Volume Traded on the Call/Put Option.*   The volume of the call/put option is the number of contracts that traded during the previous day. Newspapers will list prices and volume on both call and put options (a call option will be designated with a "c" or "call" header, a put option with a "p" or "put" header). It is possible that no contracts were traded during the previous day, which will often be designated by dashes, hyphens, periods, or "no tr" (meaning "no trade").

F/H. *The Last Price at Which the Call/Put Traded.*   This is the price at which the call/put option traded during the last transaction of the day. If no contracts were traded, this spot will be filled with hyphens, dashes, periods, or "no tr."

Options Symbols and Codes.   All options have stock ticker symbols. Options symbols contain the following components: the stock ticker symbol, the expiration month code, and the striking/exercise price code. Each of these components is explained below.

The *stock ticker symbol* is merely a set of letters an exchange uses to represent the underlying stock. For NASDAQ stocks with more than three letters in the stock code, the option ticker symbol will be shortened to three letters, usually ending in Q. For example, Microsoft's stock symbol is MSFT, so its option ticker symbol is MSQ.

Each *expiration month* has a separate code for both calls and puts (see table A.1). In addition, each *striking price* has a separate code, which is identical for calls and puts (see table A.2). In an option listing, the ticker symbol leads, followed by the expiration month code, and then the striking price code. For example, the Microsoft January 90 call would have the code MSQAR, and the Microsoft January 90 put would have the code MSQMR.

Out-of-the-Money.   A call option is considered out-of-the-money when the striking price is greater than the market price of the underlying security. A put option is considered out-of-the-money when the market price of the underlying security is greater than the striking *price* of the option. Out-of-the-money calls and puts have *no* intrinsic value, only time value. You need to know if the option you are buying is at-the-money, in-the-money, or out-of-the-money, because this affects the pricing of your option, the potential returns on the investment, and the odds of a successful trade.

Premium.   Options buyers must pay a certain price to have the right to buy an option, whereas options sellers must receive compensation

Table A.1	**EXPIRATION MONTH CODES**

Month	Call Code
January	A
February	B
March	C
April	D
May	E
June	F
July	G
August	H
September	I
October	J
November	K
December	L

Month	Put Code
January	M
February	N
March	O
April	P
May	Q
June	R
July	S
August	T
September	U
October	V
November	W
December	X

Table A.2	**STRIKING PRICE CODES**	

Code	Striking Prices	
A	5	105
B	10	110
C	15	115
D	20	120
E	25	125
F	30	130
G	35	135
H	40	140
I	45	145
J	50	150
K	55	l55
L	60	160
M	65	165
N	70	170
O	75	175
P	80	180
Q	85	185
R	90	190
S	95	195
T	100	200
U	$7\frac{1}{2}$	$37\frac{1}{2}$
V	$12\frac{1}{2}$	$42\frac{1}{2}$
W	$17\frac{1}{2}$	$47\frac{1}{2}$
X	$22\frac{1}{2}$	$52\frac{1}{2}$
Y	$27\frac{1}{2}$	$57\frac{1}{2}$
Z	$32\frac{1}{2}$	$62\frac{1}{2}$

for selling this right to an options buyer. This price is called the option premium. The option premium is exchanged from the option buyer to the option seller (also called the writer). In return, the writer of a call option is obligated to sell the underlying security (at the strike price per share) to the option buyer if the call is exercised. The same is true for a writer of a put, who is obligated to buy the underlying security from the put option buyer at the strike price if the put is exercised. Option premiums are quoted on a per contract basis. Thus, an option premium of ¾ amounts to $75.00 per option contract ($0.75 × 100 shares per contract).

Put Options. A put option is a contract giving the buyer the right, but not the obligation, to sell an underlying security at a specified price on or before a given date. As a purchaser of a put option, the buyer expects the stock will move lower prior to the expiration date of the option.

Striking Price. All equity options have a specified price at which a stock can be bought or sold if the option is exercised. This is called the striking price, or exercise price. A holder of a call (or put) option can exercise the right to buy (or sell) 100 shares of a particular underlying stock at this specified strike price. Instead of exercising the option contract and buying or selling 100 shares of stock, the holder will usually seek to exit the option position on the options exchange before the expiration date.

Styles of Options. In the United States, there are two styles of exercise available for options: *American* and *European.* An *American contract* may be exercised at any time prior to expiration. Equity options are American style. A *European contract* is exercisable only on the expiration date, also known as the settlement date. For example, options on the Standard & Poor's 500 Index (SPX) are European style, whereas options on the S&P 100 Index (OEX) are American style.

Underlying Security. Options are a derivative instrument whose value is "derived" from the performance of an underlying security. The two most popular securities underlying options are stocks and indexes, but these are not the only types of securities to have options. Commodity futures, foreign currencies, and government debt securities also have options traded on them.

Appendix B

Glossary of Important Options Trading Terms

All or none. An order that must be completely filled or not at all filled.

Asked price. *See* **offering price**.

At-the-market order (also **market order**). An order to purchase or to sell at the best available price. At-the-market orders must be executed immediately, and therefore take precedence over all other orders. Market orders to buy tend to be executed at the asked price, and market orders to sell tend to be executed at the bid price.

At-the-money (also **on-the-money**). An option for which the underlying stock sells at the same price as the exercise price of the option.

Bearish. An outlook anticipating lower prices in the underlying security.

Bearish spread. An option spread designed to be profitable if the underlying security declines in price. A bearish debit spread involves purchasing a put and writing a further out-of-the-money put. A bearish credit spread involves writing a call and buying a further out-of-the-money call.

Bid price. The highest price any potential buyer is willing to pay for a particular option.

Bid/asked quotation. The latest available bid and asked prices for a particular option contract.

Bid/asked spread. The difference in price between the latest available bid and asked quotations for a particular option contract.

Bullish. An outlook anticipating higher prices in the underlying security.

Bullish spread.   An option spread designed to be profitable if the underlying security rises in price. A bullish debit spread consists of purchasing a call and writing a further out-of-the money call. A bullish credit spread involves writing a put and buying a further out-of-the-money put. See also **option spread**.

Calendar spread (also **time spread**).   An option spread consisting of the purchase and the simultaneous sale of options with different expiration dates, on the same security. The purpose of a calendar spread is to profit from the accelerated loss in time value of the shorter-term option that is written, relative to the option that is purchased. Calendar spreading is often a neutral strategy, but it can also be bullish or bearish, depending on the options involved. See also **option spread**.

Call.   An option contract that entitles the holder to buy a number of shares (usually 100) of the underlying common stock at a stated price (see **striking price**) on or before a fixed expiration date.

Called away.   The process whereby a call option writer is obligated to surrender the underlying stock to the option buyer at a price equal to the striking price of the call written.

Cash settlement option.   An option through which exercise is accomplished by a payment in cash, rather than by the delivery of the underlying security. The amount of cash settlement is determined by the difference between the option striking price and the price of the underlying security. Stock index and industry group options are cash settlement options.

Class of options.   A group of puts or a group of calls on the same security.

Closeout date.   The date by which an options trader decides to close a position if it has not achieved its profit objectives. Using such "time stops" is a key component of *The Option Advisor's* overall strategy of risk/reward management.

Closing price.   The price of a stock (or option) at the last transaction of the day.

Closing purchase.   A transaction in which an investor who had initially sold an option intends to liquidate his written position by buying, in a closing purchase transaction, an option having the same terms as the option he wrote.

Closing sale.   A transaction in which an investor who had initially bought an option intends to liquidate his purchased position by selling, in a closing sale transaction, an option having the same terms as the option he purchased.

Contract. A call or put issued by The Options Clearing Corporation.

Covered call writing. A form of option writing in which the writer owns a quantity of the underlying security equivalent to the number of shares represented by the option contracts written. A covered call position is less risky than an outright long stock position and is equivalent in its profit/loss profile to selling naked puts.

Credit spread. A strategy by which the investor collects a credit upon initiating a spread. Bullish credit spreads typically involve selling an out-of-the-money put and buying a farther out-of-the-money put for protection. Bearish credit spreads use out-of-the-money calls in a similar manner.

Day order. A limit order entered through a broker that, if not executed on the day it is entered, is automatically canceled at the close of business on that day.

Debit spread. Investors can buy a call (put) and sell a farther out-of-the-money call (put) to create a spread at an initial debit in the investor's account. This more conservative approach limits both the dollar risk and reward relative to a straight option purchase.

Deep discount broker. A broker offering stripped-down services in exchange for very low commission rates.

Delta (also **neutral hedge ratio**). The percentage of the price movement in the underlying stock that will be translated into price movement in a particular option series. For example, a delta of 50 percent indicates that the option will move up (down) by ½ point for each 1 point rise (decline) in the underlying stock. Call options have positive delta; put options have negative delta. Deltas increase as the stock price rises and decrease as the stock price declines. The delta is also an approximation of the probability that an option will finish in-the-money.

Discount broker. A broker whose commission rates are lower than the norm. Discount brokers usually provide little in additional services such as investment research and/or advice.

Diversification. An investing or trading strategy in which positions are maintained in a variety of underlying stocks or stock options for the purpose of reducing risk and increasing bottom-line profits.

Execution. The actual completion of a buy or sell order on the exchange floor.

Exercise. The procedure whereby the holder of an option notifies The Options Clearing Corporation (through the holder's broker) that he wishes to purchase the underlying stock (in the case of a call) or deliver the underlying stock (in the case of a put) at the exercise price.

Exercise price. *See* **striking price**.

Expectational analysis. An investment analysis approach that takes into account and measures the beliefs of the investors and speculators relative to the prevailing technical trends and fundamental facts, in order to best gauge the future direction of stock prices.

Expiration day or **date** (also **maturity date**). The last day on which the option may be exercised. Listed options cease trading on the third Friday of each month. They expire the next day.

Forward price. The price at which a security is expected to be trading at a defined point in the future, as a function of the expected interest rate environment during that time period.

Free market price. The price established by buyers and sellers in the free market, with no restrictions placed on market participants. This price is a function of the level of demand versus the level of supply in the market at any time.

Full fungibility. A right of options ownership in which an options buyer is free to sell his contract at any time on an options exchange, up to and including its expiration date.

Full-service broker. A broker who provides investment research, information, and advice, as well as the services involved in purchasing and selling securities. Full-sevice brokers usually charge the highest commission rates.

Fundamental analysis. An assessment of a security's valuation, based on the underlying asset values and earnings trends of the firm; usually measured as a function of the current share price, such as price/earnings ratio, price/book value, price/replacement value, and so forth.

Gamma. The unit change in the delta of an option for each $1 change in the price of the underlying stock or index. For example, assume stock XYZ is at 60, and its 55-strike call option has a gamma of 0.05 and a delta of 75. If the stock moves to 61, the new delta will be 80, for an increase of "5 deltas."

Good-till-canceled order. A limit order entered through a broker that remains on the books of the exchange trading floor until executed or until canceled by the originator of the order (abbreviated GTC).

Implied volatility. The assumption of the stock's volatility that helps determine the options price. Since all other factors in the options pricing model are assumed to be known, the implied volatility is calculated last as a plug factor after other options pricing components are computed.

Index option. An option whose underlying security is a stock index. This includes options on the overall market (such as the S&P 100 Index options) as well as options on narrower-based industry groups. Index options are cash settlement options.

Internet. An electronic means by which individuals can find virtually any information they desire, including information on stocks and options, via the World Wide Web.

Internet broker. A broker offering on-line trading over the World Wide Web. Commission rates are typically very competitive, in line with deep discount brokers.

In-the-money. An option with intrinsic value. A call is in-the-money when the market price of the underlying stock is greater than the option's exercise price. A put is in-the-money when the market price of the underlying stock is lower than the option's exercise price.

Intrinsic value. The difference between an in-the-money option strike price and the current market price of a share of the underlying security.

Last sale price. The price of a stock or option at the most recent transaction consummated.

LEAPS. An acronym for Long-term Equity AnticiPation Securities. LEAPS are put or call options with expiration dates set as far as two and one-half years in the future. Like standard options, each LEAPS contract represents 100 shares of the underlying stock.

Limit order. An order to purchase at or below (or to sell at or above) a specified price (the limit price). Limit orders can be immediately executed only when the limit price is consistent with the bid/asked quotation at any point subsequent to entering the order. Limit orders can be either good-till-canceled or day orders.

Limited risk. An investment in which the possible loss cannot exceed a predetermined amount. For option purchases, this amount is the initial cash outlay plus commissions.

Liquid or **liquidity**. The ease with which a purchase or sale can be made without disrupting existing market prices.

Listed options. Options traded on one or more of the option exchanges. Unlike over-the-counter or unlisted options, which must be exercised to have any value, listed options are fully fungible and have an active secondary market on the options exchanges. Most traders in listed options close their positions in this secondary market prior to exercise.

Longer-term option. An option contract having more than a few months until expiration. The longest-term options are known as LEAPS, which usually have one to two and one-half years until expiration.

Market maker. Those who maintain the best bid and asked prices on the option floors of the Chicago Board Options Exchange and the Pacific Stock Exchange. Market makers can compete with each other on the same underlying security's option pricing to provide the best bid and asked prices at any time.

Market order. *See* **at-the-market order**.

Maturity date. *See* **expiration day** or **date**.

Money management principles. The principles involved in creating a plan to manage losses as well as gains, to withstand market fluctuations.

Multiply listed options. Options on the same underlying security traded on more than one options exchange.

Naked writing. A form of option writing in which (using puts as an example) the writer owns neither the underlying security nor a different option on that same security with the same (or later) expiration date and higher striking price. Naked put writing is equivalent in its profit/loss profile to **covered writing** for calls.

Neutral hedge ratio. *See* **delta**.

Neutral spread. An option spread created to profit from little net price movement of the underlying stock in either direction. Neutral spreads are most often calendar spreads. *See also* **option spread, calendar spread**.

Offering price (also **asked price**). The lowest price any potential seller is willing to accept for a particular option.

On-the-money. *See* **at-the-money**.

Open interest. The number of outstanding options contracts in the exchange market in a particular options class or series.

Opening price. The price of a stock or option at the first transaction of the day.

Opening purchase. A transaction in which an investor becomes the holder of an option.

Opening sale. A transaction in which an investor becomes the writer of an option.

Opportunity cost. A factor in the pricing of an option, as a function of the prevailing level of interest rates.

Option. A contract that entitles the holder to buy or sell a number of shares (usually 100) of a particular common stock at a predetermined price (*see* **striking price**) on or before a fixed expiration date.

Option spread. A position that results from the purchase of an option and the simultaneous sale (or write) of a different option on the same security. *See also* **bullish spread, bearish spread, credit spread, debit spread, neutral spread**.

Options Clearing Corporation, The. The issuer of all options contracts traded on the American Stock Exchange, Chicago Board Options Exchange, Pacific Stock Exchange, and Philadelphia Stock Exchange.

Options exchange. Any or all of the following markets where options contracts are traded: American Stock Exchange, Chicago Board Options Exchange, Pacific Stock Exchange, Philadelphia Stock Exchange.

Options pricing model. The conventional method to assess options prices is the options pricing model. This model incorporates six factors into its pricing assumptions: the underlying security price, the striking price, the time until expiration, any dividends to be paid, the level of interest rates, and the volatility of the stock. This model assumes that stock price movement is random with no directional bias except for a slight upward bias related to carrying costs.

Options-specialized broker. A broker that focuses on options trading and options strategies. Often such firms will have one or more Registered Options Principals on staff. Provides in-depth services related to assessing different options strategies.

Options writing. The result of selling options in an opening transaction. *See also* **covered writing, naked writing**.

Order. An instruction to purchase or sell an option, first transmitted to a brokerage office, and then submitted to the exchange floor for execution.

Oscillators. Indicators of the movement of a stock's price relative to an assumed cycle of highs and lows.

Out-of-the-money. An option with no intrinsic value. A call is out-of-the-money when the exercise price is higher than the market price of the underlying stock. A put is out-of-the-money when the exercise price is lower than the market price of the underlying stock. The entire premium of an out-of-the-money option is due to its time value.

Overbought/oversold. A condition in which a stock has reached the top of its cycle (overbought) and is now likely to turn down, or has declined to the point where the selling is over (oversold) and buyers will likely step in and push the stock higher.

Position. Established when an investor makes an opening purchase or sale of an option, or establishes an option spread.

Premium. The price paid by a buyer to the seller of an option. It is quoted on a per-share basis. The premium will usually exceed the intrinsic value of the option because of its time value.

Put. An options contract that entitles the holder to sell a number of shares (usually 100) of the underlying common stock at a stated price (*see* **striking price**) on or before a fixed expiration date.

Registered Options Principal. A broker who has passed the NASD Series 4 exam, proving in-depth knowledge related to options.

Return if called. The percentage gain that a covered writer would achieve if the underlying stock is called away (*see* **called away**). The components of this return are the original option premium plus any dividends plus any appreciation to the striking price. This is the maximum return achievable by a covered writer (*see* **covered writing**).

Risk/reward management. The complete trading approach developed by *The Option Advisor*. It results in risk being reduced and reward (or profits) being increased, thereby maximizing the target risk/reward ratio.

Rolling out. Substituting a call option of the same class and striking price, but with a later expiration.

Rolling up. Substituting a call option of the same class and expiration, but with a higher striking price (a lower striking price in the case of puts).

Sentiment. The sum total of all bullish and bearish outlooks among all market participants on a particular stock, index, or market.

Series. Options of the same class having the same exercise price and expiration date.

Short-life option. An option contract having from several weeks to a few months until expiration.

Slippage. Cost to investors that results from buying at the asked price and selling at the bid price.

Specialist. Those who provide the best bid and asked prices on the options floors of the American Stock Exchange and the Philadelphia Stock Exchange. Specialists typically do not compete with each other, but rather focus on certain underlying stocks' options.

Straddle. The purchase or sale of an equivalent number of puts and calls on a given underlying stock with the same exercise price and expiration date. The straddle purchaser seeks to profit from relatively large movements in the price of the underlying stock, regardless of direction.

Strangle. The purchase or sale of an equivalent number of puts and calls on a given underlying stock, with the same expiration date but with different exercise prices. The strangle purchaser seeks to profit from large movements in price of the underlying stock, regardless of direction.

Striking price (also **exercise price**). The price per share at which the holder of an option can purchase (in the case of call options) or sell (in the case of put options) the underlying stock upon exercise.

Target exit point. The predetermined price at which options holdings would be sold at a lucrative, yet achievable profit. It is a key component of *The Option Advisor's* overall strategy of risk/reward management.

Technical analysis. Examination of moving averages, standard deviation bands, and other price and volume indicators to identify stocks in trending situations or in trading ranges and to predict future stock prices.

Theta. Represents the loss in value an option will experience due to the passage of time. Theta is usually expressed on a per day basis. For example, if an option has a theta of –0.25, the option will lose about $0.25 a day, provided the underlying stock price and volatility hold constant.

Time decay. The nonlinear loss of value of an option over time when all other factors are constant.

Time premium or **time value.**   The difference between the total cost of an option and its intrinsic value.

Time spread.   *See* **calendar spread.**

Trading floor.   The location at the options exchange where the contracts are actually bought and sold.

Truncated risk.   The ability of an investment to resist additional loss. Truncated risk is of particular relevance to options. For example, one cannot lose more than the premium paid for an option. Profits, however, are theoretically unlimited on an option and are equal to the intrinsic value of the option less the premium paid (assuming there is no longer any time value remaining).

Two-dimensional diversification.   An option trading strategy developed by *The Option Advisor* consisting of purchasing calls and puts to obtain diversification to minimize the impact of overall market movements.

Underlying stock or **security**.   The security that would be purchased or sold were the option exercised. Underlying securities can include stock, futures, and indexes.

Vega.   The change in an option's price based on the change in its implied volatility expressed in dollar terms. For example, if stock XYZ has an option with a vega of 0.25, the option's price will change by $0.25 for each one percentage point change in the option's implied volatility.

Volume.   For options, the number of contracts that have been traded within a specific time period, usually a day or a week.

Appendix C

Recommended Reading

OPTIONS

Bittman, James B. *Options for the Stock Investor.* Burr Ridge, Ill.: Irwin Professional Publishing. 1996. Shows stock investors how to broaden their opportunities and limit their risks with options. Solid coverage of basic option strategies, including covered call writing and protective puts.

Gross, LeRoy. *The Conservative Investor's Guide to Trading Options.* New York: New York Institute of Finance. 1989. Tested techniques for lowering risk and increasing performance when trading options. Covers option pricing; buy, write, and defensive strategies; and more.

McMillan, Lawrence G. *McMillan on Options.* New York: John Wiley & Sons. 1996. A look at options in actual trading situations, with case histories. Offers fundamental definitions, outlines option strategies, covers essential trading tactics, examines neutral strategy theory, and discusses money management and trading philosophy. The author places an emphasis on option volume, volatility, and put/call ratios.

Thomsett, Michael C. *Getting Started In Options.* New York: John Wiley & Sons. 1993. An introduction that explains options and defines terms, to clear up the confusion a newcomer can experience. The book separates the real risks from the imagined ones and offers guidance for formulating a plan to fit specific investment needs.

Walker, Joseph A. *How the Options Markets Work.* New York: New York Institute of Finance. 1991. A complete introduction to options and the market, covering what options are and are not, how they are created and traded, and their uses, rewards, and risks.

Wasendorf, Russell R., and Thomas A. McCafferty. *All About Options from the Inside Out.* Chicago: Probus Publishing Co. 1994. A step-by-step tour of the option-trading world, with coverage of floor action and strategies to use under various market conditions.

OPTIONS STRATEGIES

Baird, Allen Jan. *Option Market Making.* New York: John Wiley & Sons. 1992. Reveals the secrets of the floor traders—how they view the markets, how they see opportunities, how they manage risk.

Balsara, Nauzer J., *Money Management Strategies for Futures Traders.* New York: John Wiley & Sons. 1992. Relevant advice on money management for futures, stock, and options traders on the best ways to commit capital.

Bookstaber, Richard M. *Option Pricing and Investment Strategies.* Chicago: Probus Publishing Co. 1991. An advanced look at options pricing and strategy selection. Examines exposure measurement, arbitrage strategies, volatility estimation, and more.

Daigler, Robert. *Advanced Options Trading.* Chicago: Probus Publishing Co. 1993. Explores numerous options strategies, with further thoughts on the options pricing model.

Eng, William F. *Options: Trading Strategies that Work.* Chicago: Dearborn Publishing Co. 1996. A book on options trading by an author who has produced interesting books on trading rules. Thirteen traders share the secrets of their success on the floor, in money management, and in private trading.

Lyons, Alan S. *Winning in the Options Market.* Chicago: Probus Publishing Co. 1994. A successful trader's profitable strategies. This book shows how to reduce risk and increase profits by selling options, how to integrate options into a stock portfolio, and more.

McMillan, Lawrence G. *Options as a Strategic Investment*, third edition. New York: New York Institute of Finance. 1993. An options reference, with comprehensive options strategy definitions and details.

Natenberg, Sheldon. *Option Volatility and Pricing.* Chicago: Probus Publishing Co. 1994. A book for professionals by a professional, containing a highly advanced discussion on the factors affecting options pricing.

The Options Institute. *Options: Essential Concepts and Trading Strategies*, second edition. Burr Ridge, Ill.: Irwin Professional Publishing. 1994. Comprehensive guide to the variety of potential strategies available to options investors. An excellent resource for future reference.

Roth, Harrison. *LEAPS—What They Are How to Use Them for Profit and Protection.* Burr Ridge, Ill.: Irwin Professional Publishing. 1993. In-depth discussion of a wide variety of ways that investors and traders can use LEAPS.

Shaleen, Kenneth H. *Technical Analysis and Options Strategies.* Chicago: Probus Publishing Co. 1992. Combines a variety of technical formations with the best options strategies to use with each pattern.

PSYCHOLOGY

Bernstein, Jake. *Why Traders Lose, How Traders Win.* Chicago: Probus Publishing Co. 1992. Discusses how individual investors' behaviors move the market and create sentiment, offering insights into trends; also shows how to measure sentiment.

Dalton, James. *Mind Over Markets.* Chicago: Probus Publishing Co. 1993. An in-depth discussion of the market analysis technique known as "market profile," and the psychological underpinnings that support this methodology.

Douglas, Mark. *The Disciplined Trader.* New York: New York Institute of Finance. 1990. Explores the psychology of investing and the internal issues faced by the trader that determine the results produced.

Goodspeed, Bennett W. *The Tao Jones Averages.* New York: E.P. Dutton. 1983. Dedicated to "everyone who has the guts to follow his gut." This book examines the intuitive, right brain side of investing, and its integration with conventional left brain analytic reasoning.

Kindleberger, Charles P. *Manias, Panics and Crashes.* New York: John Wiley & Sons. 1996. Analysis of a variety of financial crises, including discussion of the common elements necessary to precipitate such declines.

Koppel, Robert, and Howard Abell. *The Innergame of Trading.* Chicago: Probus Publishing Co. 1994. Details the internal traits and state of mind needed to be a successful trader; includes interviews with top traders.

LeBon, Gustave. *The Crowd.* Burlington, Ver.: Fraser Publishing Co. 1982. A classic treatise on the elements of crowd behavior.

LeFèvre, Edwin. *Reminiscences of a Stock Operator.* New York: John Wiley & Sons. 1994. Documents the trading exploits of the legendary Jesse Livermore. This book can be read multiple times as a refresher for how market trends work. While set in the early 1900s, this book teaches us that the more things change in the markets, the more they remain the same.

Mackay, Charles. *Extraordinary Popular Delusions and the Madness of Crowds.* New York: Random House. 1995. Explores by studying the evolution of mass psychology, Tulipmania, the South Sea Bubble, and the Mississippi Scheme, among other phenomena.

Mehrabian, Albert. *Your Inner Path to Investment Success.* Chicago: Probus Publishing Co. 1991. Techniques for controlling the roller-coaster of emotions that trading can arouse.

Neill, Humphrey B. *The Art of Contrary Thinking.* Caldwell, Ida.: Caxton Printers. 1985. An in-depth look at the high value of watching what the crowd is doing, and knowing when to bet the crowd is wrong. The original bible for contrarians.

Peters, Edgar. *Chaos and Order in the Capital Markets.* New York: John Wiley & Sons. 1996. One of the trailblazers that explores chaos theory, the nature of trends, and how markets are nonlinear (yet still very structured).

Pring, Martin J. *Investment Psychology Explained: Classic Strategies to Beat the Markets.* New York: John Wiley & Sons. 1995. Shows how to avoid distorted decision making, resist expensive fads, and stick with your system.

Schwager, Jack D. *Market Wizards.* New York: Harper & Row. 1990. Interviews with top traders, including Paul Tudor Jones and Jim Rogers. Many lessons to be learned, with some common themes among a variety of successful approaches.

Schwager, Jack D. *The New Market Wizards.* New York: John Wiley & Sons. 1995. More interesting interviews with leading traders.

Vaga, Tonis. *Profiting from Chaos.* New York: McGraw-Hill. 1994. Details the benefits of chaos theory. This book also includes useful summaries of numerous successful investment strategies over time.

TECHNICAL/FUNDAMENTAL

Chande, Tushar S., and Stanley Kroll. *The New Technical Trader*. New York: John Wiley & Sons. 1994. Innovative twists on conventional technical indicators. Includes the VIDYA moving average, by which the author shows how to make moving averages more responsive to existing market conditions.

Edwards, Robert D., and John Magee. *Technical Analysis of Stock Trends*. Paramus, NJ: Prentice Hall. 1997. The original bible for technical analysis. Learn how to interpret gaps, flags, triangles, and numerous other technical patterns.

Fosback, Norman G. *Stock Market Logic*. Ft. Lauderdale, Fla.: The Institute for Econometric Research. 1984. In-depth study of technical, fundamental, monetary, and sentiment indicators. Shows how well stocks performed historically when certain conditions existed.

Murphy, John J. *Technical Analysis of the Futures Markets*. New York: New York Institute of Finance. 1986. Relates more to understanding technical trends than to futures. The CNBC market analyst discusses numerous technical patterns and formations.

Niemira, Michael P., and Gerald F. Zukowski. *Trading the Fundamentals*. Chicago: Probus Publishing Co. 1993. Examines a variety of economic releases and the best strategies to benefit from historically significant fundamental data.

O'Neill, William. *How to Make Money in Stocks*. New York: McGraw-Hill. 1988. Outlines the "C-A-N S-L-I-M" method of analyzing and predicting stock performance. Numerous examples of big winners in the stock market based primarily on strong earnings momentum and relative strength.

Rubenfeld, Alan. *The SuperTraders*. Burr Ridge, Ill.: Irwin Professional Publishing. 1992. Lessons from top traders, plus a look at their backgrounds and what led them to trading. First chapter details a well-known options trader.

Soros, George. *The Alchemy of Finance*. New York: John Wiley & Sons. 1994. Details how Soros has outperformed the market, and his theory of reflexivity. This book is not quick reading, but highly informative.

Sperandeo, Victor, with T. Sullivan Brown. *Trader Vic—Methods of a Wall Street Master*. New York: John Wiley & Sons. 1993. Highly readable look at investing as a key component of life. This book takes big-picture view of economics and markets and then focuses on methods to spot big moves.

Vince, Ralph. *The Mathematics of Money Management*. New York: John Wiley & Sons. 1992. Explains Vince's "optimal f" asset allocation philosophy, and the implications of overcommitting or undercommitting capital to each trade.

Appendix D

Ten "Ignore at Your Peril" Rules for Successful Short-Term Options Trading

If you are buying options for the short term, which optimally is a holding period of five to fifteen trading days, you should follow my ten "ignore at your peril" rules.

1. *Don't trade front-month options.* These options should be used purely for scalping purposes, that is, for holding periods of a day or two. Instead, trade options with a minimum of six weeks of life remaining. Yes, front-month options are "cheap" in dollar cost and offer huge leverage. But if you expect a position to take a couple of weeks to work out in your favor, you need to avoid the extreme time decay of front-month options. And the "leverage" afforded by front-month options is often illusory. Sure, that front-month IBM 170-strike call will produce a 1,500 percent gain if the stock reaches your goal of 175, but if IBM is currently at 160, the chances of a move of this magnitude occurring are effectively "zero" if this option expires in two days. Finally, front-month options are rarely priced at implied volatility levels lower than their back-month counterparts, and are often priced at much higher levels of implied volatility. This is due to the fact that front-month options attract unsophisticated "roll the dice" speculators who are attempting to make the "big score" in a single trade, and it also attracts speculators (sometimes sophisticated, sometimes not) who are betting on such external events as an earnings report and who want to maximize their leverage if they are correct about the outcome. My advice is to leave these overvalued and risky front-month options to the crapshooters and the professionals.

2. *Be a contrarian.* But don't let a contrarian viewpoint be the immediate driver for a trade. I have at times in the past succumbed to the temptation to immediately react to a news story or a magazine article that I found particularly compelling from contrarian perspective by taking a position in the options market. Perhaps a stock that I believe is overly recommended relative to its true prospects releases earnings that are disappointing, but analysts are tripping over themselves in the media to put a positive "spin" on the report. My immediate reaction would be to want to buy a put on this "high expectation" stock, but unfortunately I have found that such trades are rarely successful. This is because a contrarian view is often early, and as such some additional time is required before the stock will behave as a contrarian would expect. It is much better in such a case to keep a close eye on the stock for signs of a technical breakdown before you jump in and buy those puts.

3. *Entry timing is critical.*   As we have seen in earlier chapters, in options trading it is not enough to ultimately be correct on the direction of the underlying stock—we must be right almost from the very beginning. And if we are trading over a five- to twenty-day period, good timing becomes even more critical to our success—so critical that I hone my technical timing tools down to the intraday level before I recommend an options trade.

4. *Don't ever let a losing position get "out of control."*   This means that you should never let an open position decline below the price level at which you still view a closeout as worthwhile. For example, you may have bought an option at $1\frac{1}{2}$. Although you may be more than willing to cut your losses by closing out this position at $\frac{7}{8}$ or even $\frac{3}{4}$ and thus conserve your trading capital, you may consider a closeout at less than $\frac{3}{4}$ to be a waste of effort, particularly when commissions are considered. The trick here is to close the position as soon as the option reaches your "line of demarcation" between a worthwhile closeout and a waste of time. Otherwise, once you cross below this price threshold, you are reduced to the position of a "hoper," as in "I sure hope this stock will reverse course so I can get out of this position with some value." Unfortunately, the market doesn't care about what you hope, so it is not surprising that passive "hopers" are invariably among the losers in the options game, and the spoils belong to those who trade proactively on both winning and losing positions.

5. *If you fail to follow rule 4, consider your trade to be "busted."*   Then look to close out your position on *any* move in the stock that results in a worthwhile closeout price for your option. Why do I call this a "busted trade"? Because your timing was obviously wrong (see rule 3), otherwise you wouldn't be in this unenviable position! And when your timing is wrong, you always look to get out of an options trade with as much of your original capital as you can. It is a "damage control" situation, so don't get greedy and play the loser's game of looking to turn a busted trade into a winner.

6. *Take the profits that the market is willing to give you.* If you were looking for a double on a position and you are at a 90 percent gain and the stock is stalling, take the profit. While you are holding out for that extra 10 percent, the stock could turn around and take away your nice 90 percent gain. Although it is true that you need to have patience and staying power to achieve big profits on your winning trades to offset the smaller losses that you are taking on your losers, don't try to force the market to give you more profit than it is prepared to extend to you.

7. *Be wary of stocks whose daily charts are in a "trading range" mode.* This is particularly true if you are buying strength or selling weakness. Betting on a breakout or a breakdown from a range is generally a low-probability strategy, and with your short holding period the chances of you correctly timing a breakout from a trading range are slim.

8. *Watch for moving average crossovers on the daily chart and don't try to fade them (that is, trade against them).* By "moving average crossover," I am referring to the situation in which a shorter-term moving average, such as the 10-day moving average, crosses above or below a longer-term moving average, such as the 20-day moving average (a cross above has bullish implications; a cross below has bearish implications).

9. *Don't take a position in the same direction that the front-month option traders are heavily playing.* This can be determined by looking at the "open interest" of the various front-month options, and seeing if there is a strong imbalance on the call side or on the put side. Why avoid siding with the very popular option bets? Because options speculators have a strong tendency to be wrong when they agree in large numbers, and you don't want to share their unhappy fate.

10. *Don't ignore areas of long-term resistance or support in your trading decisions.* This rule should be followed in spite of what I have said about the importance of timing to your short-term options trading and my emphasis on daily and even intraday charts. Always check out the monthly charts and look for levels of long-term resistance or support, and in particular check out the 10- and 20-month moving averages. Don't buy puts, even for the short-term, on stocks that are at long-term support levels, and don't buy short-term calls on stocks that are at long-term resistance levels. Such levels often take a long time to ultimately penetrate—far longer than the maximum of fifteen days that you will be in a trade.

Appendix E

Myths about Options

Despite the tremendous expansion in the awareness in the investment community of the workings of the options market, myths about options are still rampant. Most of them date from the old "cottage industry" days, and the fact that they are still with us is a testimony to the resilience of folklore.

The vast majority of options myths are in one of two polar-opposite categories. The first category is the "gee-whiz, options are the world's greatest invention, as they are a license to print money" mythology. The myths underlying this category are of the "options are great because" variety, and include:

1. You can lose only your original investment, and no more.
2. By using naked option selling strategies, you can be just like the "house" at a gambling casino and profit on virtually every trade.
3. If you buy a portfolio of very cheap, "out-of-the-money" options, your profits from the big winners are bound to more than offset your losses from those that expire worthless.

The belief in any one of these myths can be extremely dangerous for the options investor, as they encourage the unwary trader to let his guard down and be less vigilant about the risks of trading options. The truth about each of these myths follows:

1. A loss "limited" to one's original investment is of little solace to someone who invests a large portion of his capital in a single options trade.
2. Naked option selling strategies were by far the most devastating source of investor losses in the 1987 stock market crash.
3. The odds of a cheap, out-of-the-money option ever achieving any substantial value are minuscule, and even a portfolio of

these options has a minuscule probability of developing any value.

The second category of myths about options is equally dangerous, as it has prevented many investors from ever participating in options trading and thus enjoying the many benefits of such participation. I would label this category as the "options are a 'rum game' and there is no way you can make any money with options" mythology. It includes the following folklore:

1. 90 percent of options expire worthless.
2. 90 percent of options traders lose money.
3. Options trading is much riskier than stock trading.
4. Brokerage commissions for trading options are too high.
5. Options trading is only for investment professionals.

The actual truth about each of these beliefs is listed below.

1. It is impossible for 90 percent of options to expire worthless, because for every call option that achieves value from a rise in the price of the underlying stock, there is a put option that achieves value from a decline in the price of the underlying stock. So when call option buyers are seeing their contracts expire worthless, put option buyers are seeing their contracts appreciate in value, and vice-versa. In fact, less than 50 percent of options expire worthless.

2. Although it is very likely the case that most options traders lose money, there are no statistics justifying this absurdly high 90 percent figure. Chapter 3 discusses the major mistakes that cause options traders to lose money, along with many simple steps you can take to avoid the mistakes of the crowd.

3. Options trading can be riskier than stock trading, but most often when the options investor overcommits his trading capital, underdiversifies his options positions, and engages in strategies at the riskiest end of the spectrum. Most beginning options traders and many intermediate traders are guilty of some or all of these "sins," which are discussed in chapter 4. Also, chapter 9 explains some very attractive yet relatively low-risk option strategies that belie the "options trading must be risky" myth.

4. Options brokerage commissions used to be relatively high. But with the explosive growth of the discount and deep-discount brokerage industry, as well as the advent of Internet brokers and brokers who specialize in options transactions, the level of options commissions has declined substantially in the 1990s (see chapter 10).

5. Options trading is for anyone who understands the rewards and the risks and who also understands the proper ways to approach the options market. The goal of this book has been to "arm you" you with this understanding so you can trade options like a professional.

Index

3 Month FREE Trial Offer

Put the same options trading strategies you've read about in this book to work for you with a 3 Month FREE Trial subscription to the nation's most widely-read options newsletter, *The Option Advisor*.

Each month, Senior Editor Bernie Schaeffer provides you with a detailed market commentary, a portfolio of six aggressive options recommendations, four longer-term LEAPS recommendations, and a put-selling portfolio. If the strategies used in this book have piqued your interest in options trading, then this 3 Month FREE Trial subscription is an ideal way to get started.

For the next 3 months you're invited to "test drive" this valuable newsletter and its options trading strategies. Just call our customer service hotline at 1-800-327-8833 today. You'll get three issues of *The Option Advisor*, plus... complete access to *The Option Advisor* weekly telephone hotline.